IMAGES
of America

GLENN COUNTY

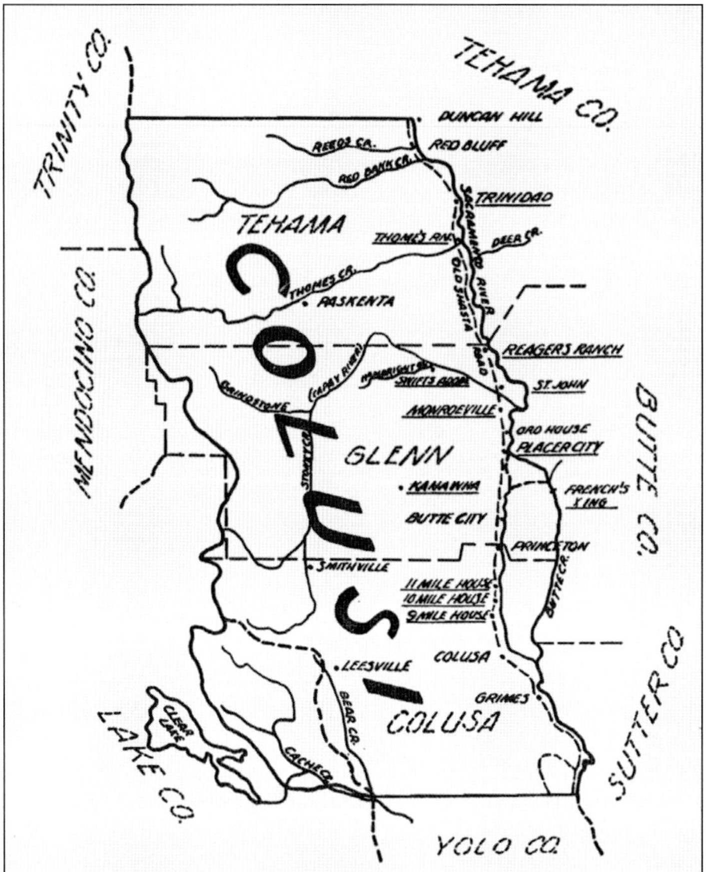

Original boundary of Colusi County, established by first California Legislature December, 1849, at San Jose and subsequent changes. — Scale — 1" is 16 miles.
Research by Frank S. Reager.
Map drawn by courtesy of Gus Hoever, Jr.

Gus Hoever Jr. drew this map based on research by Frank S. Reager. It depicts the original Colusi County boundaries, which were established in 1849, and the more recent changes delineating Glenn, Colusa, and Tehama as separate counties. This is the go-to map for any discussion or research on the parent county of Colusi and the division of the counties mentioned above. (Colusi County Historical Society.)

On the Cover: Picnics were an enjoyable way to spend a warm afternoon. This group appears to be just removed from a Chrome baseball game. Note the picnic blankets and the metal eating utensils, including pails and large bowls. From left to right are (first row) Jim Powell, Bert Hull, and Mertie Millsaps Hull; (second row) Francis Squires Niesen and Francis Mendinghall Hull; (third row) Isabell Niesen and John Hull; (fourth row) Nora Niesen Drew, Emma Hull Niesen, and Louis Niesen; (fifth row) Chase Haskell, Jim Drew, Walter Niesen, Will Niesen, Inez Niesen Haskell, Bessie Manson Niesen, Nolan Niesen, Laura Niesen, Orley Niesen, Mary Hull, Bud Niesen, and Roy Hull. (Hollis Burrows Spurlock.)

IMAGES
of America

GLENN COUNTY

Anna Canon

ARCADIA
PUBLISHING

ISBN 978-1-4671-3184-1

Published by Arcadia Publishing
Charleston, South Carolina

Printed in the United States of America

Library of Congress Control Number: 2013954828

For all general information, please contact Arcadia Publishing:
Telephone 843-853-2070
Fax 843-853-0044
E-mail sales@arcadiapublishing.com
For customer service and orders:
Toll-Free 1-888-313-2665

Visit us on the Internet at www.arcadiapublishing.com

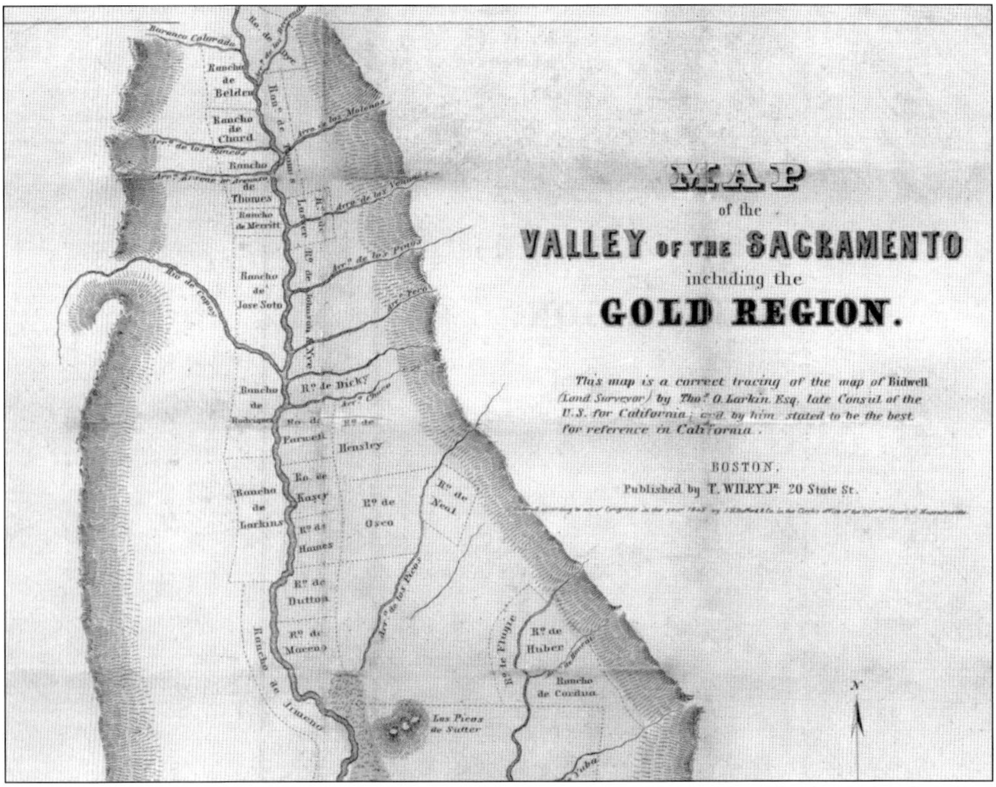

In 1844, Thomas O. Larkin, consul to the United States for California, hired John Bidwell to find him a tract of 10 leagues. As Larkin never received Mexican citizenship, he was unable to own the land. However, his children were eligible, so he secured the land in their trust. This map is a correct tracing of the map that John Bidwell was commissioned to draw for Larkin. This map was used in other land-grant proceedings. (David Rumsey Collection.)

Contents

ACKNOWLEDGMENTS

The pictorial history of Glenn County that has been compiled here is a tribute to many deep-rooted families whose descendants were willing to allow a non-native Glenn Countyian into their homes, lives, and ancestries.

Those whose family photos you will see here are Steve Ansel, Laura Blevins, Sherrie Cooper, Diana Domingo, Robert Wesley Johanningsmeier, Jesus Rodriquez, the Rumiano family, Hollis Burrows Spurlock, Greg Steel, and Lana Trovao. Each family represents a different part of the county.

Several historic photo collections were opened to the author as well, including the Bancroft Library, Glenn County Fair, Hamilton City Community Services Office, Donna Klobas, Library of Congress, Orland Historical and Cultural Society, and the David Rumsey Map Collection.

These photos will allow the viewers to travel to an earlier time in Glenn County, which the author has been doing vicariously through the pioneer ancestors of Eletta Walker Jacobsen and the research and writing of Dr. Gene Russell. Through the guidance and direction of these two amazing individuals, a love for the history of the county has been seeded, watered, and sometimes fertilized. The reader is now partaking of the harvest.

The historic works of Colusa and Glenn County historians laid the foundation for the information found herein. Thanks must be given to them for their forethought to compile the information when the county and state were young. Included here are all the authors who have contributed their time and research to write for the Colusi County Historical Society's publication *Wagon Wheels* from its inception in May 1951 to today. Also included are the comprehensive works of Sima Baker, Al Ball, Cynthia F. Davis, Elizabeth Eubank, Will S. Green, W.S. Guilford, Rebecca T. Lambert, Milly Latta, Charles Davis McComish, Justus H. Rogers, Ann Foley Scheuring, and Thelma B. White.

In regards to the content of this compilation, an excerpt from a paragraph taken from Will S. Green's *The History of Colusa County, California and General History of the State*, is as fitting today as it was in 1880:

> I am well aware of the fact that there are many and important omissions and, perhaps, some mistakes. Out of some forty letters, written to different persons, I was enabled to get answers to but three, and, in fact, to but one that gave me any material aid . . . It is much easier to criticize than to execute, and hence I shall expect to have many critics but as I have not had the means or the opportunity of gathering up facts outside my own knowledge, I ask for an indulgent criticism.

This work could not have been completed without Bruce Chapman, who has been extremely instrumental in allowing time to be carved out of busy lives and creating sustenance; Jamie Jo Canon, who served as an editor and a support-team chairman; and Logan Chapman and Travis Chapman, who endured many trips to historic places and gave up their adolescent time to be more informed about the history of Glenn County and California.

INTRODUCTION

One of the very first documented accounts of present day Glenn County was by General John Bidwell. As he wrote in a letter to the *Colusa Sun* dated January 6, 1877:

> I first saw that portion of Colusa County lying west of the Sacramento River in 1843, at which time I passed through its entire length. It did not then contain a white inhabitant. No one had ever thought then of obtaining a grant of land there. No Mexican had ever lived there, and I have some doubts if one had ever been there. The territory comprised the present county of Colusa, so far as settlement, or the least sign of civilization was concerned, was as new as when Columbus discovered America.

General Bidwell mentions meeting a group of travelers in the fall of 1843. With the Feather River as their final destination, the party followed the west bank of the Sacramento River and crossed at the mouth of Stony Creek. Maj. P.B. Redding was with this party. He sketched the land around the mouth of Stony Creek and gave the map to the wife of Dr. Stokes, who was from Monterey, so that she could obtain a grant, as she was a Mexican citizen. This was the first grant made within the limits of Colusa County.

The next grant was made for the children of Thomas O. Larkin, a merchant and US consul at Monterey. In 1844, Larkin employed General Bidwell to find him a tract of land. With an Indian guide, he traveled the west side of the valley (west of the current town of Colusa), camped overnight, and then headed west across the plains of the valley and into the foothills. He traveled what was called the Stony Creek Valley from south to north and followed the creek down to the Sacramento River just below present-day Hamilton City. The map Bidwell drew can be found opposite the table of contents.

General Bidwell also wrote, "Granville P. Swift and Frank Sears settled on Stony Creek, I believe, in 1847." Other authors have written much about these two men. They used stone and adobe corrals to hold their cattle in the Maxwell area at Kanawha Corners (west of present day Willows) and built several adobes throughout Glenn County. The first known structure to be built in Glenn County was Swift and Sears's rancho on Hambright Creek, one mile north of present-day Orland.

A fringe of settlers along the Sacramento River, from the mouth of Stony Creek to below Grimes, is noted in 1851. These entrepreneurs established "road houses" to accommodate travelers up and down the river. Two very small towns could be found at that time on the river: Colusa, known as Colonel Semple's town, and Monroeville, founded by U.P. Monroe, south of the mouth of Stony Creek.

The adventures of Will Semple Green and his uncle Robert Baylor Semple, along with Robert's youngest brother Charles, are documented in various *Wagon Wheels*, historic biannual publications published by the Colusi County Historical Society. Green and Semple are noted as instrumental in the formation of the town and county of Colusa. In *The History of Colusa County, California and General History of the State*, Will S. Green notes that the name of the original county was of Indian origin: "The name of the tribe was pronounced "Colus." He does note that this was not the pronunciation used by the Indians. The "a" was added in 1850 because it "gave a very euphonious name."

A short time after the formation of the town of Colusa in 1850, the first state legislature convened and gave a boundary and name to the county, Colusi. It was not until 1854 that the name was officially changed to Colusa.

The rivalry between the counties began with the original formation of the county. Although the legislature created the boundaries and the name, they did not provide for a county seat. At that time, the state was divided into judicial districts, and the newly formed county of Colusi was under the jurisdiction of Butte County.

U.P. Monroe of Monroeville and Robert Semple of Colusa each utilized the judicial system to attempt to win the location of the county seat. There were five elections held in 1851, allowing the citizens of Colusi County to vote often. The two towns continued to quarrel for the honor until the fall of 1853, when Colusa was finally victorious and won the county seat by 310 votes to Monroeville's 52.

When the legislature plotted out the counties in 1850, much of it was based on guesswork. Colusa County, as it was first laid out, was almost 100 miles long from north to south. Boundaries were changed by cutting off a 36-mile-wide strip from the northern end and adding it to Tehama County. In 1864, a boundary change was proposed to put Bear Valley and Stonyford into Lake County. Again, the county citizens fiercely opposed this bill and killed it in the senate. In 1866, a bill to add the areas of Afton and Butte City to Butte County was introduced. Again, the citizens vehemently opposed the bill and it was defeated.

In January 1887, a bill providing for county division was introduced in the assembly. A petition bearing 800 signatures for division was presented. When the roll was eventually called, the results reflected 19 ayes for division and 20 nays against division.

The Glenn County Bill, as it had come to be known, was labeled "one of the liveliest of the sessions" for the state legislature in January 1889, when the division was reintroduced. Former senator K.E. Kelly presented a petition signed by hundreds of residents supporting division. The issues of unfair taxes due to the size and population of the county and the distance residents had to travel (over 90 miles in some cases) to settle matters at the county level were the heart of the desire for division. Sen. John Boggs was in charge of those opposed to the division.

Large delegations for both sides swarmed to Sacramento to plead with Governor Waterman once the bill was on his desk. The speeches and presentation of a "living petition" were not enough. Governor Waterman vetoed the division.

The third time the Glenn County Bill was presented, it passed both houses and was signed by Governor Markham on March 11, 1891. Although Markham was not in favor of county division, he wanted to put "an end to the fierce contests" between the north and south portions of the county. This, however, was not the end of the battle. The newly formed Glenn County had to vote to ratify the division as well as set up the new county government. The election was highlighted in the newspapers as the "Glenn County Election Fraud" case. Several court cases were created out of the discord of the citizens, including stuffed ballot boxes, fraudulent voters, constitutionality, and bribery, to name a few. The allegations and trials continued through 1893, when the California Supreme Court declared the creation of Glenn County constitutional.

The name of the county was proposed and financially supported by the family of Dr. Hugh James Glenn, a prosperous wheat farmer who came with his family to the Jacinto area in 1868. His business savvy, agricultural advancements, open hiring practices, and ambition created a solid foundation for those who unknowingly followed in his footsteps.

To adequately represent the whole of what has been (and is) Glenn County would take much more space than has been provided here. The author gathered information and compiled it in brief captions. As the reader progresses through the compilation, they will note other historical documents, books, and collections referenced. The hope is that readers will be inclined to visit their local library or peruse the internet for some of the fine collections of historical information that are available, including the Arcadia Publishing books *Land of Orland* and *Willows*. Enjoy.

One

River

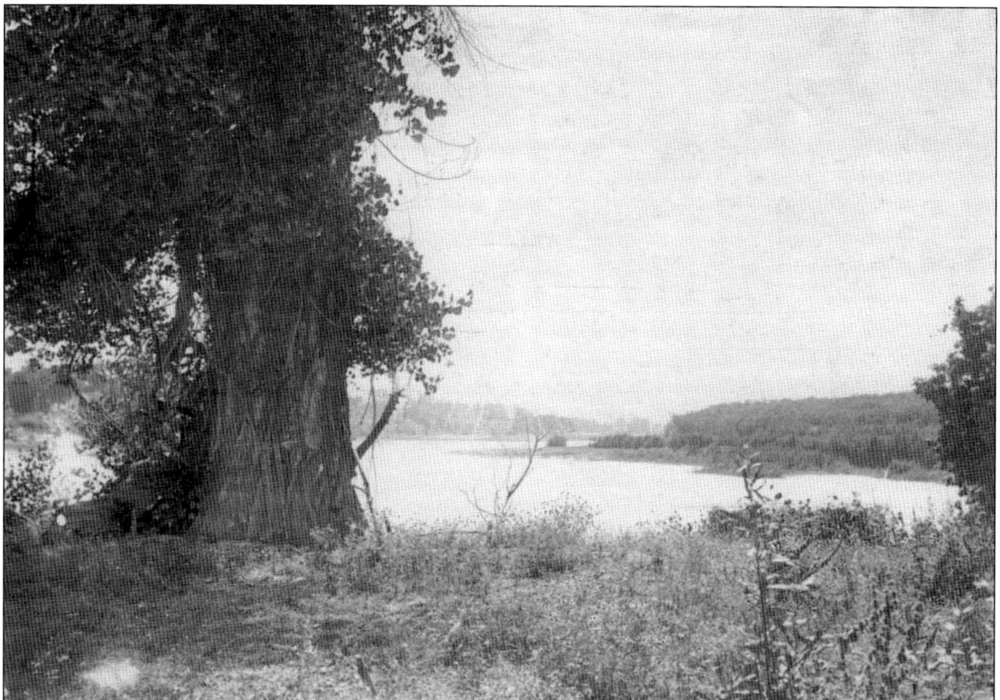

The Sacramento River defines much of the eastern border of Glenn County. The Native Americans encamped upon its shores and partook of its bounty. Early explorers followed its course on foot and vessel. Steamers and barges forged its shallow depths and sandbars. Traders traveled its route in search of business and pleasure. Towns were dreamed of, laid out, populated, and abandoned. Agriculturalists diverted its water. It has been low and high. Even with modern dams and levees it frequently flows over its own banks. It continues to provide all of this for current and future generations. (Greg Steel.)

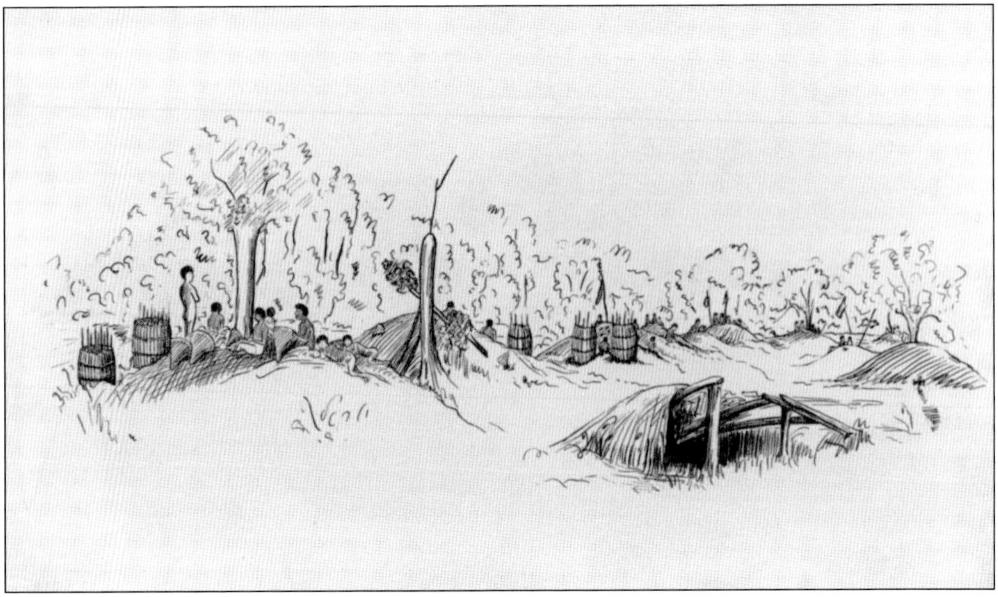

There were many tribes of Native Americans in all parts of what is now known as Glenn County. A firsthand encounter by John Bidwell in 1843 was published in the *Colusa Sun* dated January 6, 1877. Henry B. Brown had been commissioned by the United States and Mexican Boundary Commission to gather information on native languages and to create drawings and sketches of the various Indian peoples and their activities. Throughout 1852, Brown traveled up the Sacramento River valley to Shasta City capturing images and local vocabularies for the commission. This 1852 pencil sketch is labeled "Chino Village near Munroe's" (Munroeville). (Bancroft Library.)

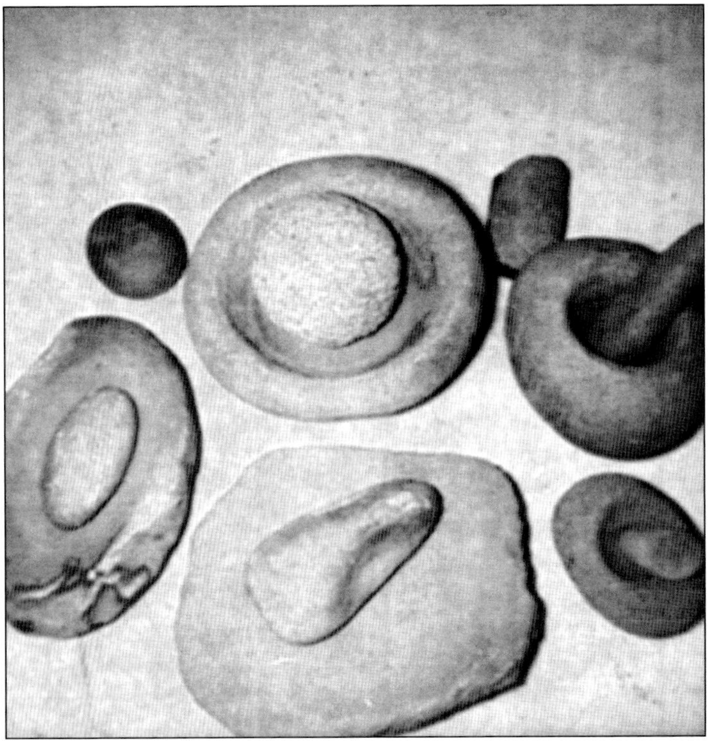

In 1845, Peter Lassen, W.C. Moon, and a Mr. Merritt filled a canoe with grindstones found along Stony Creek and paddled them along the Sacramento River to San Francisco. Will S. Green saw the canoe leave Sacramento and noted that it looked "anything but safe." The grindstones pictured here were recovered from the Baker Ranch east of Artois, according to Ethel A. Baker in the February 1958 issue of *Wagon Wheels*. (*Wagon Wheels*, February 1958.)

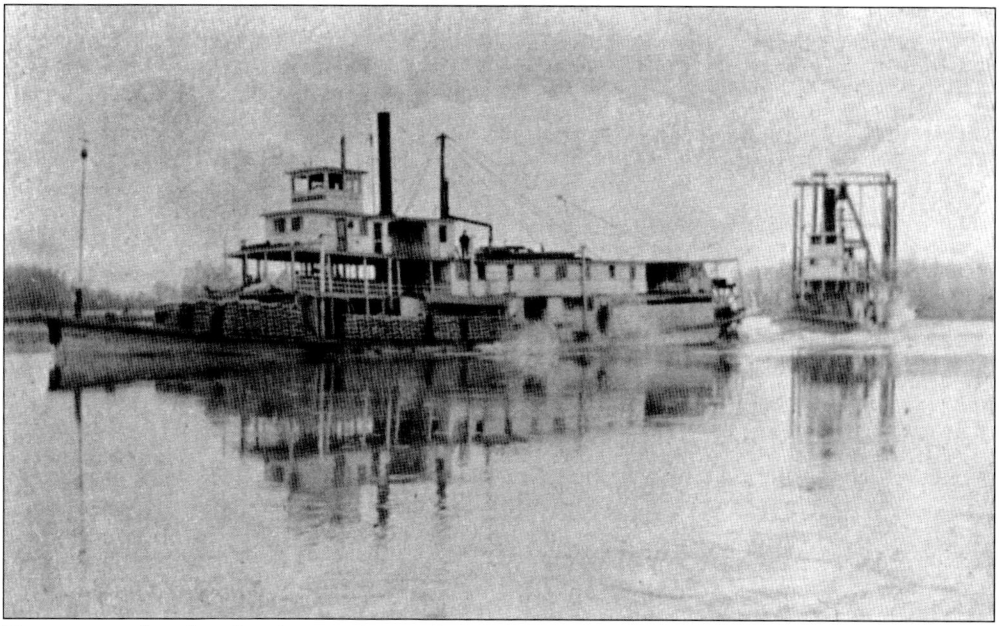

Teamsters and packers heading to the northern mines traveled up the west side of the Sacramento River. The heavily traveled route was dusty in the summer and muddy in the winter. Steamboats began to run on the Sacramento River in 1850. Here the steamers *Dover* and *San Joaquin No. 3* are towing the *Gerber*. Note the sacks of grain and the paddlewheel. (*Wagon Wheels*, spring 1985.)

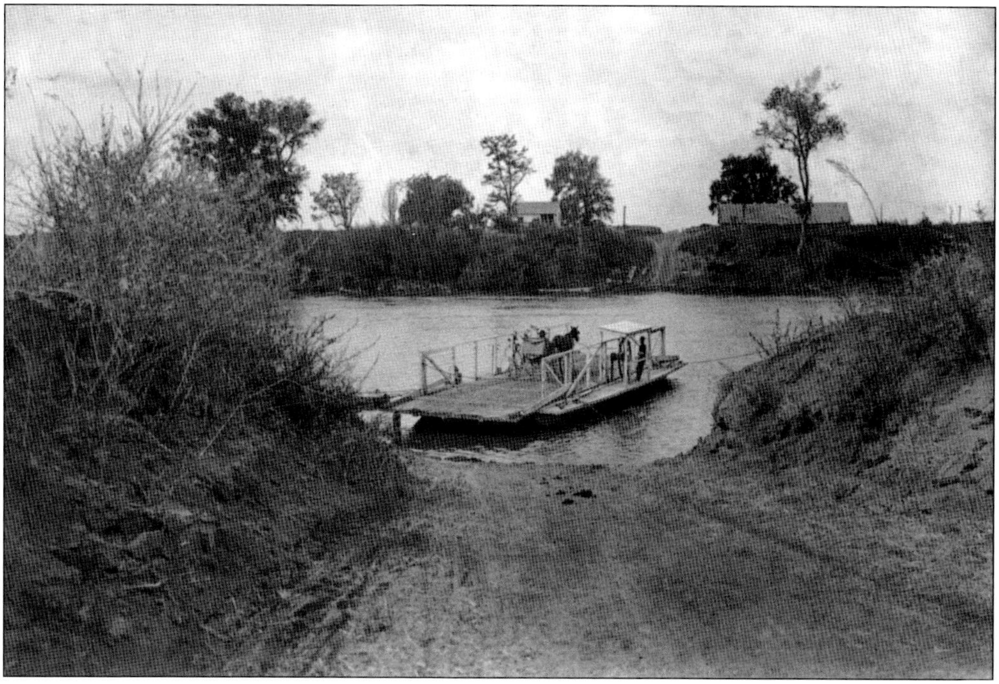

An early foot crossing on the Sacramento River was at Swift's Point (above the current Gianella Bridge). Ferries soon became a necessity to transport people, vehicles, and livestock with reduced travel times. Samuel Picknell and his partner Joseph Bounds operated this ferry in Butte City beginning in 1876. Note the ferry operator and the carriage. (Greg Steel.)

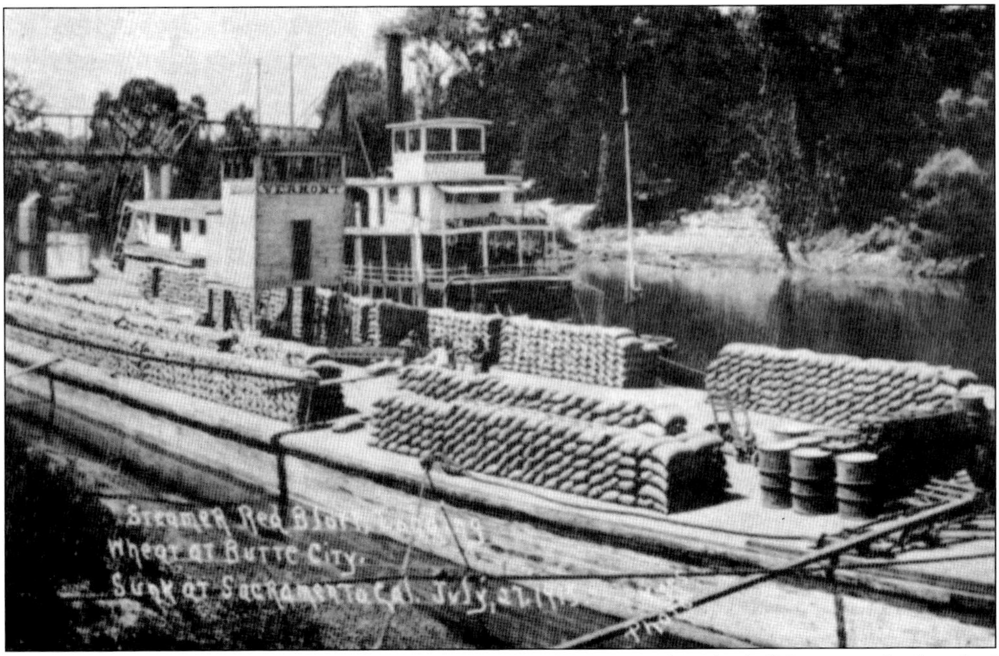

Once snag-clearing boats began clearing the river, the town of Red Bluff became the head of navigation. According to John Quincy Adams Warren, editor of the *American Stock Journal*, a trip up the river was slow because of the crooked course of the river, shallow water, and many snags. He credited the boat pilots for being skillful at maneuvering their vessels and for being very courteous. Here the barge *Vermont* is moored at Butte City while wheat is loaded. The steamer *Red Bluff* sits to its west. The *Red Bluff* was sunk on July 27, 1915. (*Wagon Wheels*, spring 1985.)

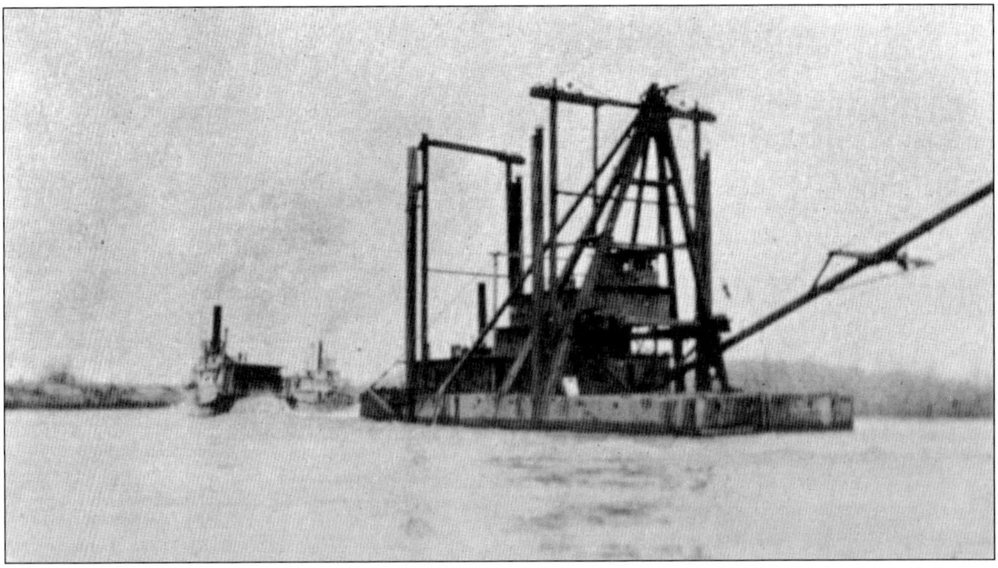

As sediment gathered on the bottom of the river with every winter flooding, dredging became necessary over time to allow steamers and barges to travel without running onto sandbars or snags. The material that was excavated was often used for reinforcement levees on the banks of the river. This 1915 photograph shows the *Gerber* dredge with the *San Joaquin No. 3* and *Dover* in the background. (*Wagon Wheels*, spring 1985.)

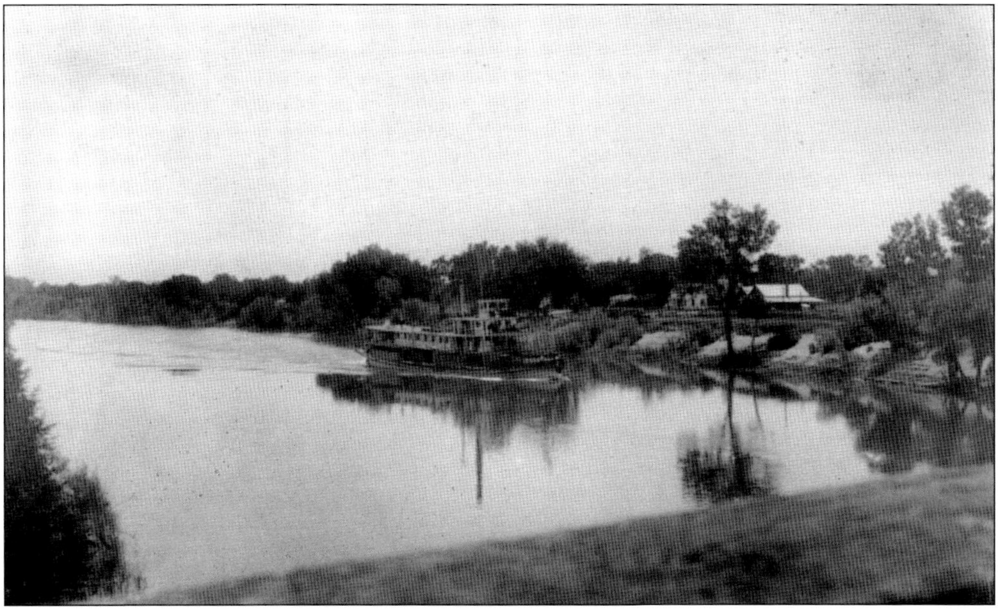

Izilla Wadsworth, a longtime resident of Butte City, wrote in her memoirs about an old trading boat that came up from Sacramento, arrived in Butte City about 1:00 p.m. on Saturday, and left at noon on Sunday. The upper deck was a store and the lower deck carried freight and wet goods. The merchants would buy goods and livestock from farmers and sell their wares, which included anything from a tin cup to a new hat. (Greg Steel.)

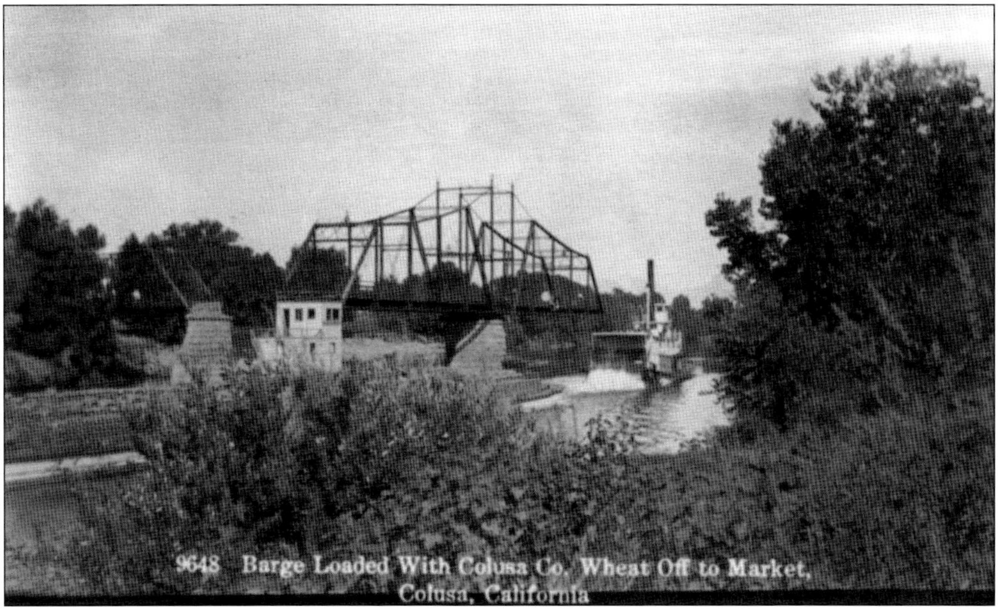

Butte City has been known as Laramie, Gouge Eye, and Pin Hook. Four bridges have spanned the Butte City section of the Sacramento River. The first was built in 1883 or 1884. According to the memoir of Izilla Wadsworth, this first bridge was dedicated on a Saturday and was washed away by the raging river the next Monday. The second was struck by a steamboat and fell into the high waters. The third was the existing bridge at the time Wadsworth wrote the *History of Butte City* in 1933. The fourth was dedicated on January 17, 1949. (Greg Steel.)

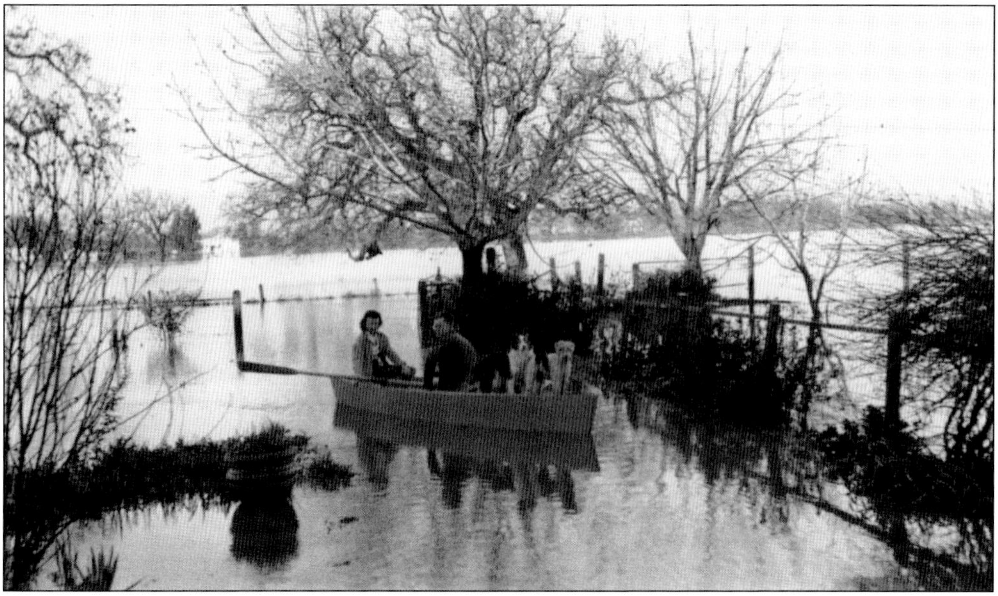

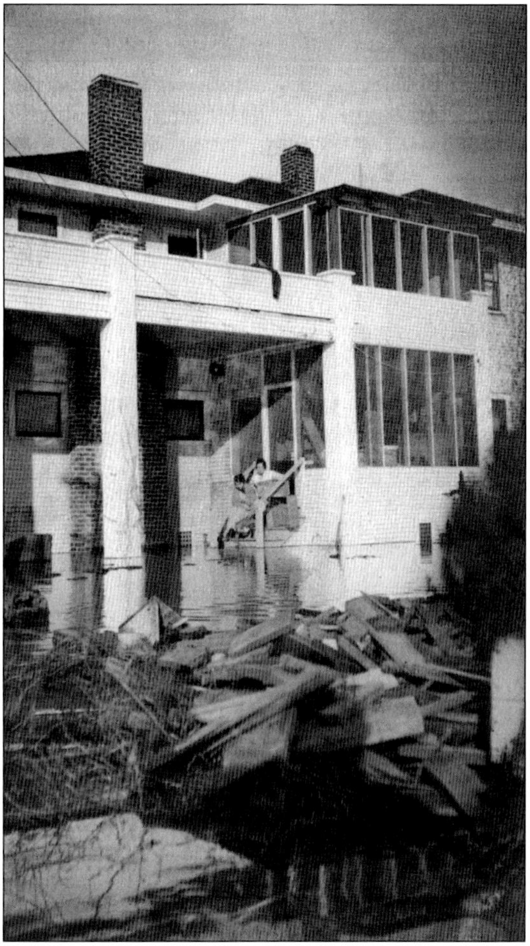

Native Americans told stories of great floods in 1805 and 1825–1826. Numerous references to these floods can be found in early newspapers such as the *Daily Alta California*, the *Sacramento Transcript*, and the *Colusa Sun*. They were described as the "highest water ever known in the county" and as "rains the worst in history." Collis and Margaret Steel, who lived in the flood plain of the Sacramento River, show how Butte City and Afton residents adjusted for the flooding. (Greg Steel.)

Many personal reports give a picture of the devastating effects of flooding. Because homes and barns would flood, people and livestock were forced to seek high ground. Levees would break, creating forceful floodwaters that tore down structures and drowned people and animals. Often, the water would not recede for days. The Steel Ranch house in Afton had to be repaired numerous times due to its proximity to the river. (Greg Steel.)

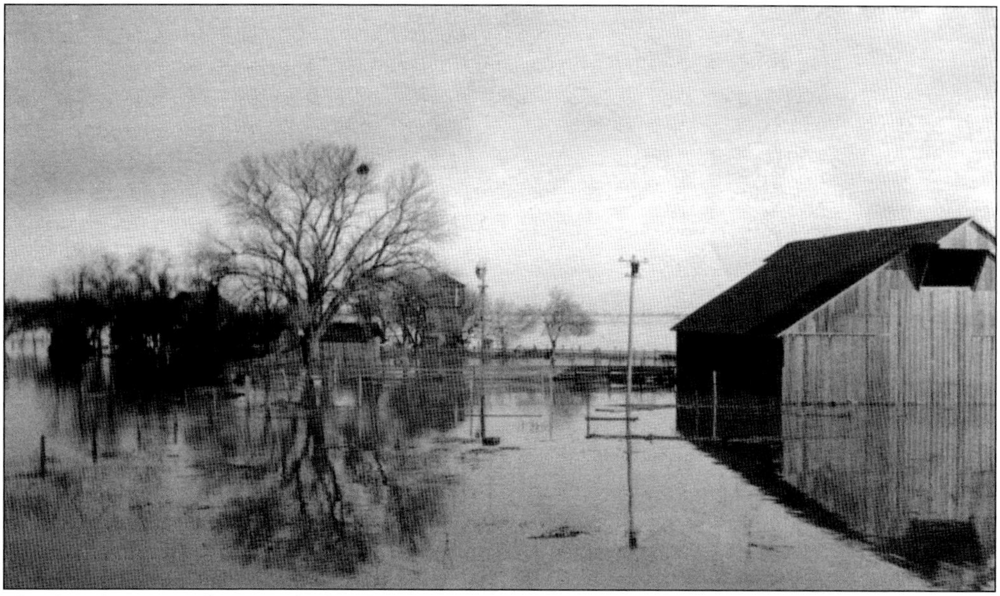

Flooding brings with it a rich, fertile soil ideal for agricultural purposes, and man has attempted to tame rivers in order to utilize their surrounding lands. However, this gamble often results in a loss of livestock and crops. Before any levees were built, the water of the Sacramento River escaped through a number of sloughs and over low banks. Levees have helped to direct the waters and have, in turn, changed the flow of the river, creating new needs for flood control. The Steel and Picknell families of the Afton and Butte City areas suffered and recovered from numerous floods. (Both, Greg Steel.)

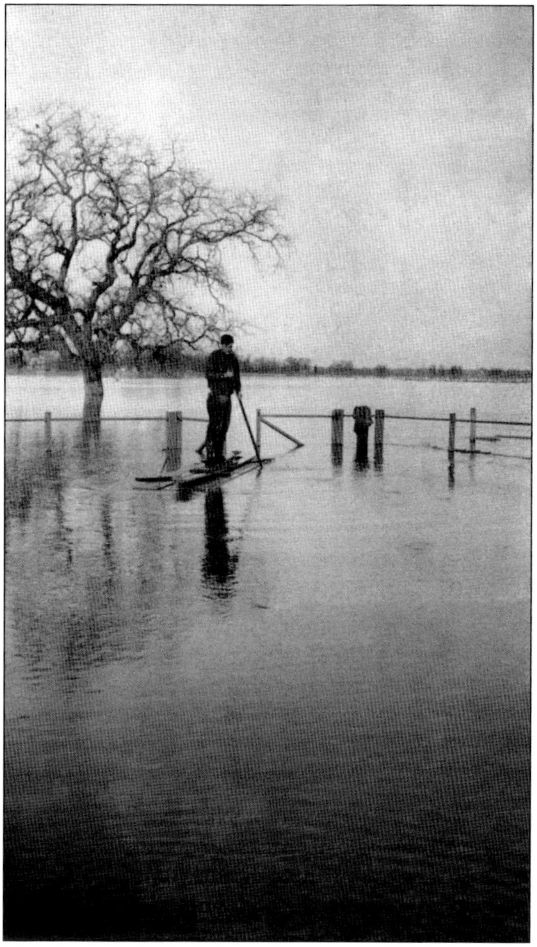

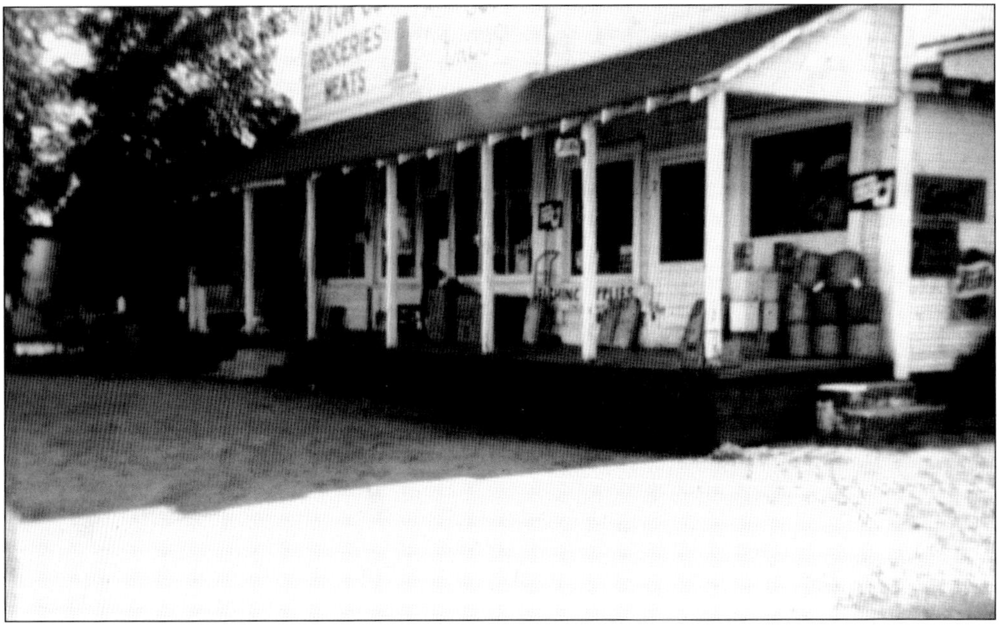

Settlement in the Afton area began in the mid-1850s. Afton pioneers developed a viable community and became prosperous farmers. The nearby Sacramento River provided a convenient way to transport products to the markets in Sacramento and San Francisco. The Afton Store was established in 1918. The storefront pictured here was probably photographed in the late 1940s. (Jesus Rodriquez.)

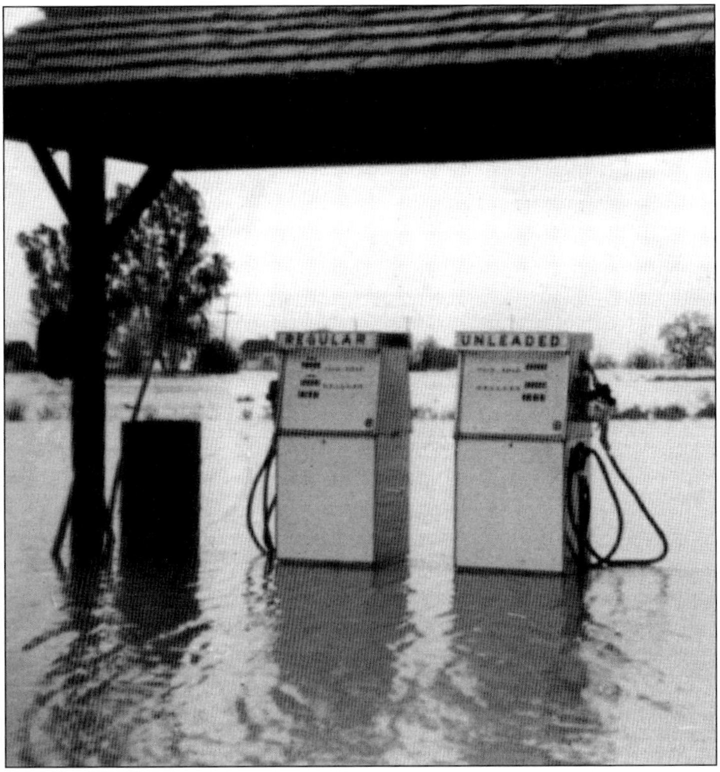

Flooding affected all travel, and preparations had to be made in order to continue to function. A record of the owners of the Afton Store has been diligently kept from 1918 to today. Their surnames include Tuburgen, Bultema, Snider, Mix, Smalls, Alyward, Ku, Volkman, and Rodriquez. (Jesus Rodriquez.)

Ranches raised hay and barley in 1851 for the purpose of supplying the teams that were heading to the mines. The winter of 1851 was extremely dry, and it was said that nothing of the kind could have been grown if planted. The overflow of the river allowed native grains, such as oats, to grow. They were utilized as hay through dry spells. The river basin was known to be either dry or soaked, with not too much in between. Butte City rancher George Wadsworth, pictured below in 1969, still had to feed his livestock regardless of conditions. (Both, Diana Domingo.)

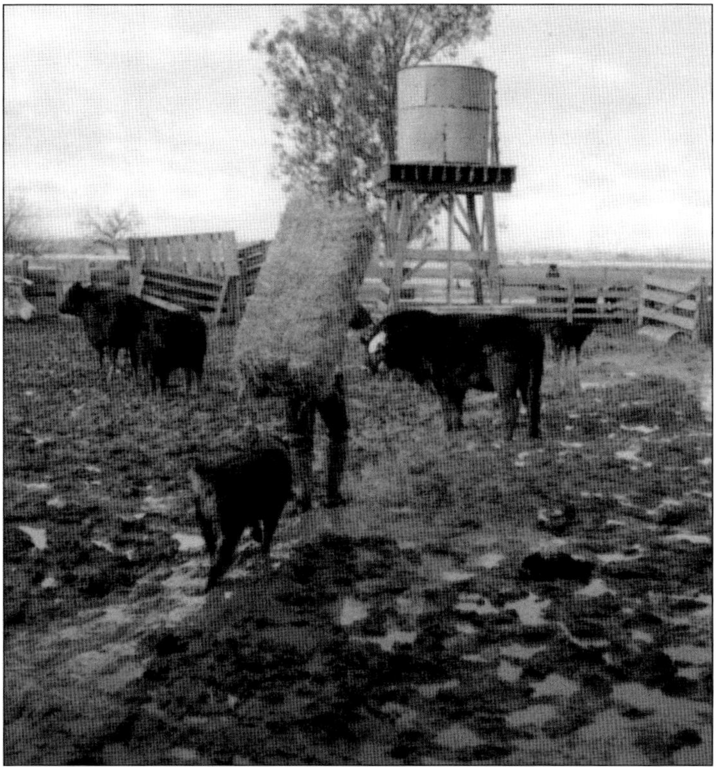

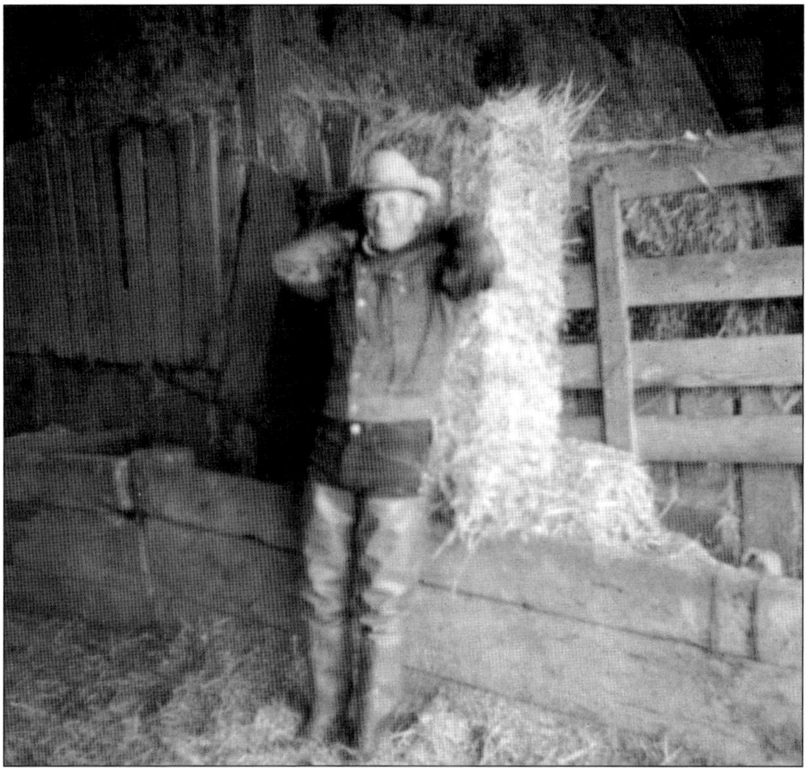

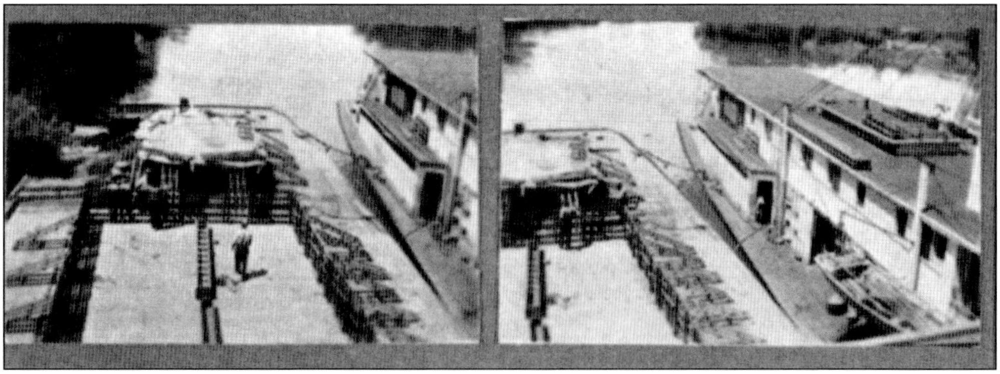

The Butte City Ranch raised registered Berkshire hogs while P.R. Cox bred Poland Chinas. The hogs foraged for food along the wood and brush in the river bottom along the Sacramento River. In the fall of the year, the hogs were fattened on Indian and Egyptian corn in order to be market ready. The hogs were shipped on boats and barges to the stockyard in San Francisco. The market price was generally higher there than anywhere else in the country. The pens were readied in advance, with the water troughs full. (Both, W.S. Guilford.)

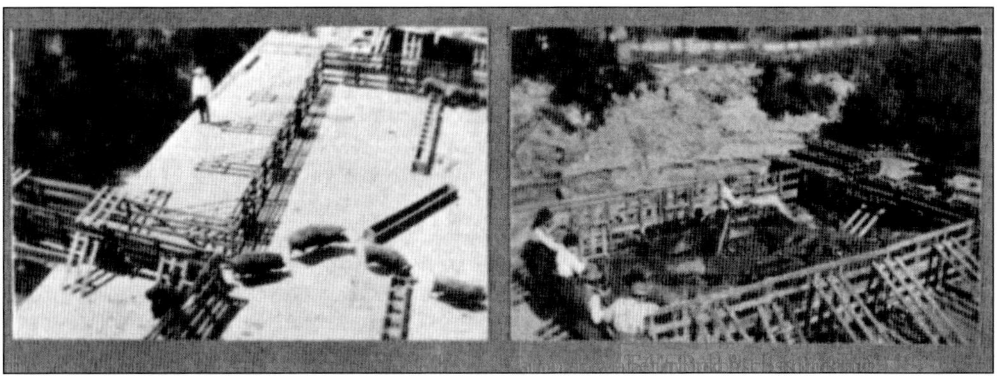

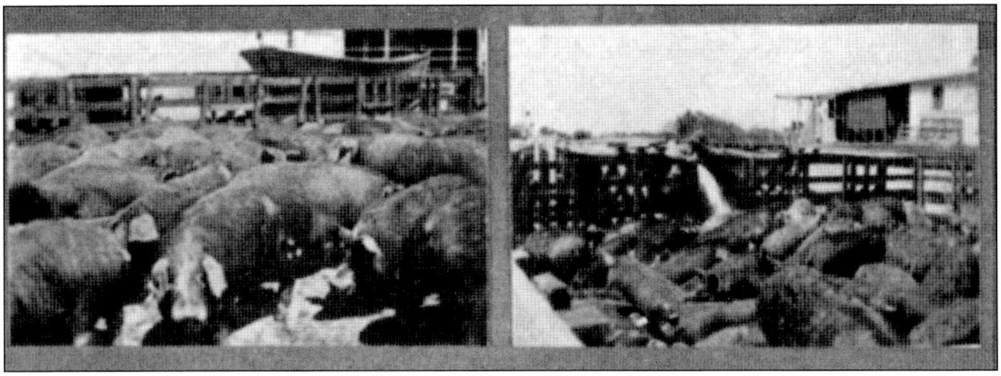

Many hogs were shipped on boats and barges because it was easy on the animal, loading was generally shaded, and it allowed the owner to accompany the shipment. Prior to loading, the hogs were wet down. If the hogs were too warm, care was taken to not put any water on their backs until they cooled down. The hogs were wet down frequently to keep them cool, and they were fed and watered in the same manner as at their pens at home. The pens on the barge were covered in heavy canvas to keep the sun off and the sides were left open for free circulation of air. If hogs were driven before being weighed at the shipping point, it might have been possible for them to arrive in San Francisco as heavy or heavier than at the point of loading. (Both, W.S. Guilford.)

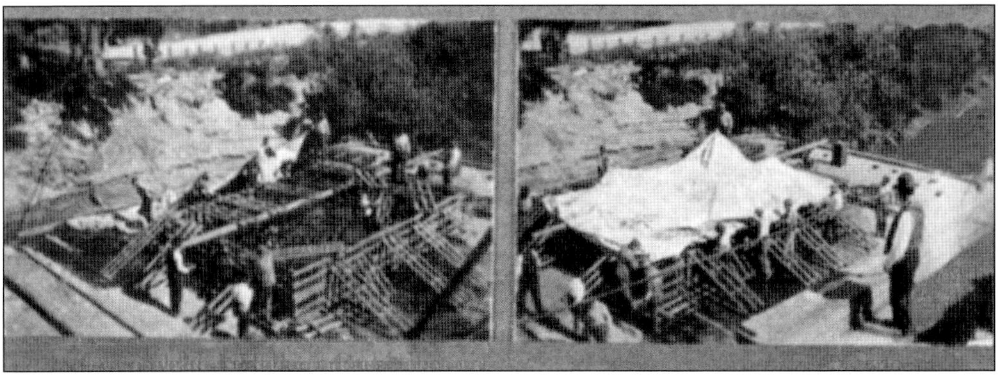

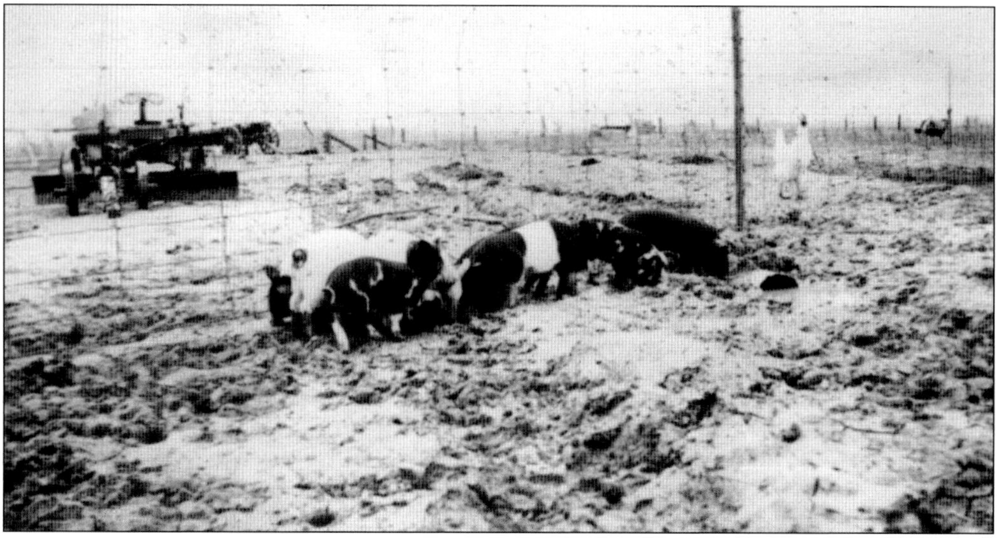

California hogs were often forced to forage for food on their own. Very few buildings were provided for them. The most abundant time for feed was after the grain was harvested in the summer, when they had the run of the stubble fields. These hogs were known as stubble hogs. Between 18 and 20 months of age, a stubble hog would make a weight of 150 to 175 pounds, which was considered market ready. (Diana Domingo.)

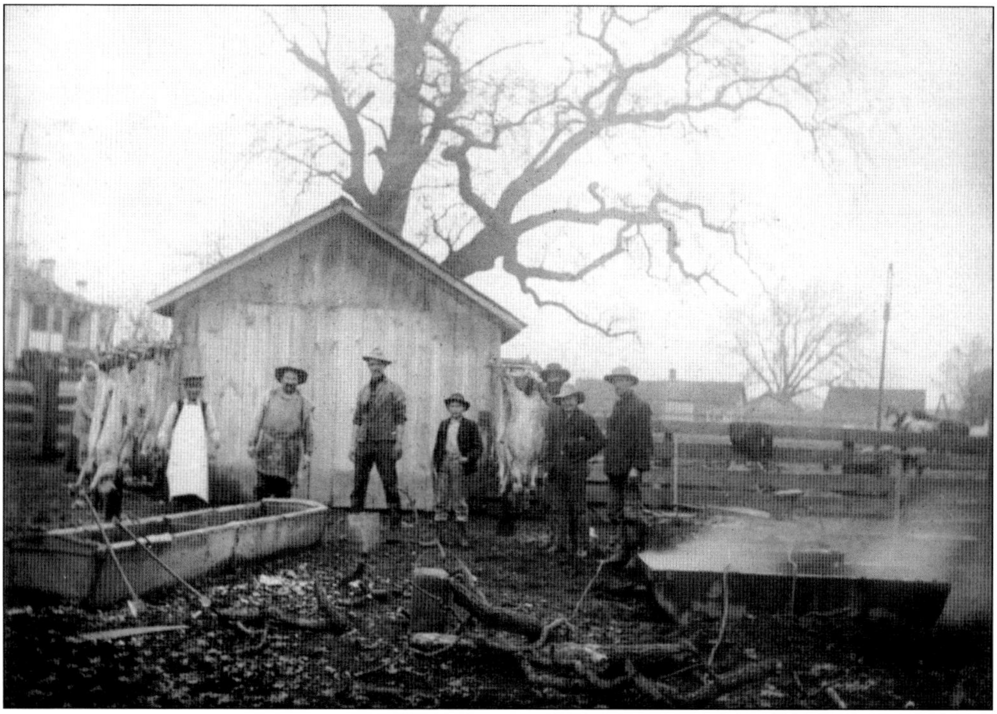

Hog-killing time was one of the big events of the year. The rancher would cure practically all of the meat used during the year, making home-cured hams, bacon, and sausages. Andrew James Lovejoy published a book that was commonplace on every hog farm. It gave practical hog-raising advice as well as recipes that could be easily used by every housewife. He advocated that farmers slaughter their own animals, which produced a better quality product than large producers. (Greg Steel.)

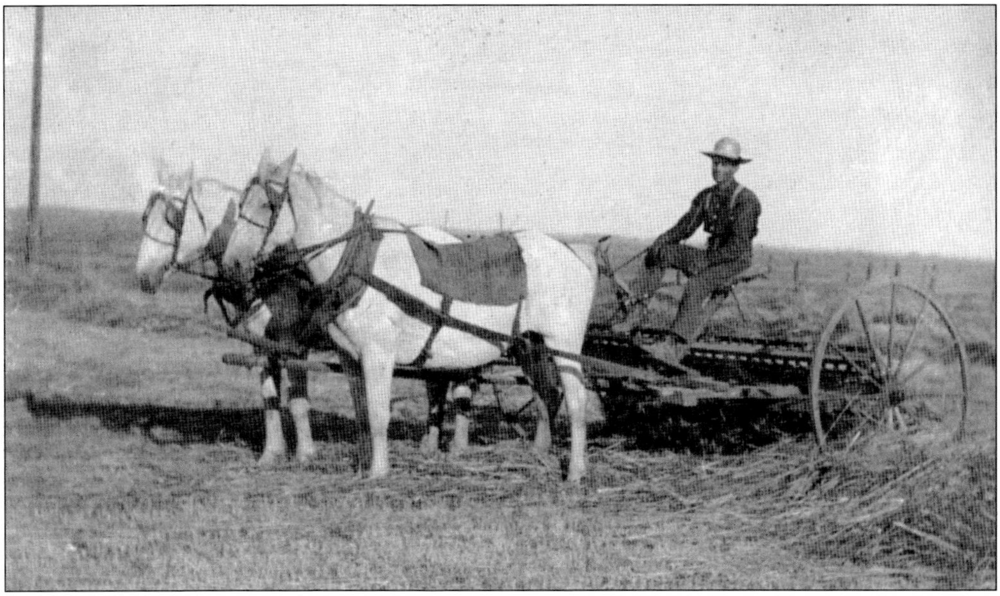

As long as farmers have been working the land and raising livestock, making hay has been one of agriculture's standard chores. In 1820, the first horse-drawn wooden rake was introduced, replacing the sickle (or scythe) and wooden rake (or fork). The rake hit a peak of popularity from 1835 to 1840. For the first time in agriculture's history, hay was not always made entirely by hand. (Greg Steel.)

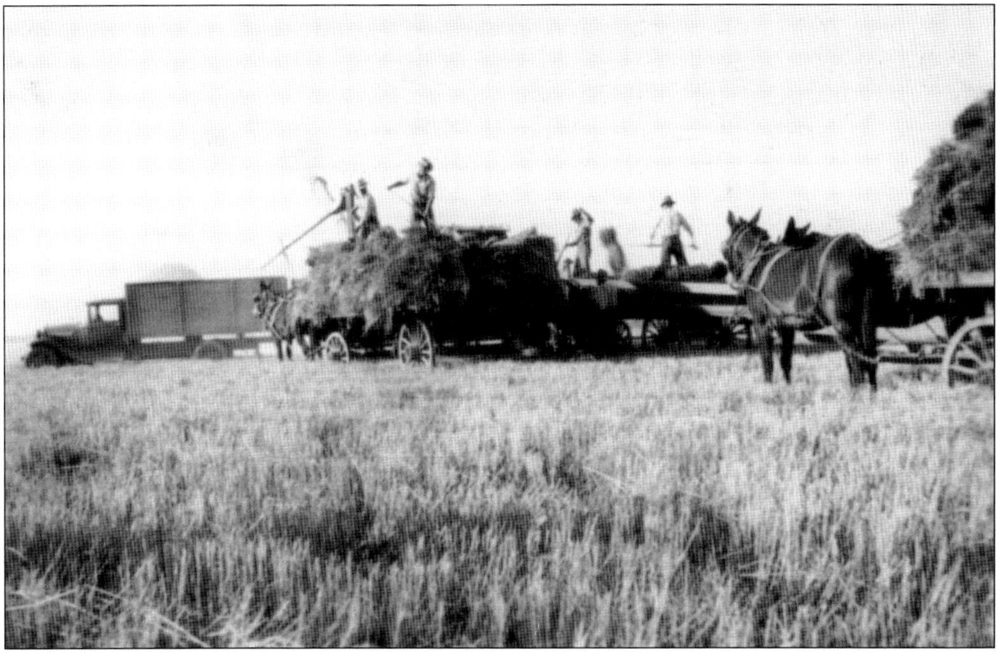

The cultivation of wheat and barley began in 1851, the year after Colusa County was started. As the need for grain for the freight teams that were hauling supplies to the mines increased, the acreage sown to grain increased very rapidly. By 1880, Glenn County produced two percent of all the wheat in the United States. A wheat harvest is depicted here on the Parrott grant in the early 1900s. (Diana Domingo.)

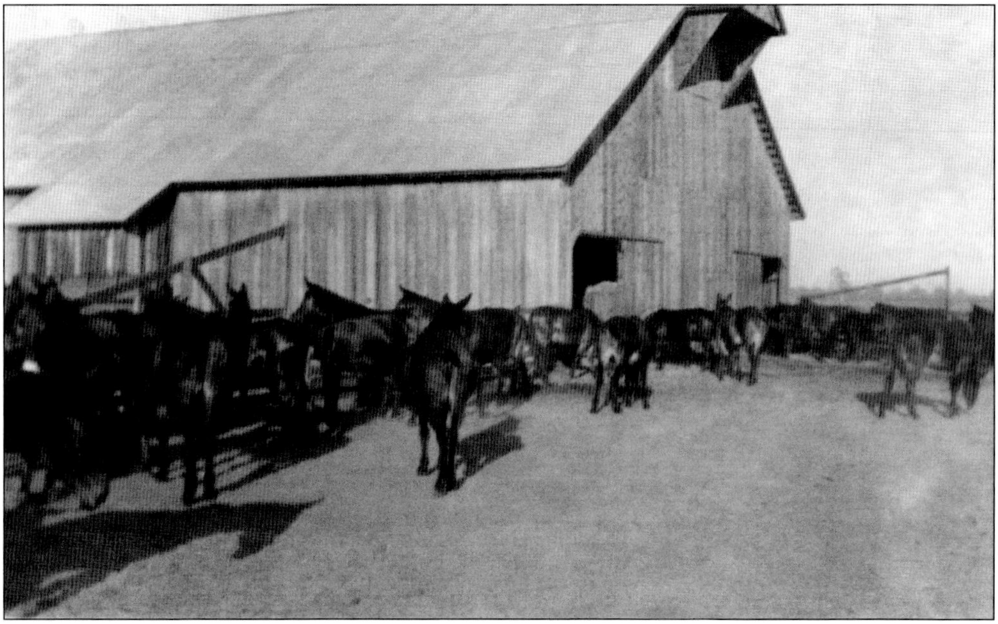

The raising and keeping of mules was an important role of early Glenn County residents. In 1879, the agriculture assessment recorded the population of mules as 3,089. If a farmer used 24 to 30 mules to pull a grain harvester and employed the use of two or three harvesters, this would equal no less than 72 mules that had to be kept and fed. Barns and pastures expressly for mules were common. (Greg Steel.)

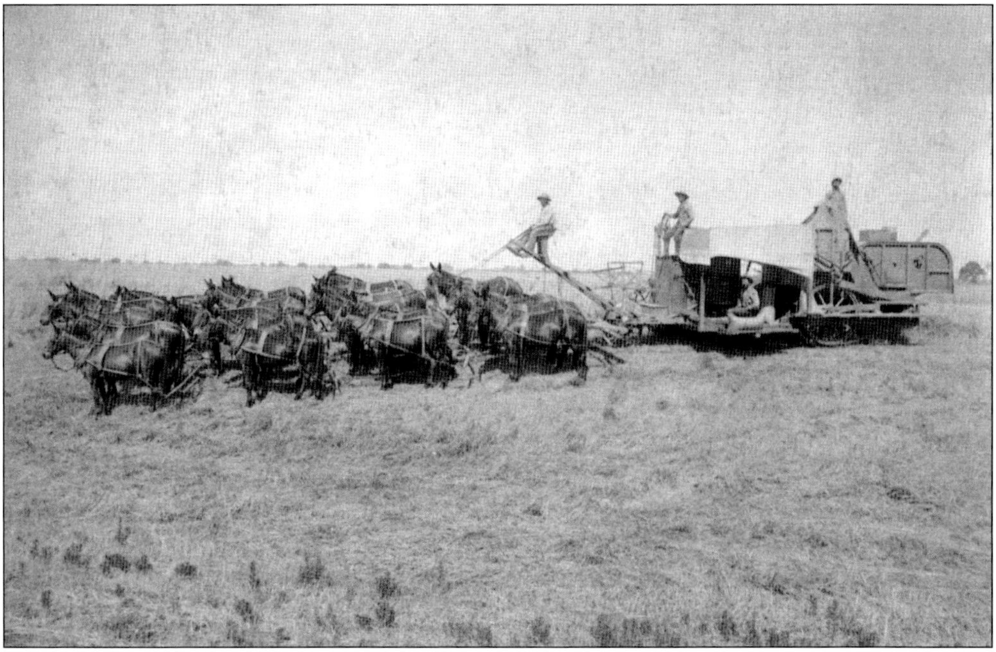

Combines cut the size of an average threshing crew from 21 to 22 men to just four or five. This harvest on the Steel Ranch near Butte City had a pilot, crew captain, teamster, and a sacker. Some pilots driving the teams used vocalization to prod the mules. Others used a long whip or small stones tossed at the collar of the slow-moving animal. (Greg Steel.)

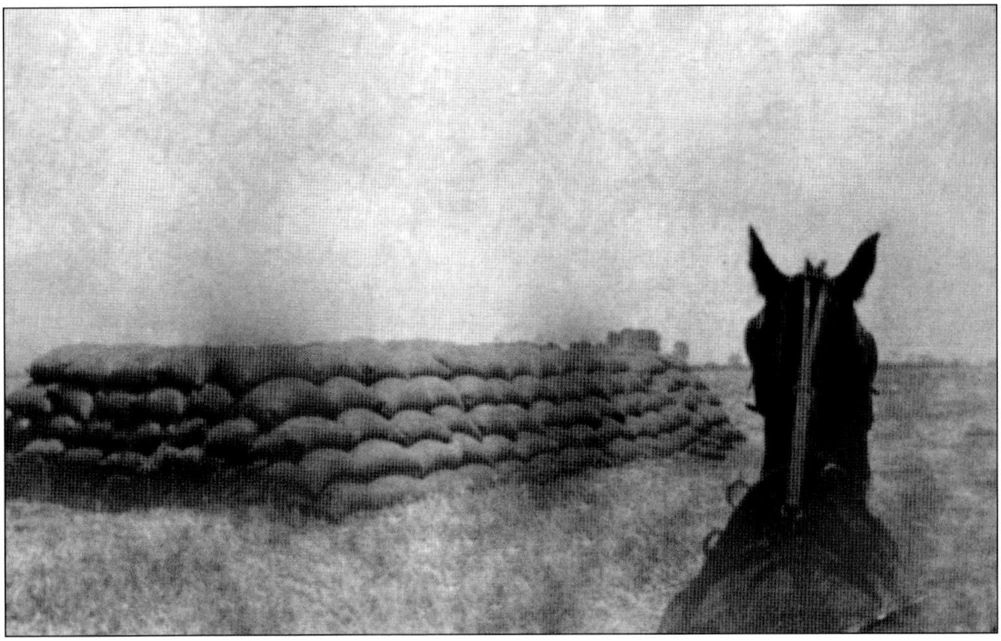

Although not commonly used in the East, the grain sack was necessary in the West. Eastern wheat farmers hauled their grain from the field using wagons that were "perfectly tight" and hauled directly to the point of shipment, usually railcars. In the West, each sack had to be handled many times before it reached the port to be shipped to the European market. (Greg Steel.)

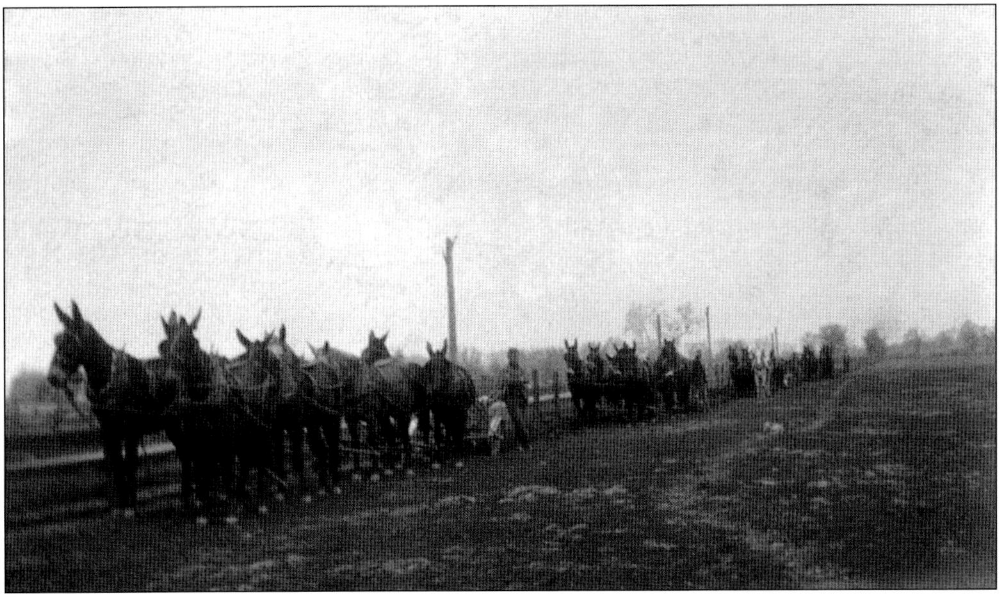

In the days of mule power, a large part of the land that should have been in cultivation was left untouched. If rains were late in the year, the mule and plow may not have been able to cultivate the whole acreage. Statistics given by the *Pacific Rural Press* in 1916 show that 25 percent of all the cultivated land in the United States was used to feed working animals. Prior to pausing for this picture, four teams of six mules pulling gangplows had made one pass on this Butte City ranch. (Greg Steel.)

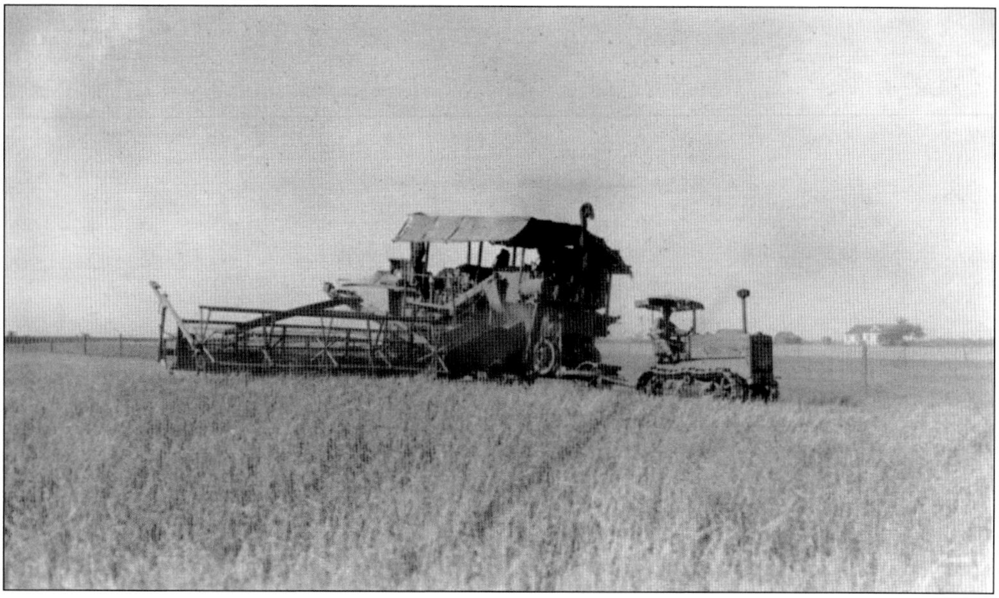

Benjamin Holt founded the Holt Manufacturing Company of Stockton, California. He was aware of "crawler" tractors powered by steam and saw their use in the soft soils of the San Joaquin Valley. Holt's first version was tested in 1904. The story of the name is that Holt's photographer Charlie Clements saw the motion of the track undulating and exclaimed that the machine crawled like a caterpillar. In 1906, gasoline-powered internal combustion engines replaced the steam versions. The C.L. Best Company began producing crawler tractors in 1912, but since Holt had patented the term "Caterpillar," they were considered "Tracklayers." As combines on the Steel Ranch became larger and more efficient, it was necessary to utilize the added horsepower and speed of a crawler. (Both, Greg Steel.)

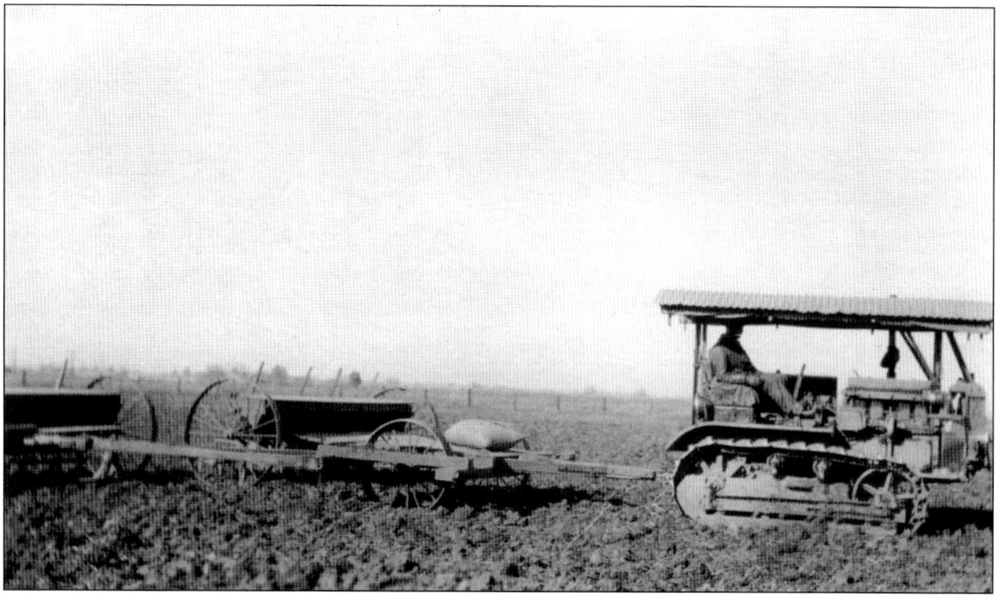

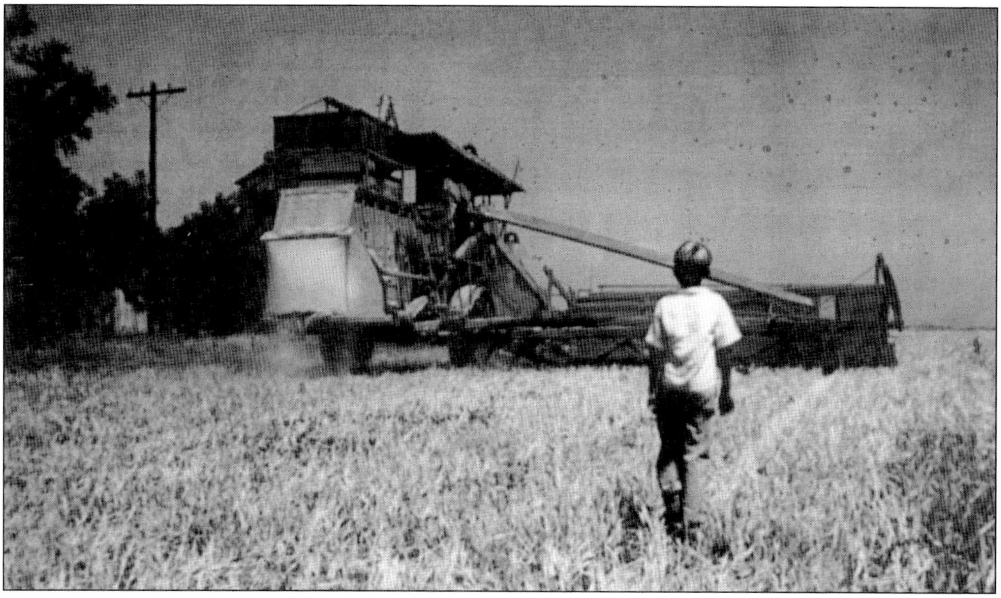

From sustenance to large production, the agrarian lifestyle has always been family oriented. The school year was built around harvest time, and not all children were able to attend school because of their farm chores and the distance to school. Here Greg Steel is relaying a message to the wheat combine operator on the Steel Ranch in Butte City in the 1950s. (Greg Steel.)

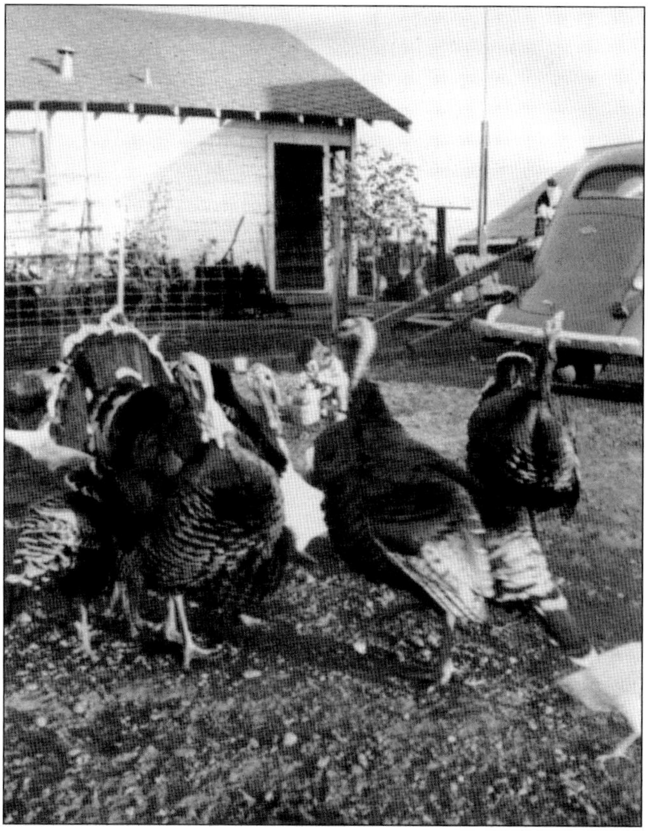

Glenn County had a thriving turkey industry from the late 1800s to the early 1900s. The outstanding weather and an increasing market allowed small farmers to increase their flock sizes and become competitive in the market. Turkey raising was a business that women and children could specialize in and make money. Prior to the Great Depression, it was not unusual for growers to receive 45¢ a pound; however, the prices soon dropped to below 13¢ a pound. (Diana Domingo.)

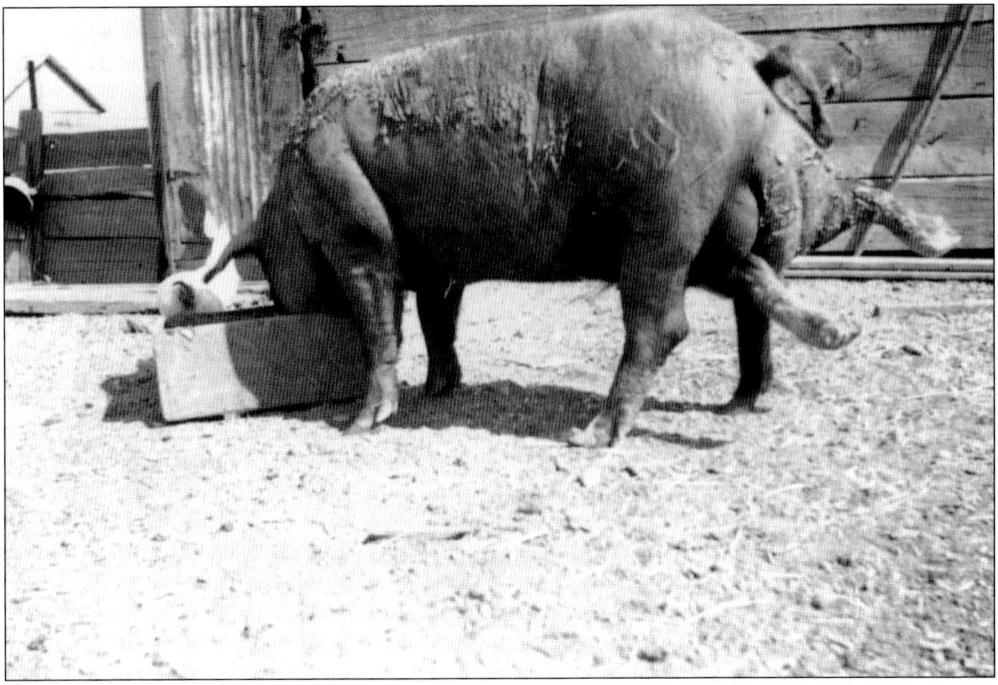

The 1937 Butte County Spring Fair and Fiesta had in its billing a "freak pig." The *Chico Daily Enterprise* advertised that one of the principal attractions was a freak pig raised at Butte City and brought to the fair by its owners, Arthur Wadsworth and his wife. "It has six legs, is fully formed, and is billed as the pig with four hams." (Diana Domingo.)

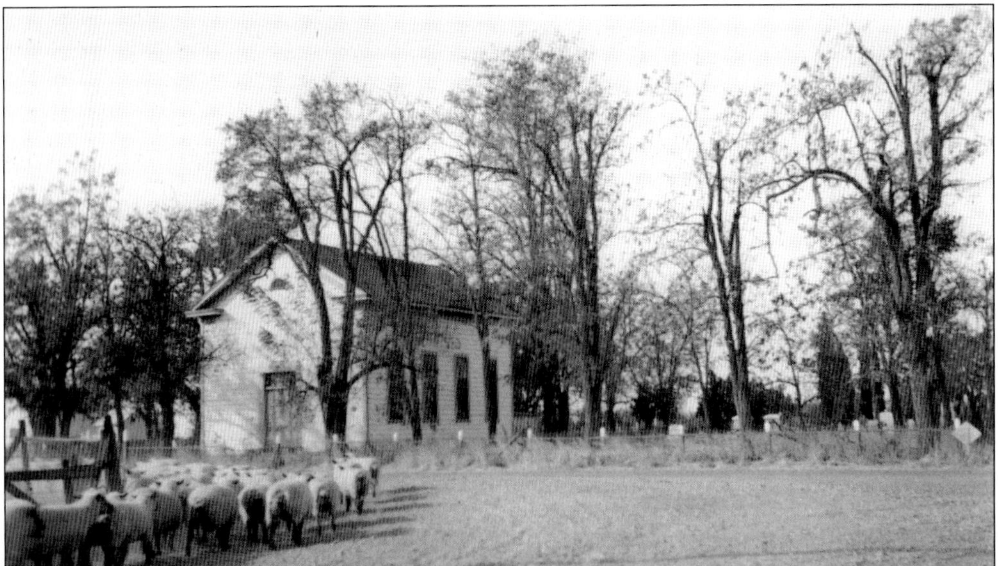

In order to find better grazing, sheep are being driven down the road toward Marvin Chapel in Afton. The pioneers of Afton decided that they needed a permanent place of worship around 1874. Afton pioneer Elijah McDaniel wrote that Bishop Enoch Mather Marvin came from San Francisco to help the congregation make its decision. The camp meeting was such a success that it was decided to name the church Marvin Chapel. (Greg Steel.)

Children on the ranches were expected to carry their own weight and had daily chores. As pictured here, they were often in charge of taking care of the babies, bucket calves or bummer lambs. George Wadsworth does not look pleased with one of his summer chores, bottle-feeding a young lamb around 1916. (Diana Domingo.)

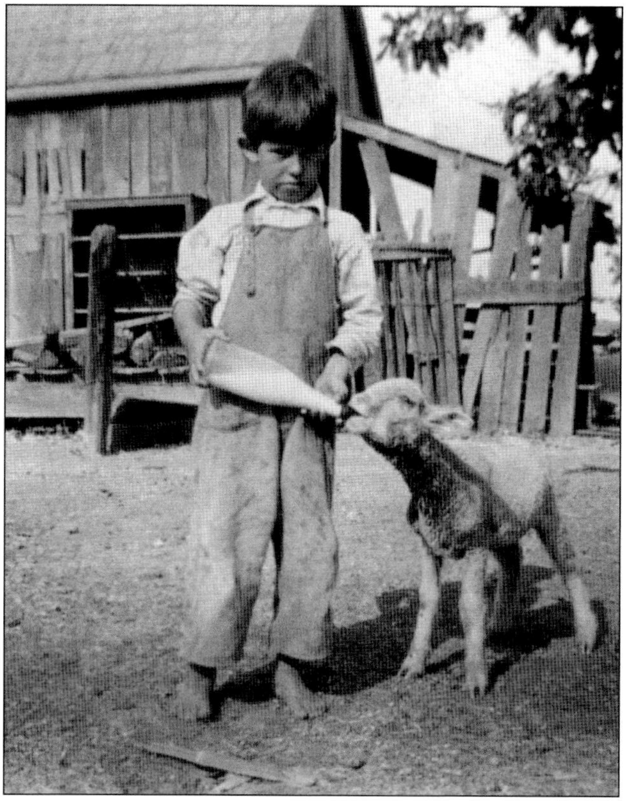

Many times, those daily chores involved some fun time as well. One of the Steel boys is pictured here diligently milking his cow while his brother sits atop another. (Greg Steel.)

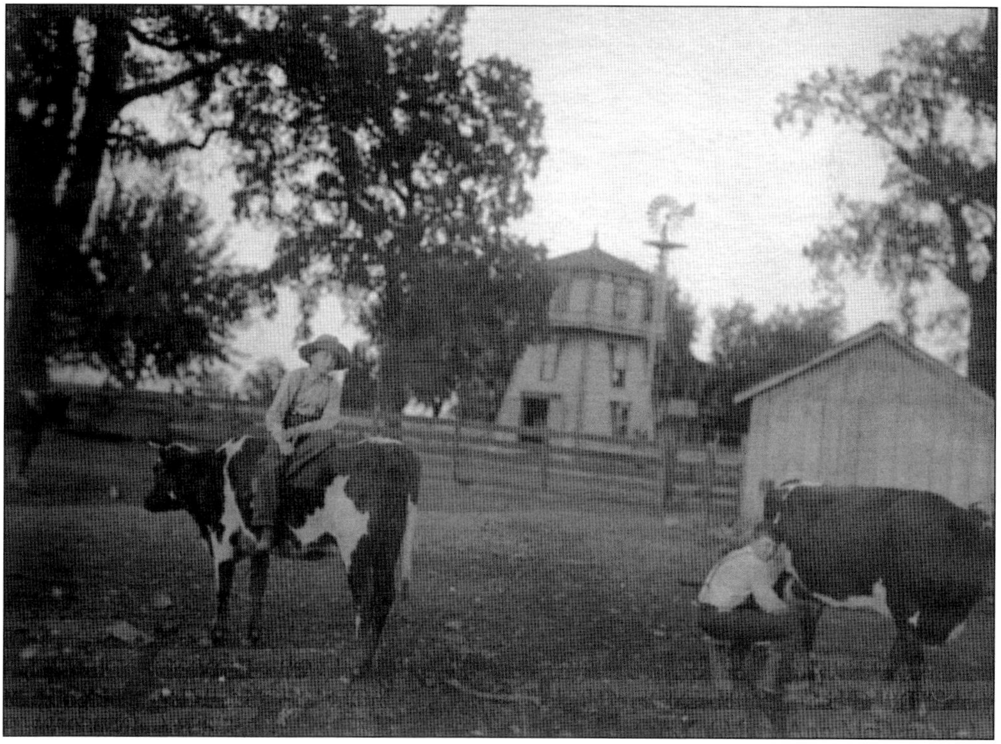

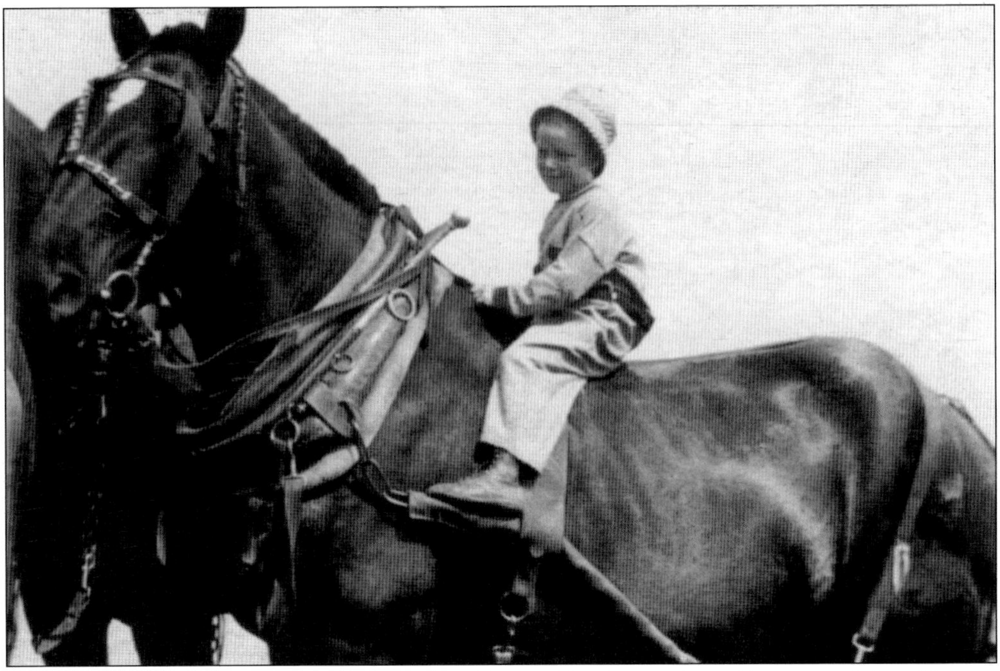

According to the assessment work of W.T. Beville in 1879, the number of horses in Colusa County was 7,280 and the number of people was 15,000. Horses were obviously an important part of every person's life. The advent of steam engines and the automobile put the working-horse population on a decline. Here, Butte City resident George Wadsworth is becoming acquainted early with the use of the horse. (Diana Domingo.)

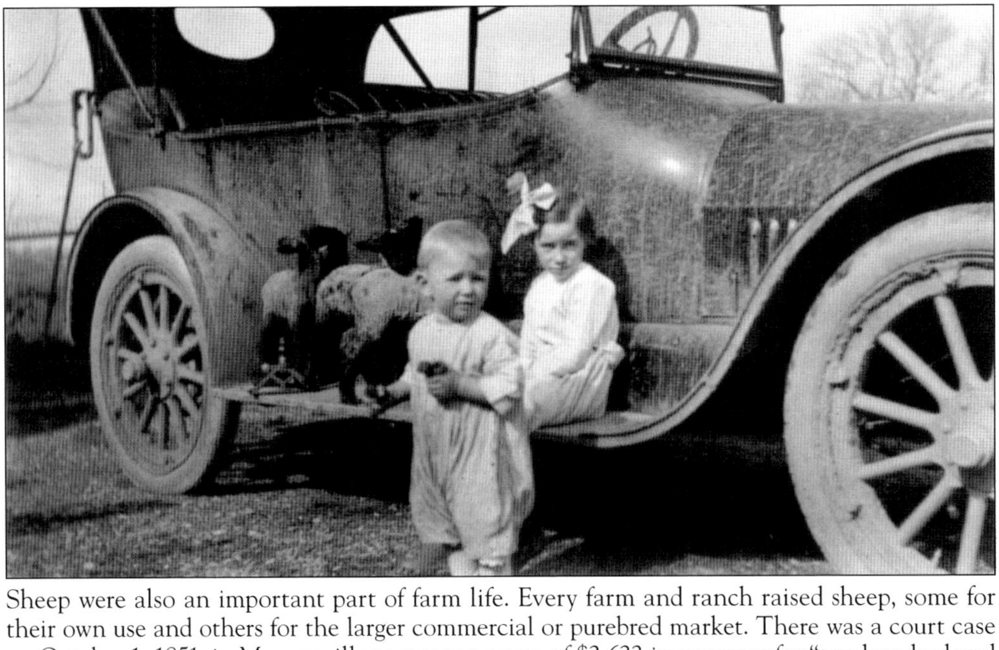

Sheep were also an important part of farm life. Every farm and ranch raised sheep, some for their own use and others for the larger commercial or purebred market. There was a court case on October 1, 1851, in Monroeville to recover a sum of $2,622 in payment for "one hundred and fifteen fat sheep." In Butte City, Collis and Catherine Steel are waiting with three lambs on the running board of the family's Buick. (Greg Steel.)

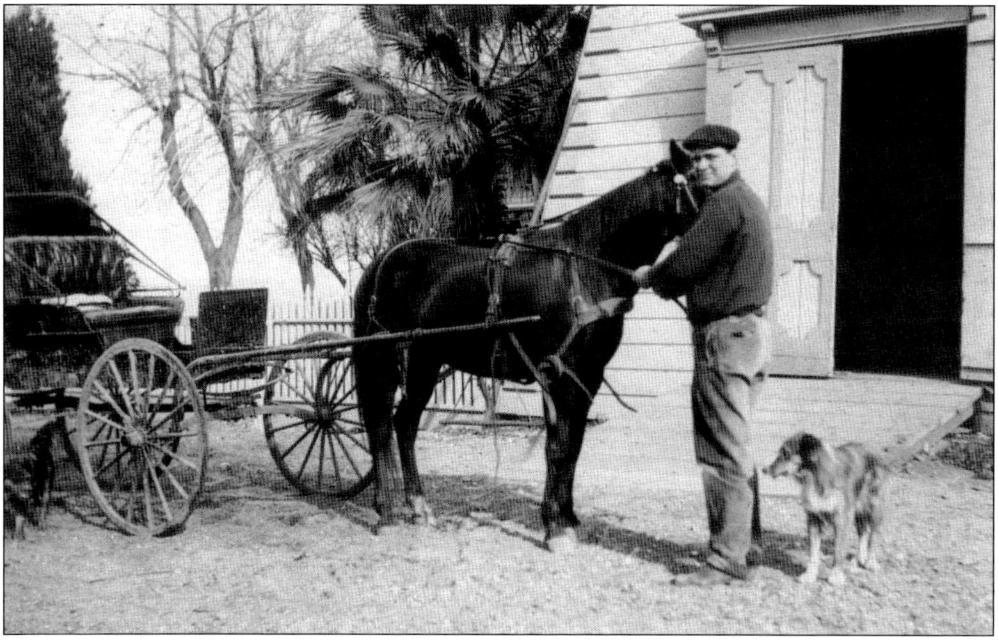

The carriage and horse are being readied for a trip to town from the Steel Ranch in Afton. They would have to take the Butte City ferry to travel to Princeton. A carriage like this could have been purchased complete with shafts and a three-quarters leather top for $68 from Sears, Roebuck and Co. in 1894. It appears that the carriage and horse are the same in both photographs. (Both, Greg Steel.)

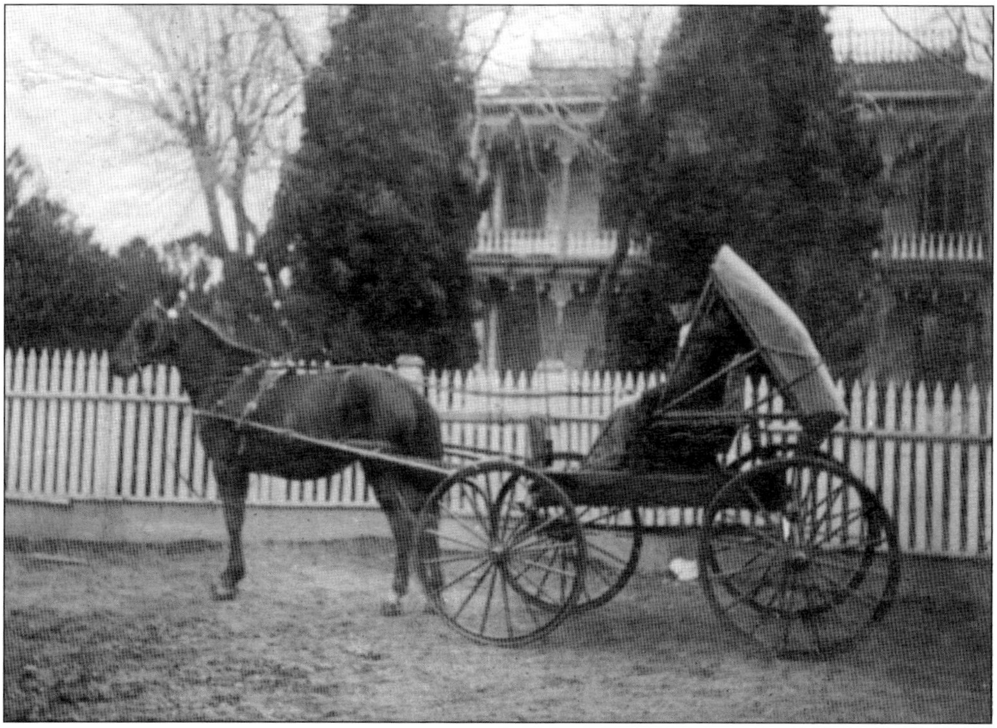

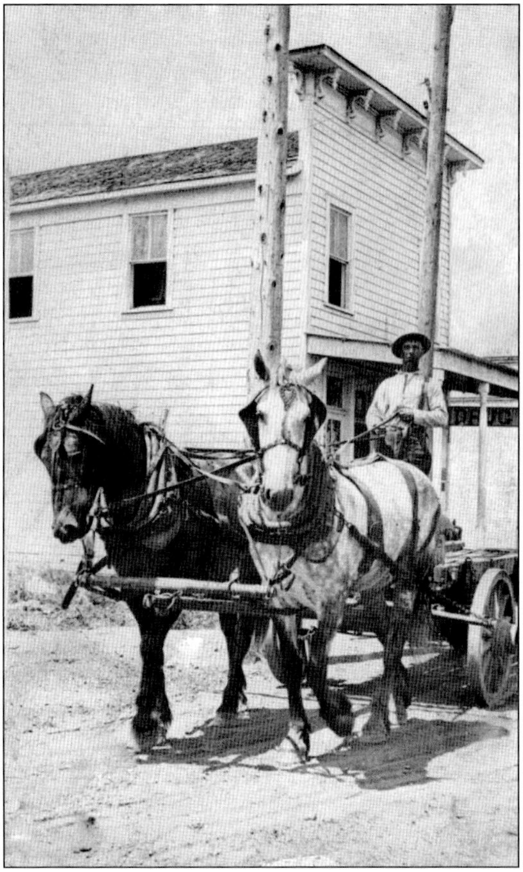

Arthur Wadsworth, originally from England, drives a pair of draft horses in front of M. Bills Drug Store in Butte City. The wagon and draft team would indicate that Arthur is heading to the river to pick up a load of freight. The heavy collars, which are a part of the horses' harness, allowed the horses to exert their full strength while pulling the freight wagon. (Diana Domingo.)

Many of the ranching families had similar carriages for transportation purposes. While they would have used a wagon to carry supplies to and from town, a carriage was used for social visits and family outings. The Wadsworth family (from left to right), Etta, George, and Arthur, lived and ranched on the plains east of the Sacramento River and north of Butte City. (Diana Domingo.)

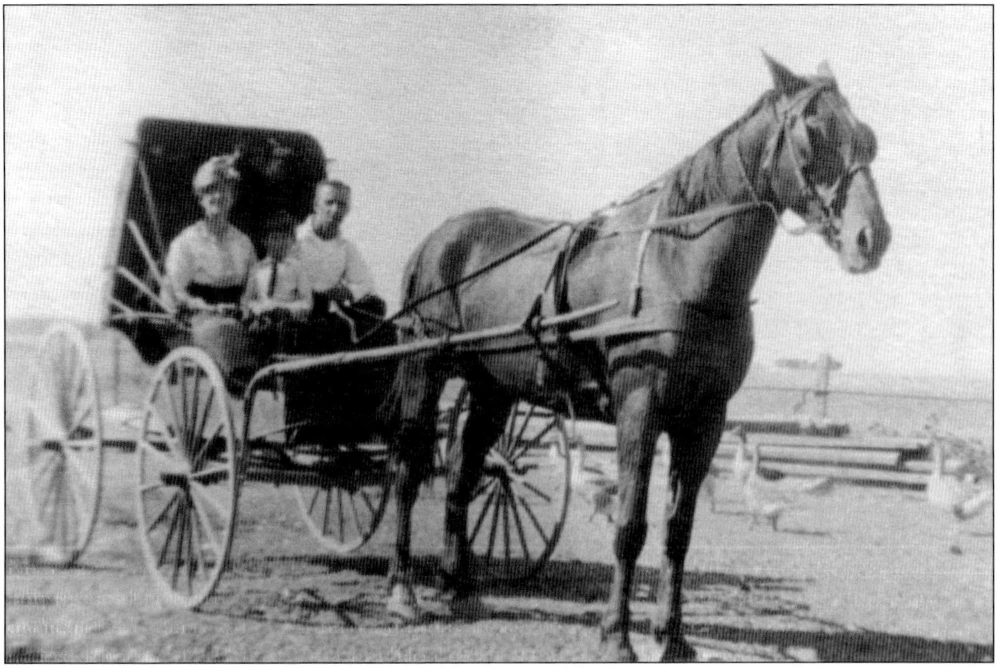

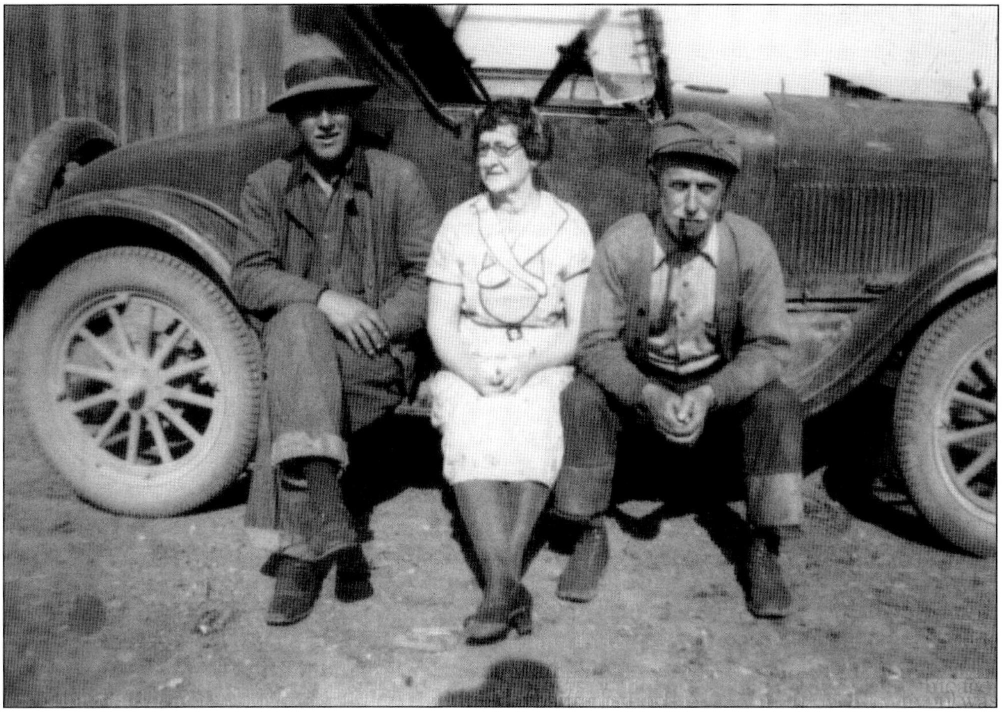

As time progressed, most farmers and ranchers sought to buy an automobile. The roads had very little gravel. They were dusty in the summer and muddy in the winter, but most people found the automobile to be worth the trouble. It did not consume hay like a horse, and fuel was affordable. From left to right, George, Etta, and Arthur Wadsworth enjoy a moment with the camera on the running board of their automobile. (Diana Domingo.)

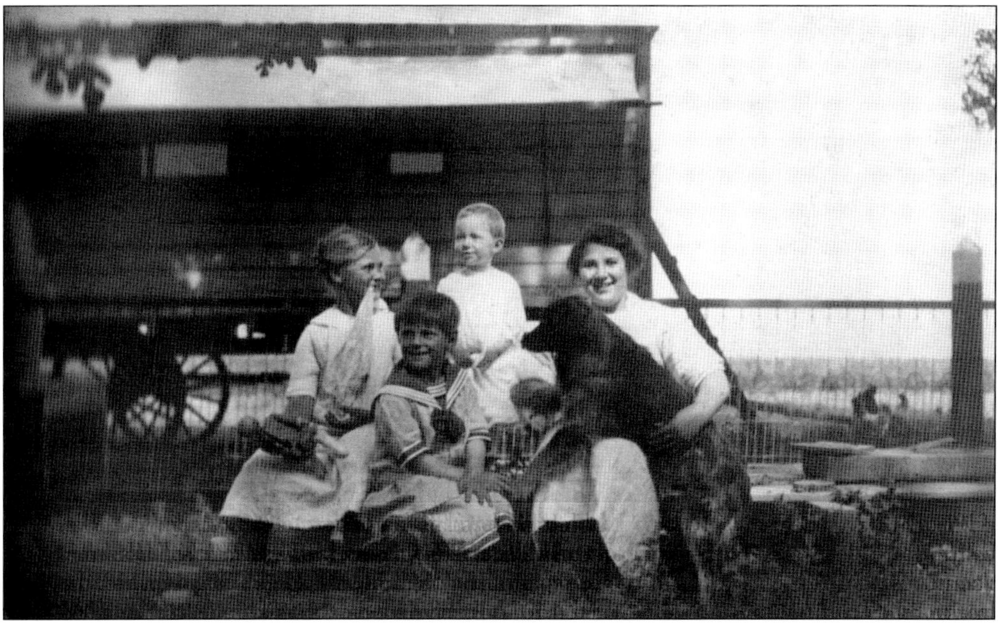

The children of Catherine M. Picknell Bound find time to play for the camera. From left to right are Alice, Stanley, Sara, and Cora. Note the cook wagon behind the children. (Greg Steel.)

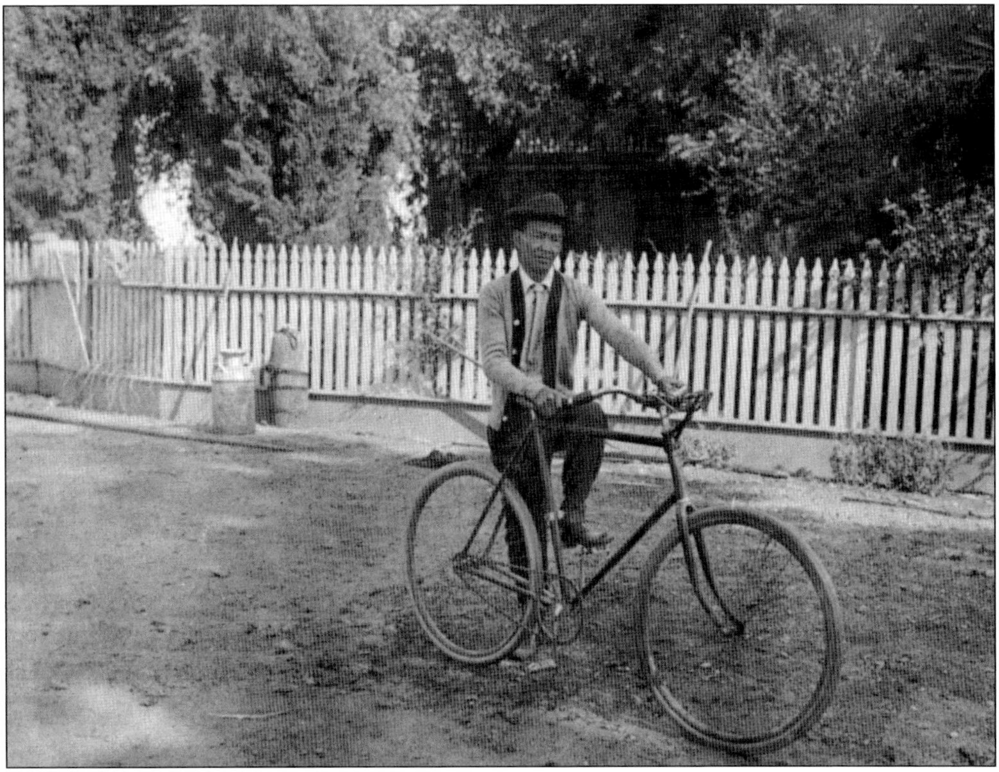

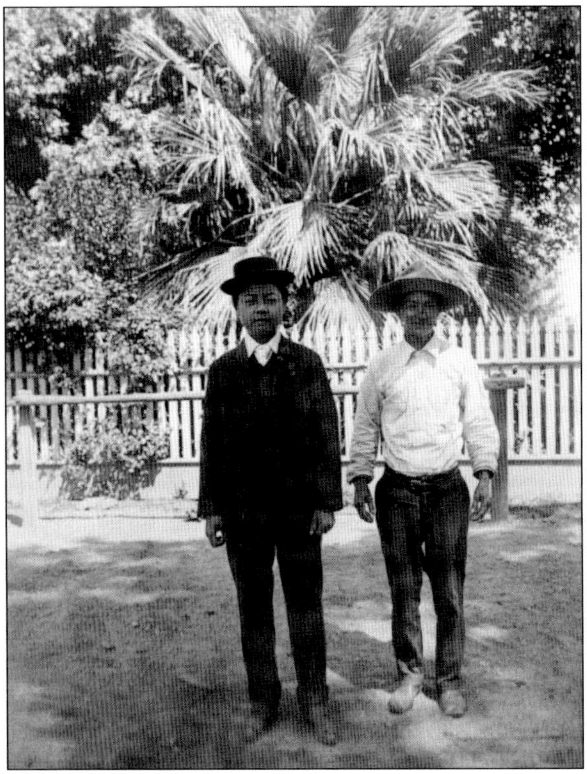

Chinese began to immigrate to California during the Gold Rush. They were hardworking, industrious, and humble. The magnates of the Central Pacific Railroad recognized these qualities and hired Chinese workers to build the railroad over the summit of the Sierras. Upon completion of the railroad, many of these same people turned to agriculture labor as their next industry. The 1870 Census of Colusa County gave the population as 5,088. This number included 271 Chinese and 424 Indians. They found employment on many of the farms and ranches both in the fields and as domestic help, serving as laundrymen, gardeners, and cooks. Each valley town had a Chinatown during the 1800s. Dr. Hugh Glenn was admonished for being an employer of Chinese, but he maintained that they were hard-working and trustworthy laborers. (Both, Greg Steel.)

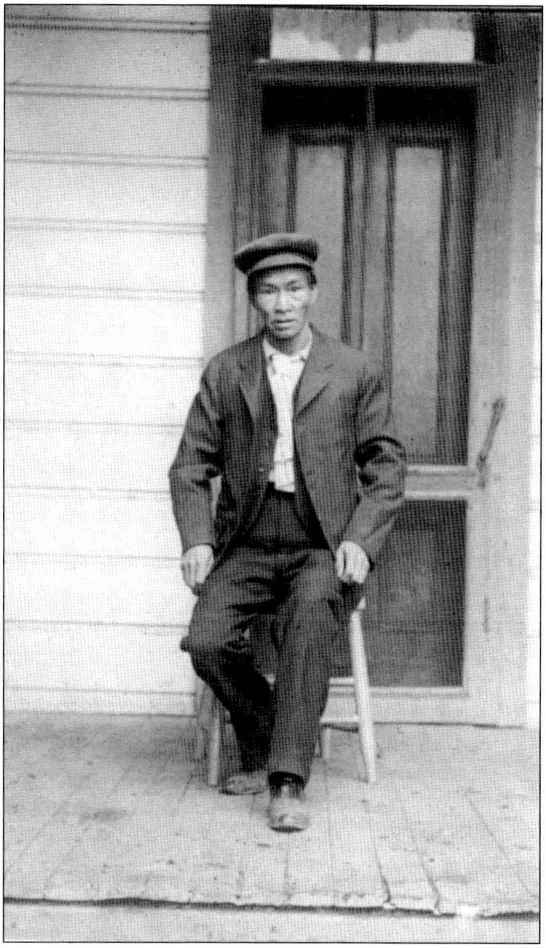

Many of the Chinese cooks were considered parts of the families. A popular cook for the foothill ranches was known as Chiney Sam. He worked for the Butlers, Neilsons, Pattons, and Julians, to name a few. Dr. Hugh Glenn employed Chinese workers to tend his fruit and vegetable gardens along the river and to work during wheat harvest. John Bidwell also hired them to work on his ranch. By the 1870s, prejudices against Chinese laborers began to grow. Many communities that once had employed them now formed anti-Chinese societies. The Chinese Exclusion Act of 1882 became the first major law restricting immigration to the United States. (Both, Greg Steel.)

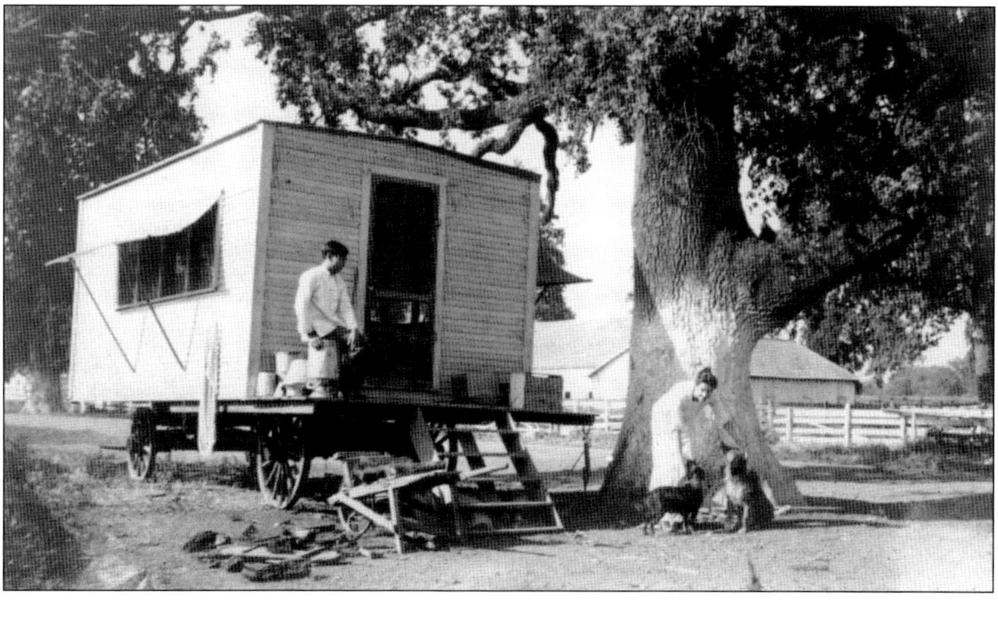

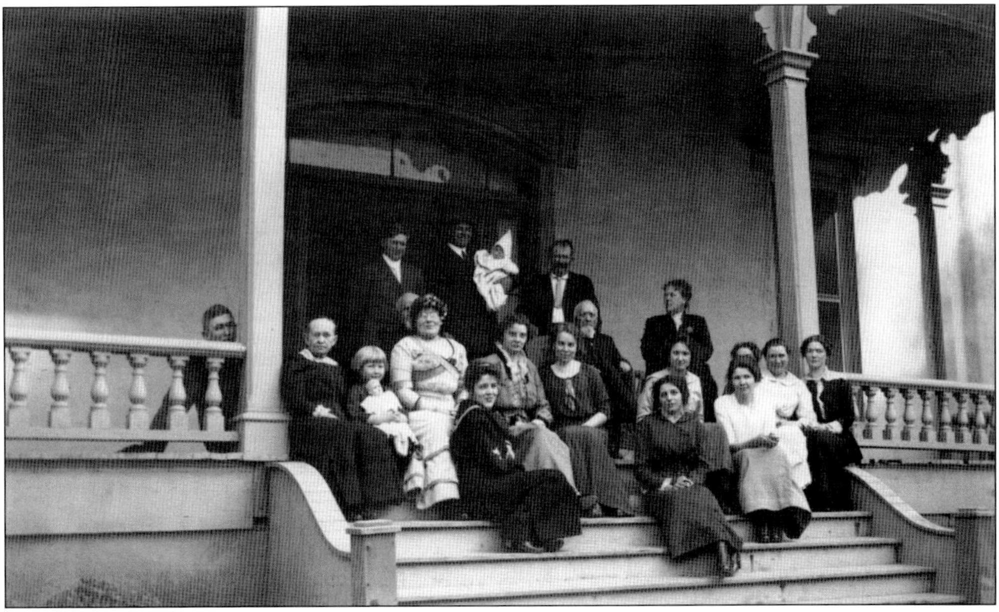

Frank Steel settled on the east side of the Sacramento River in 1853. Samuel Picknell came to the area around the same time. The Steel and Picknell families intermarried and had two beautiful homes in the area. The two families are pictured here at a holiday gathering in February 1915. (Greg Steel.)

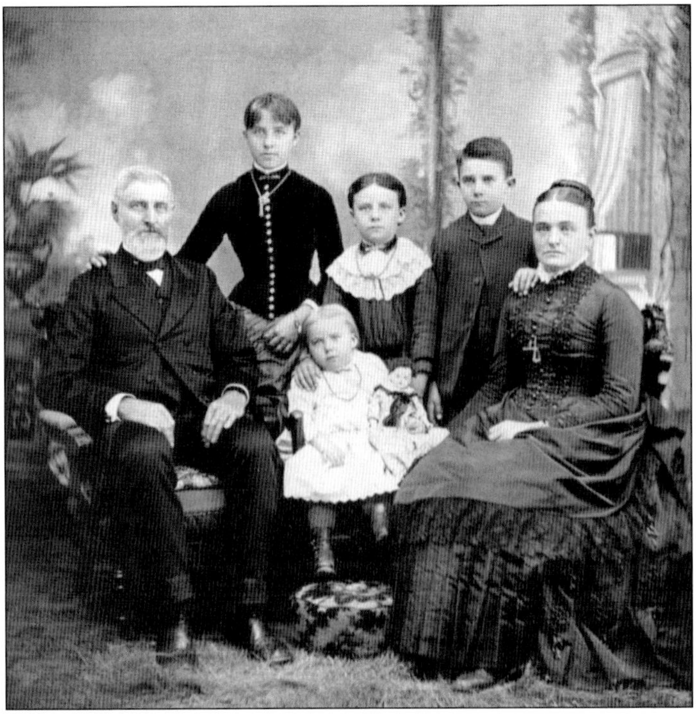

The marriage of Catherine Picknell and Joseph Bounds was a matter of convenience, according to family history. Bounds had been Samuel Picknell's partner in the Butte City ferry and other enterprises. Pictured here, from left to right, are (seated) Joseph Bounds, Sara Bounds, and Catherine Picknell Bounds; (standing) Cora Bounds, Alice Bounds, and Stanley Bounds. (Greg Steel.)

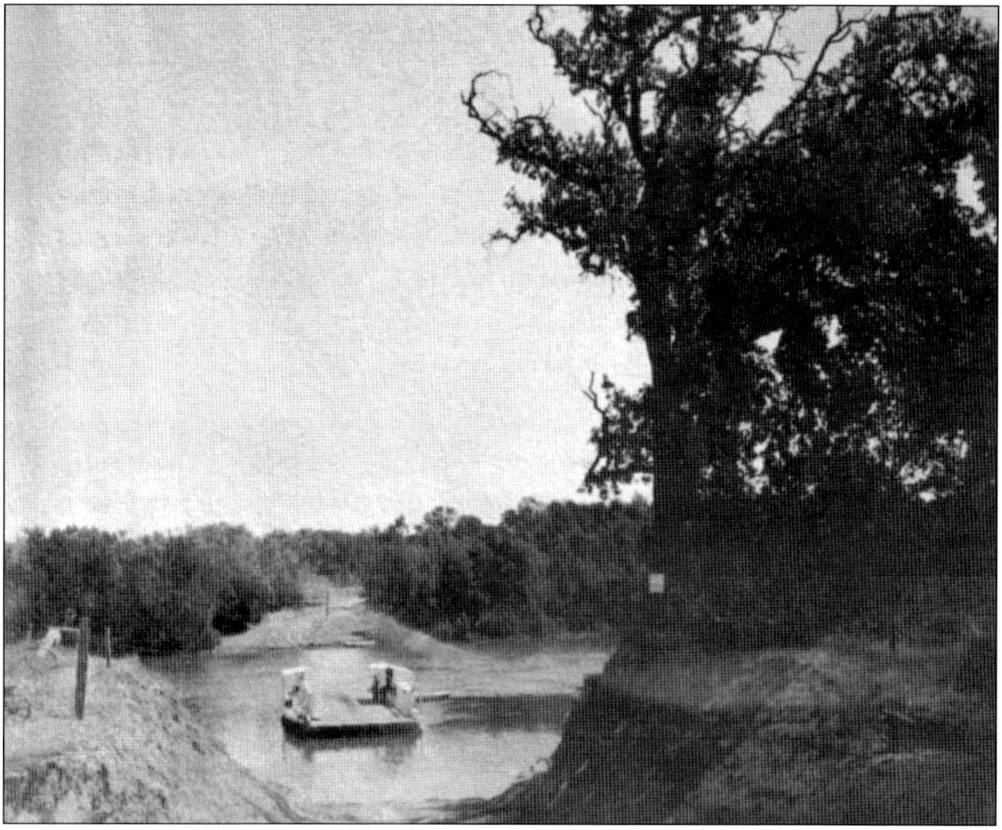

The Ord Ferry was built in May 1914. Because the ferry had no engine, it was controlled by attachment to a cable and the current of the river. The first ferryman was Jim Ryan, the second Frank Deck, and the third Joe Scharsch, who operated the ferry for 24 years. This picture was taken from the Glenn County side. (*Wagon Wheels*, February 1961.)

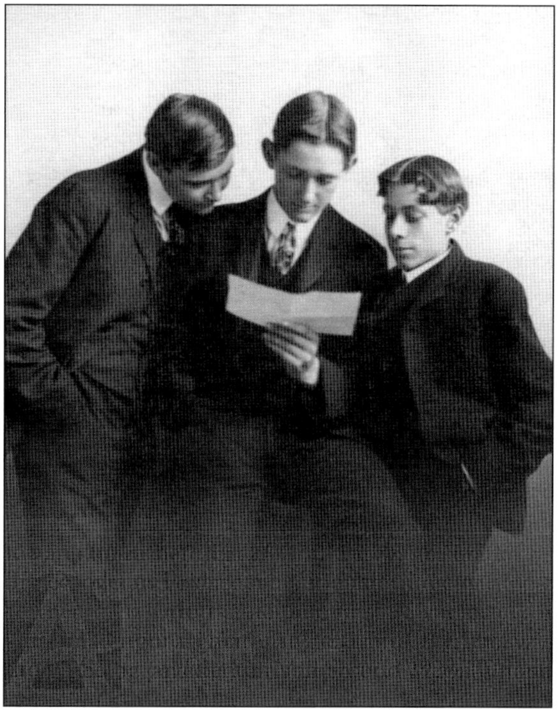

From left to right, Edward, Walter, and Oscar Steel posed to reflect their intelligence and mischievousness on this cabinet card from the early 1900s. Both Walter and Oscar married and remained in the Butte City area. They each ran farms, and Oscar became president of the bank in Princeton. According to the 1920 and 1930 US federal censuses, Edward, a landscape artist, lived in Alameda with his mother and farmed fruit. (Greg Steel.)

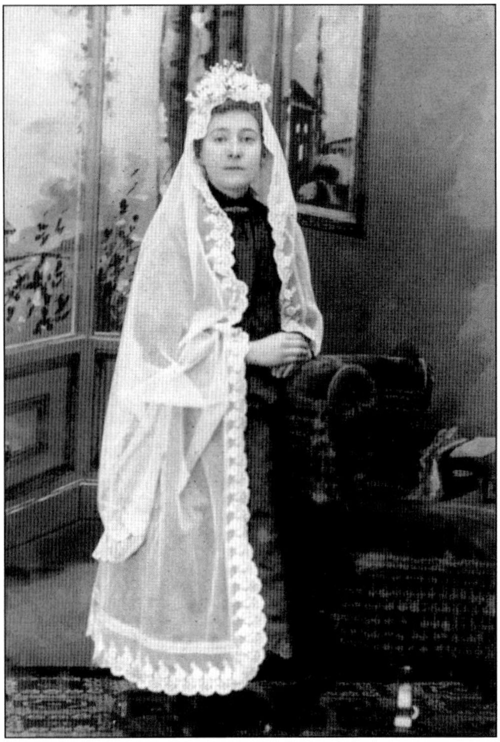

This cabinet card from the late 1880s shows Etta Elicia Kenrick in her communion dress and veil. She was born on June 3, 1877, in Butte City, California, to parents who had immigrated to the United States from Ireland in 1867. She remained in Butte City most of her life and married Arthur Wadsworth in October 1907. They raised one son, George. (Diana Domingo.)

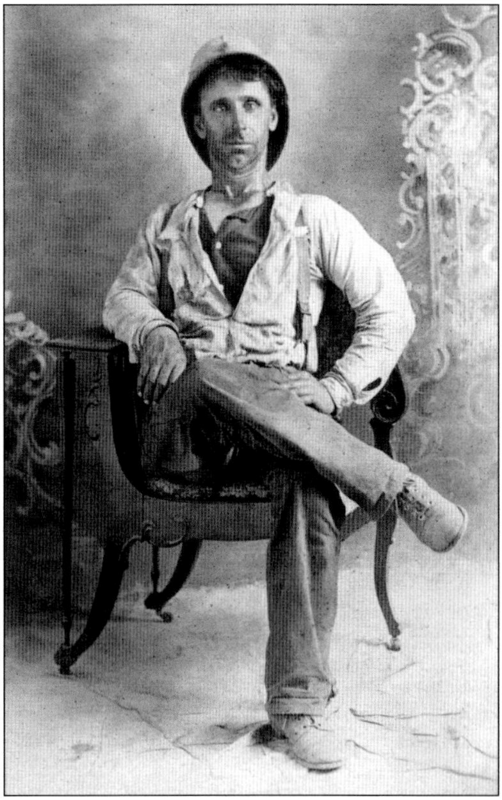

Arthur Wadsworth was born on November 7, 1876, in England. He came to the United States at the age of 10. By 1900, he had become a farm laborer in Butte City. He married Etta Elicia Kenrick in October 1907. Arthur and Etta had one son, George, in 1910. The family ranched in Butte City for over 60 years. It appears that Arthur Wadsworth is enjoying having his picture taken in the 1890s. (Diana Domingo.)

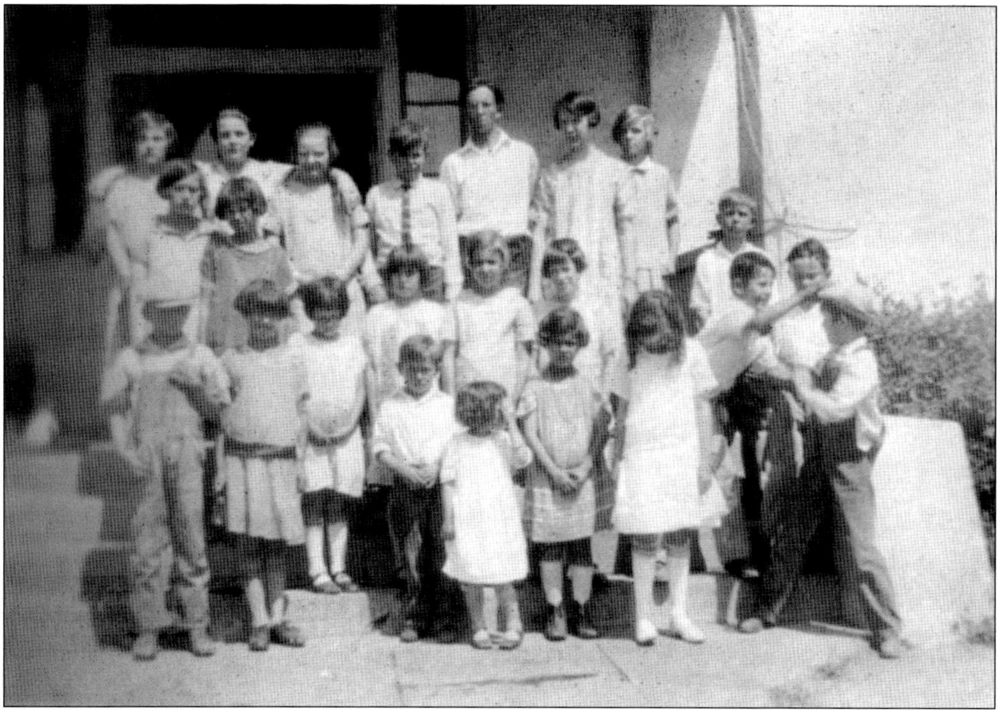

The Union School was the first school established on the east side of the Sacramento River in 1862. According to "Early Schools of Glenn County" published in the spring 1994 *Wagon Wheels*, the original school site was "between the grocery store and the Eastern Star building" in Afton. The school pictured here in 1925 was located north and east of that location. The Union School became one of the five schools in the Princeton Joint Union District. It closed at the end of the 1962 school year after 100 years of service to area children. (Both, Greg Steel.)

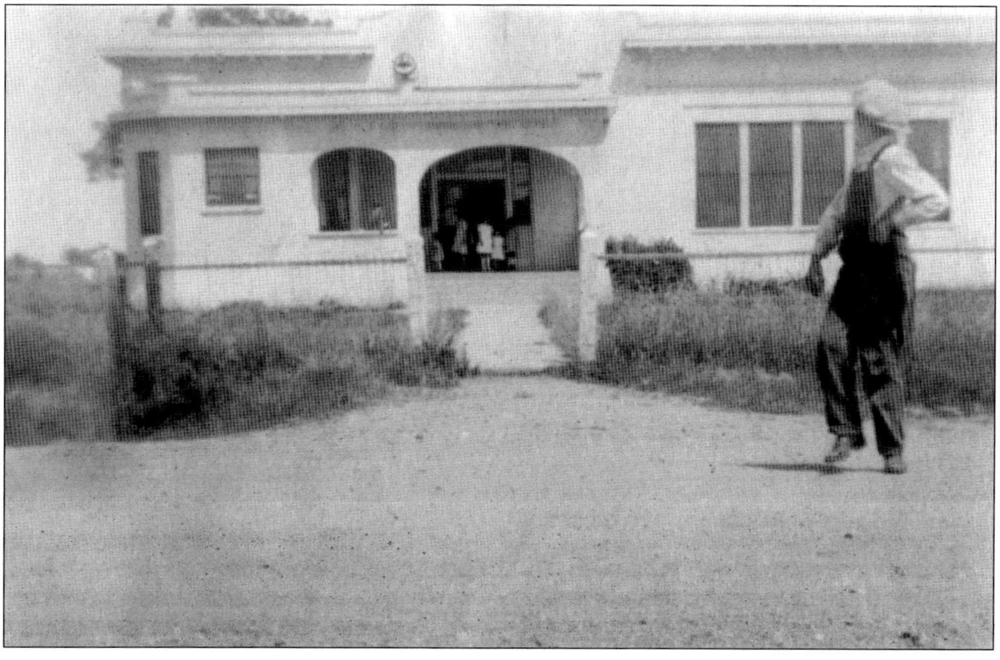

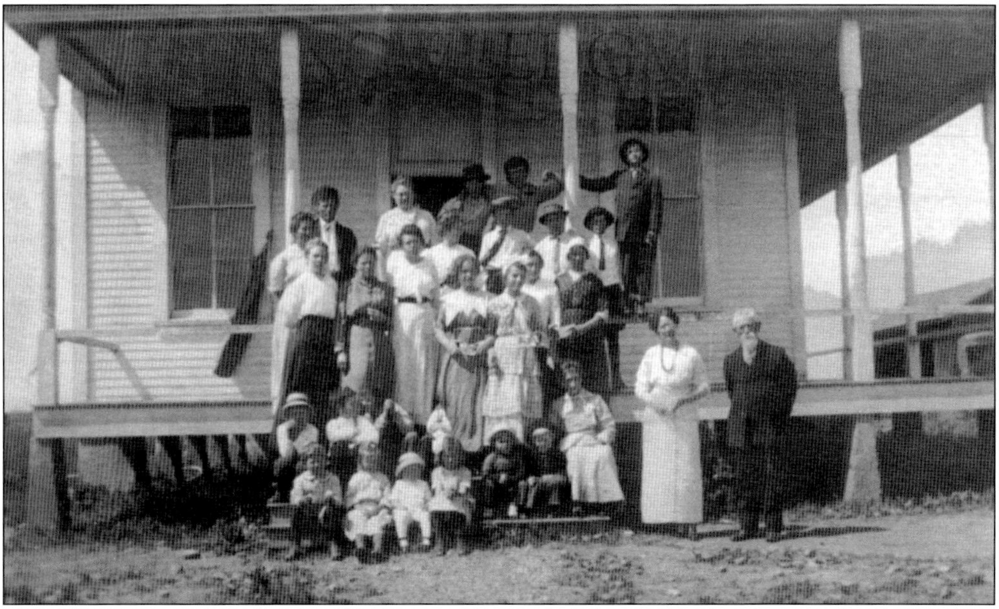

Both of these photographs of the Agua Fria School were taken in the spring of 1920. Although the names of the individuals pictured are not listed, the surnames of the families who had children that went to this school are Wadsworth, Warnick, Young, Owens, McKee, Nuckles, and Decker. (Diana Domingo.)

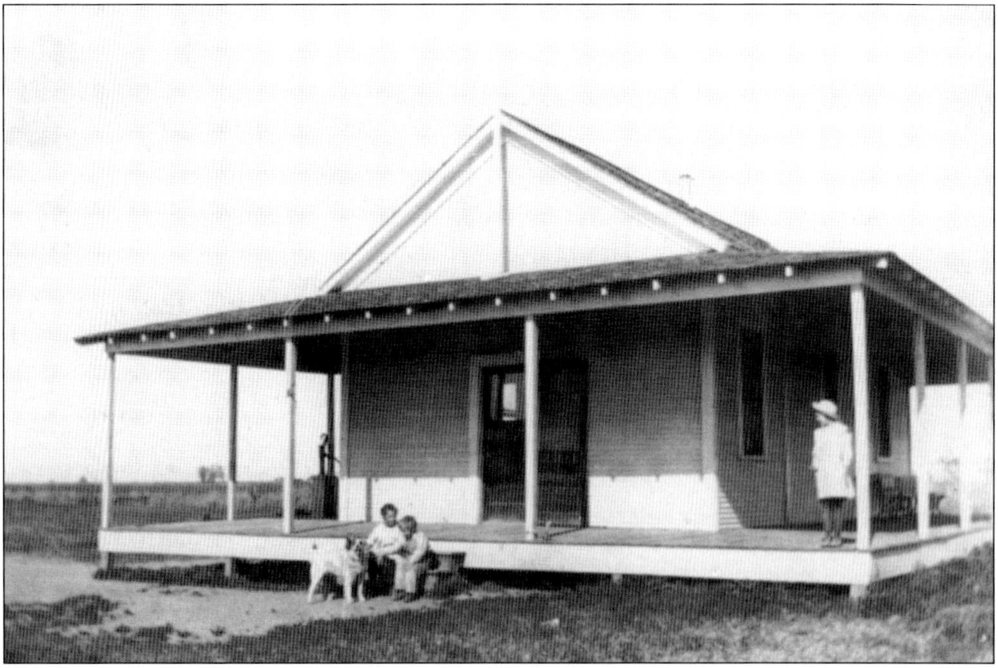

The Agua Fria School was located on County Road 4, about four miles northeast of Butte City. Built on property owned by the Goodman family, it opened in 1906 and contained one room. It closed at the end of the 1942 school year. The students from that area then attended the Butte City School. (Diana Domingo.)

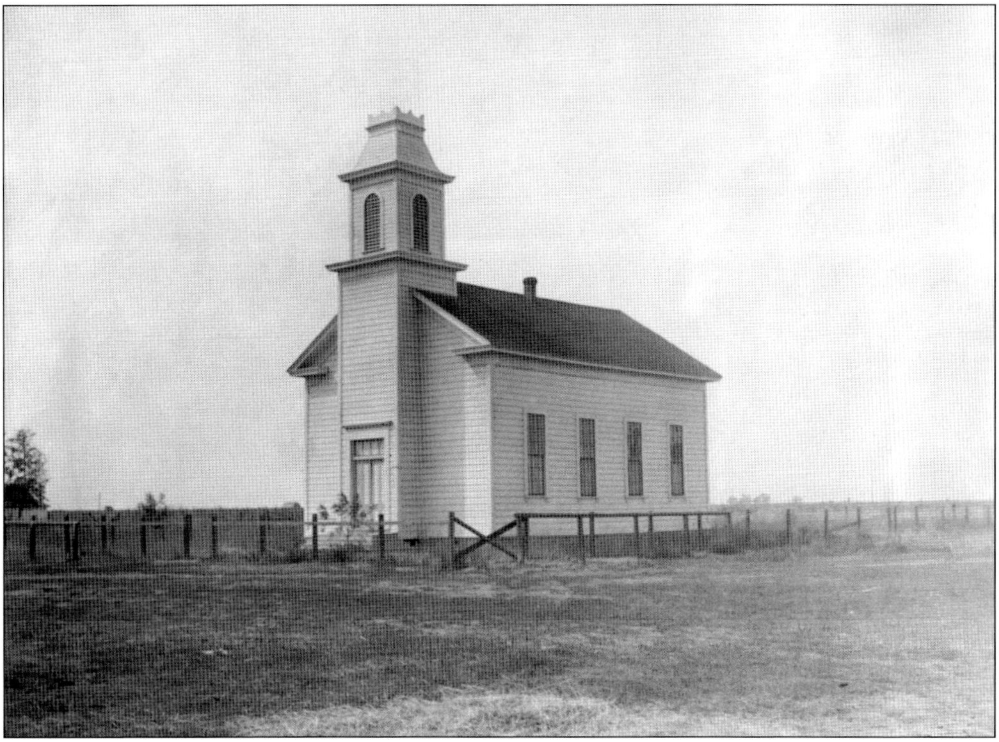

Afton resident Mayberry Davis donated several acres for the Methodist Episcopal church to be built. The deeds book in Colusa County contains the handwritten document deeding the land from Mayberry Davis to E. McDaniel, H.C. Wilson, and L.N. Helphinstine, acting trustees for the Princeton Circuit Methodist Episcopal Church, South. The deed was dated July 25, 1874, and the transaction was for one dollar of gold. Services were held twice a month. (Greg Steel.)

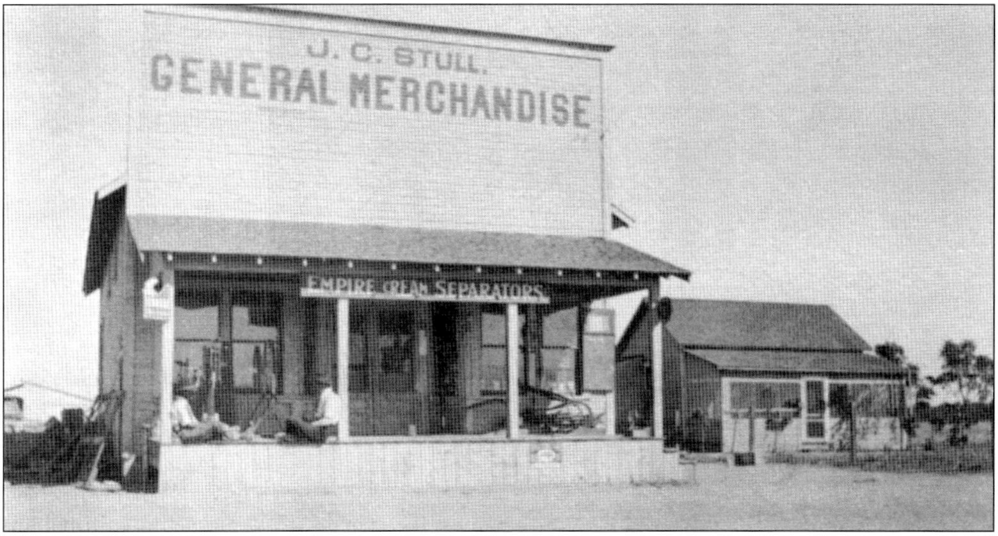

The Ordbend Store was built in 1910 and operated by J.C. Stull until 1918. At that time, Junius Van Scyoc took over operations, and it was run by members of the Van Scyoc family through the 1960s. The little house on the right had been relocated from the Reed ranch. (*Wagon Wheels*, February 1961.)

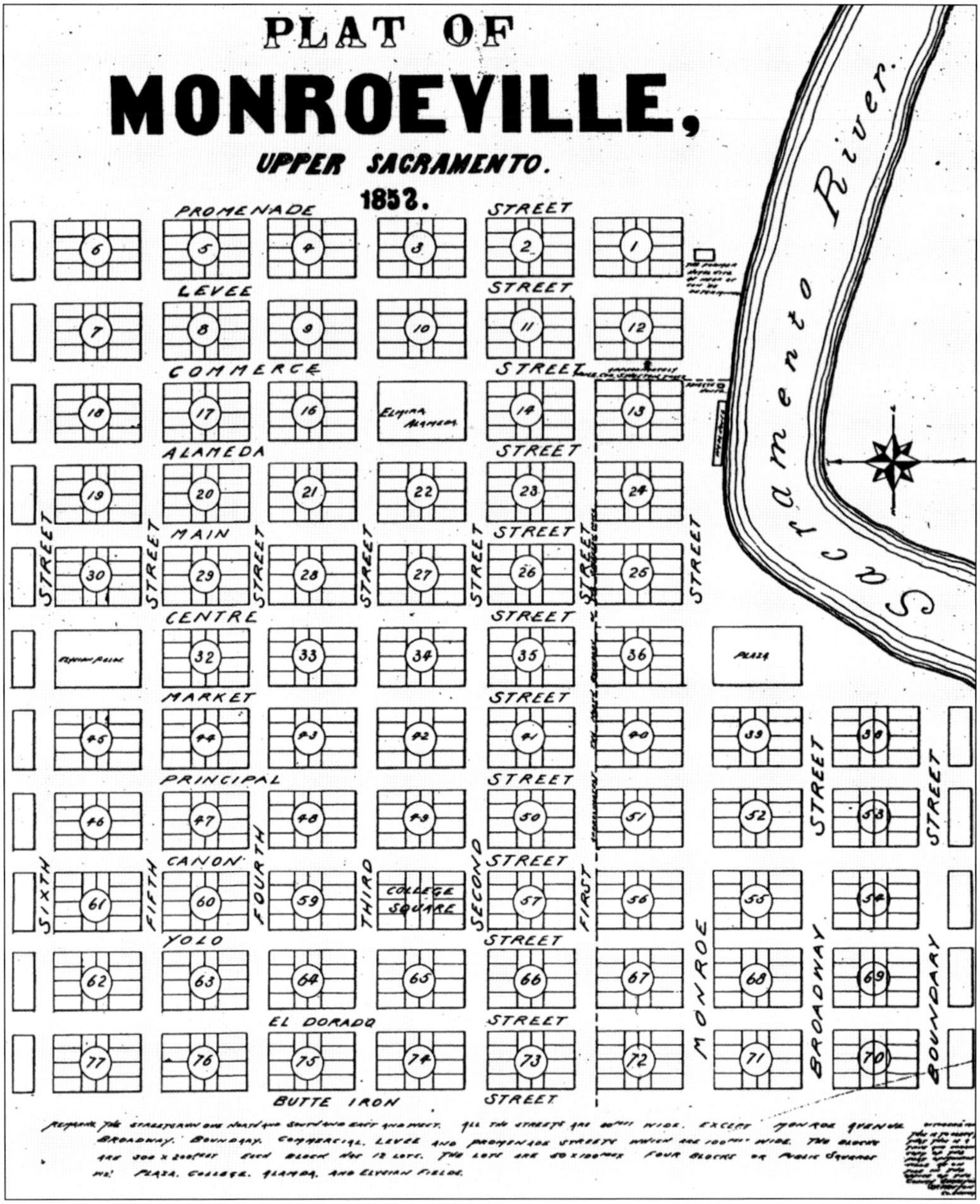

In 1850, Uriah P. Monroe had visions of grandeur. He owned property on the west side of the Sacramento River and, with the Shasta mining road and river travel bringing commerce, he began a town and named it after himself. Monroeville was located just south of the mouth of Stony Creek and became Colusi County's first county seat in 1851. It held this distinction until 1853, when the county seat moved to Colusa. The town consisted of the Monroe House, William B. Ide's cabin, some other cabins, and a warehouse at nearby Monroe Landing. Once the county seat moved and the river traffic flowed past to Tehama County, this town, once so important, faded into history. The county surveyor, Joshua Francis Weston, drew this plat map of Monroeville in 1900. (*Wagon Wheels*, May 1953.)

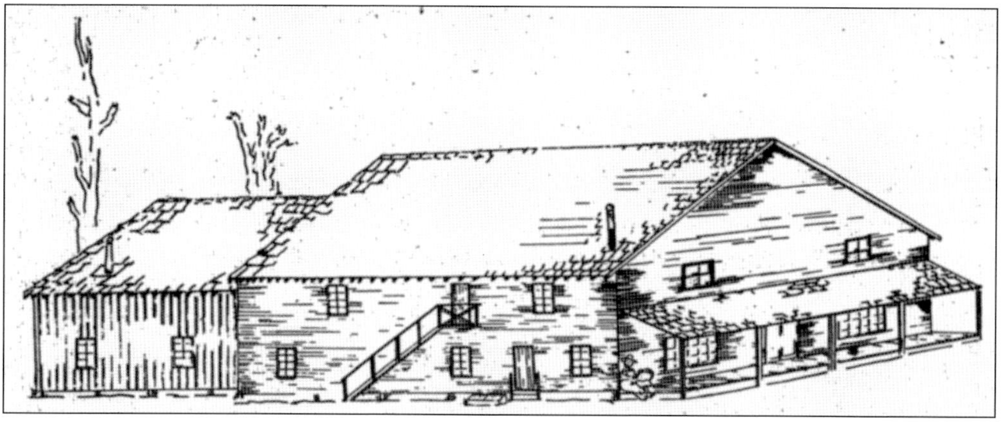

J.F. Weston drew this picture of the Monroe House from memory in 1951. He was born in Monroeville in 1868. Built mostly from the remains of the steamer *California*, which had wrecked in the Sacramento River about one mile above the mouth of Stony Creek, the Monroe House was constructed as a hotel. A store, saloon, post office, dining hall, and the first Colusi County courthouse were also housed there. (*Wagon Wheels*, May 1953.)

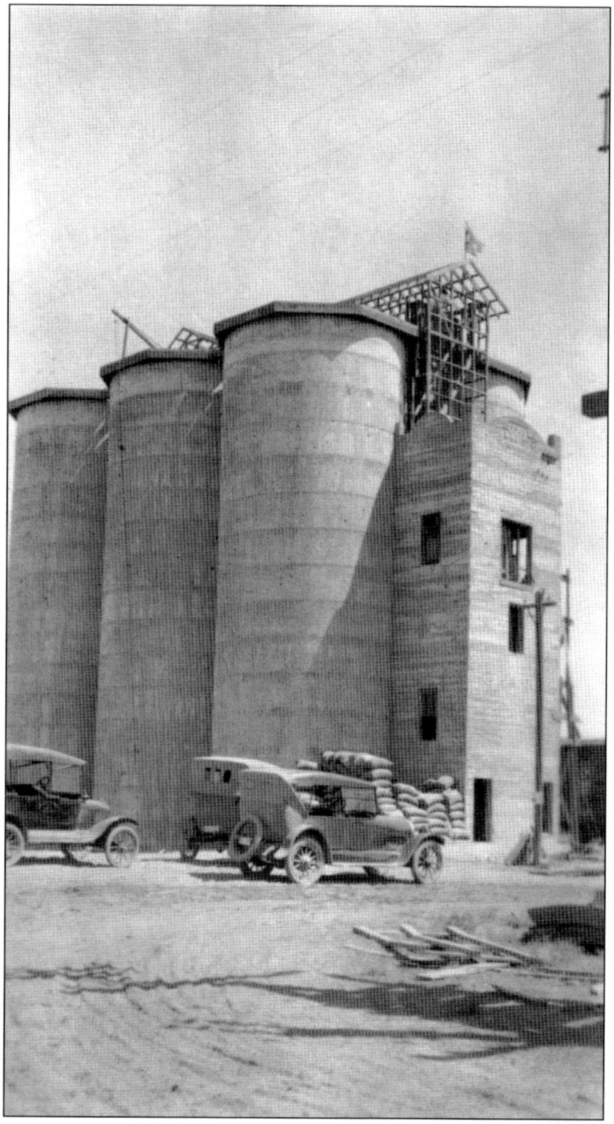

According to a clipping from an unidentified newspaper, Andrew Kaiser "established a bulk system of grain handling." He was instrumental in building a large grain elevator at Monroeville near where his ranch was located. This photograph was loaned to the Orland Historical and Cultural Society. (Orland Historical and Cultural Society.)

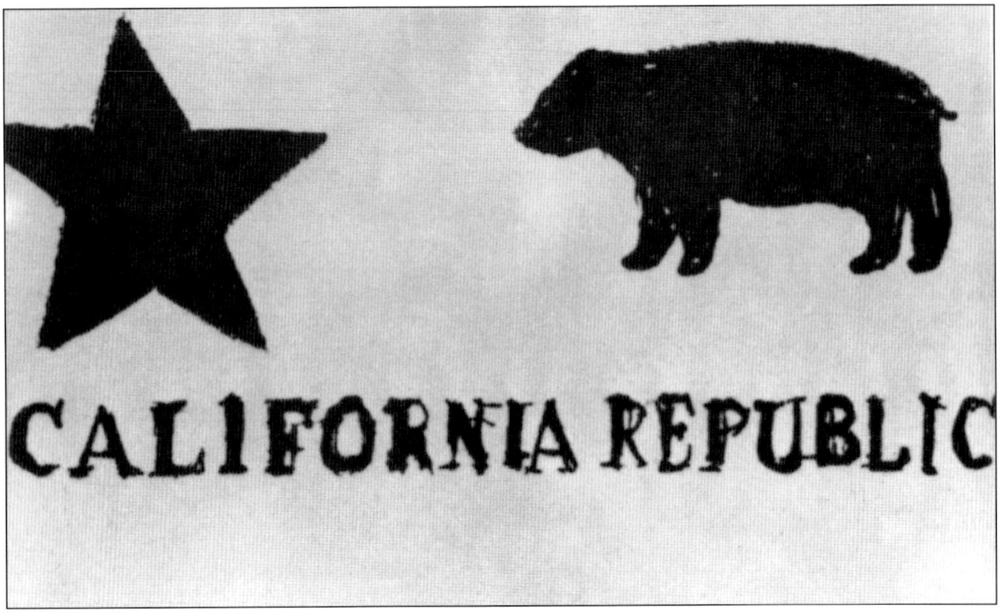

William L. Todd, Granville P. Swift, Peter Storm, and Henry L. Ford designed the bear flag shown here. They used a piece of "cotton domestic" not quite a yard wide. A four inch piece of flannel was used as a wide stripe. The star and grizzly were painted. As the Bear Flag Revolt Party was not authorized to raise the American flag to declare California a republic, this flag was raised in Sonoma on June 14, 1846. It remained the state flag for about 26 days. (*Wagon Wheels*, February 1978.)

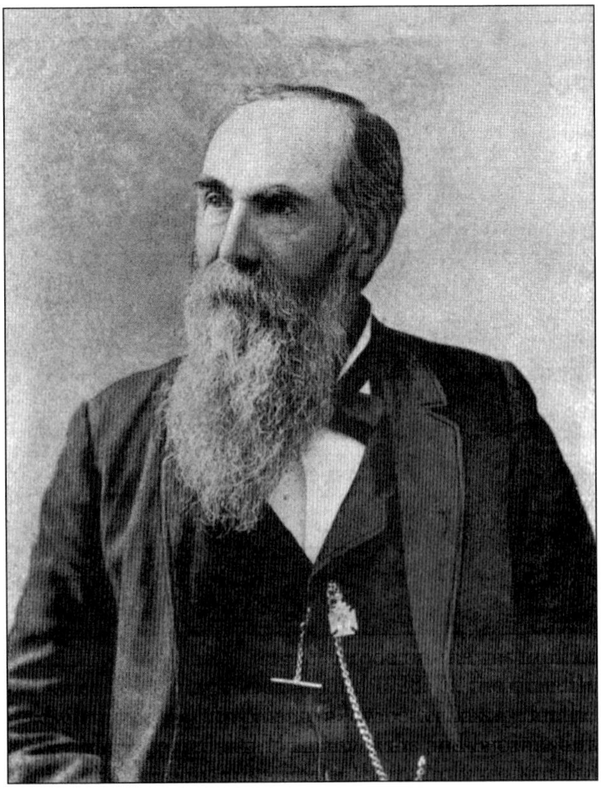

Jubal Weston was born on November 13, 1824, in East Adams, Connecticut. He arrived in San Francisco in April 1849. He married Sarah Frances Richardson and they settled in Monroeville, where he managed the hotel. Post office records show Jubal Weston as postmaster for 1856–1859. In 1868, he purchased a strip of land that reached from the plains to the river. It was considered worthless agriculturally, but it was profitable as a "drive-way" for livestock. (Justus H. Rogers.)

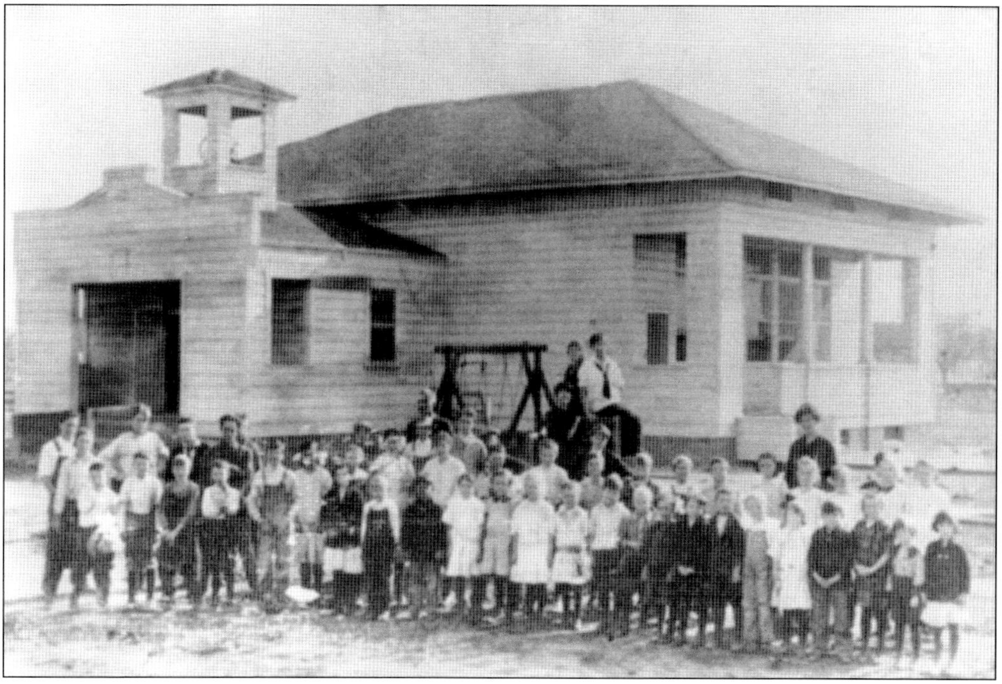

In 1858, the earliest school in Glenn County was located in a settlement north of Jacinto known as Placer City. The school served an area larger than that of the present Glenn County. As the county became settled, other schools were established. Placer later became known as Plaza Elementary. Walsh Elementary was in St. John until 1942. Hamilton Elementary School is shown here in 1913. (Hamilton City Community Services District.)

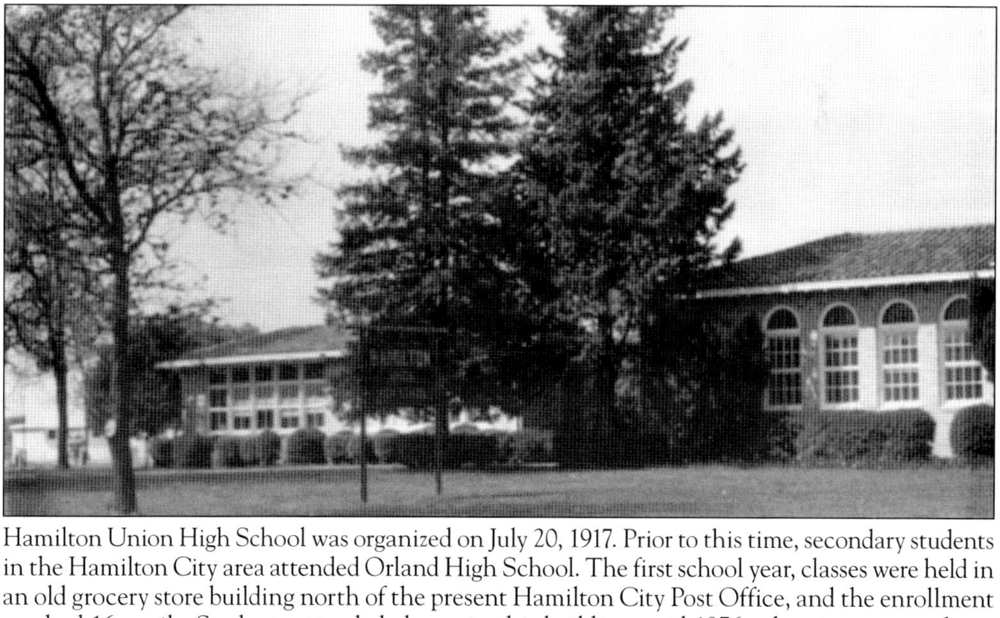

Hamilton Union High School was organized on July 20, 1917. Prior to this time, secondary students in the Hamilton City area attended Orland High School. The first school year, classes were held in an old grocery store building north of the present Hamilton City Post Office, and the enrollment reached 16 pupils. Students attended classes in this building until 1976, when it was torn down and replaced with the current facility. (Hamilton City Community Services District.)

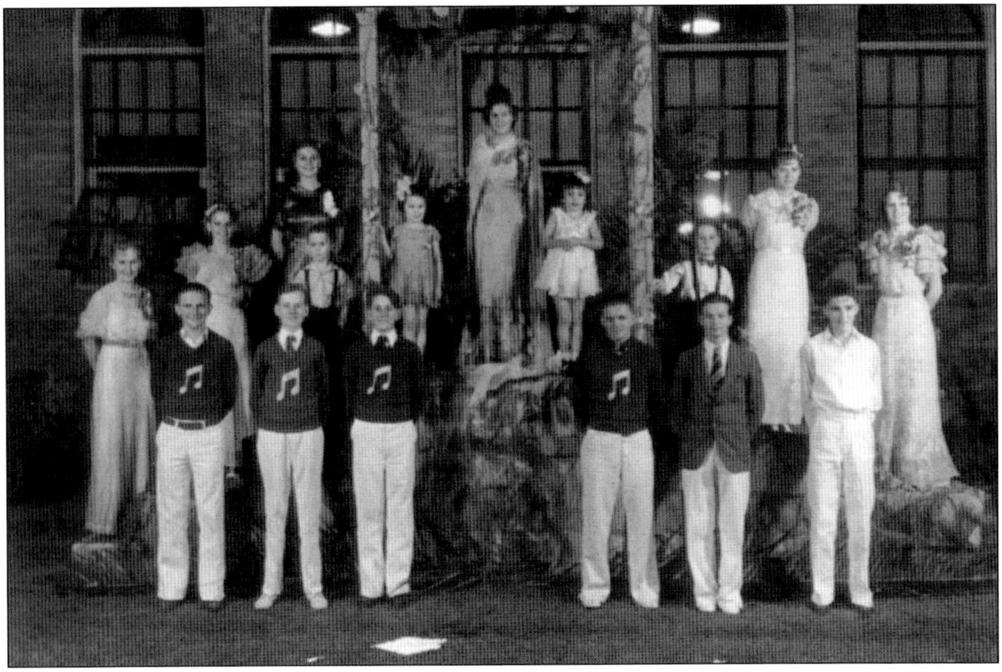

The Hamilton Women's Club sponsored a carnival each year. Organizations sponsored a girl to run for the honor of queen. This photograph shows the Hamilton High School Queen and her entourage from 1936 to 1937. From left to right are (first row) song leaders Harold Beck, Harold Worktime, Howard Schaffert, Orland Ennis, Layne Porter, and Ralph Gunn; (second row) Luella Boone and Lorretta Cornelius; (third row) Norma Scott, two unidentified boys, and Mary Ellen Ferry; (fourth row) Martha Compton, unidentified girl, Queen Clarie Price, and unidentified girl. (Hamilton City Community Services District.)

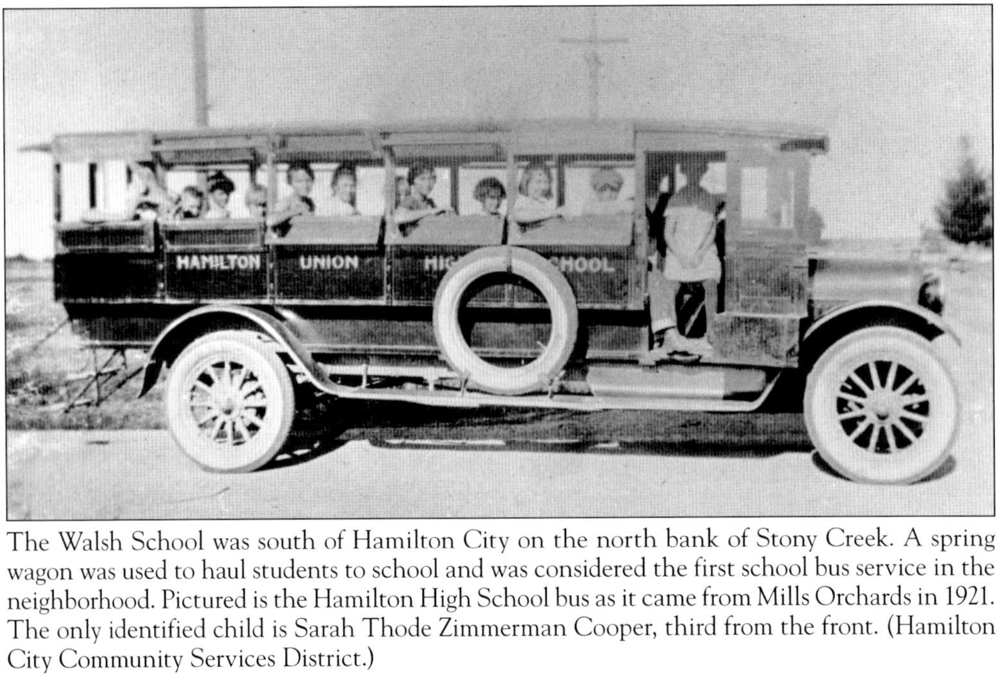

The Walsh School was south of Hamilton City on the north bank of Stony Creek. A spring wagon was used to haul students to school and was considered the first school bus service in the neighborhood. Pictured is the Hamilton High School bus as it came from Mills Orchards in 1921. The only identified child is Sarah Thode Zimmerman Cooper, third from the front. (Hamilton City Community Services District.)

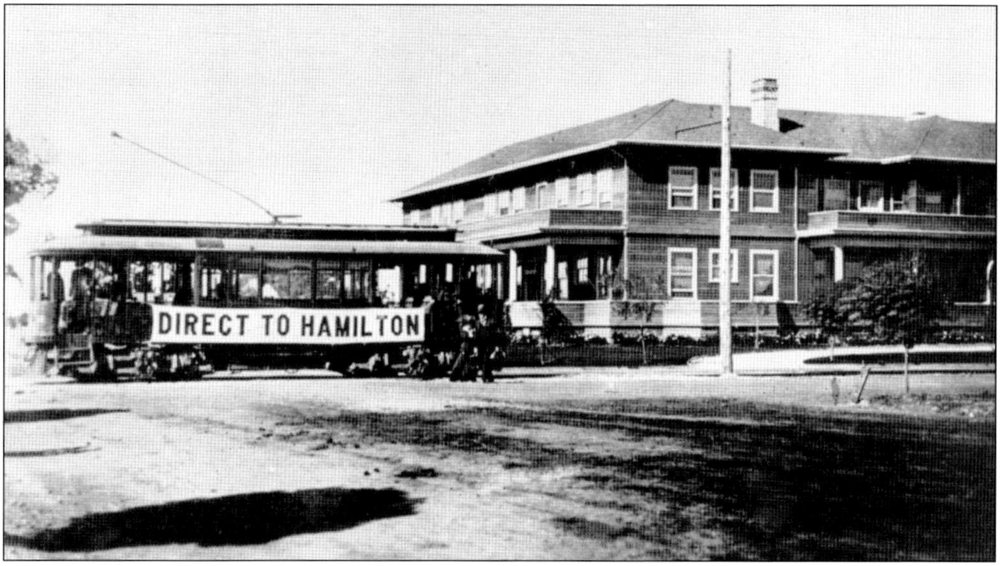

The Shotover Inn was built in 1906 at a cost of $40,000. The top floor contained mostly single rooms and a few double rooms with baths. There were two public restrooms, one at each end of the building. The kitchen was located downstairs and contained all the modern appliances of the era. A large dining room contained mostly round tables covered in white linens. There were many special dinners, parties, and dances hosted at the inn that drew crowds from Chico via the Chico-Hamilton stage (pictured below in 1910) or on the Northern Electric street car. Visitors from Willows would travel by train. Many of the employees of the sugar beet factory lived at the inn. In 1942, the building was converted into apartments. They rented furnishings for $30 and $40 a month. Although the building has been renovated several times, it is still used as apartments. (Both, Hamilton City Community Services District.)

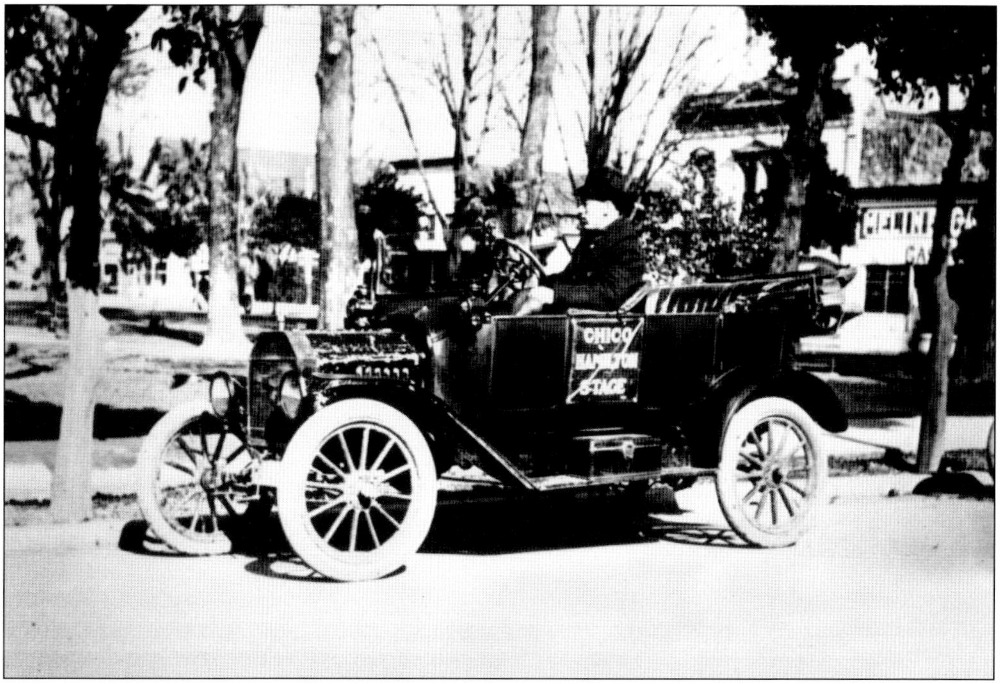

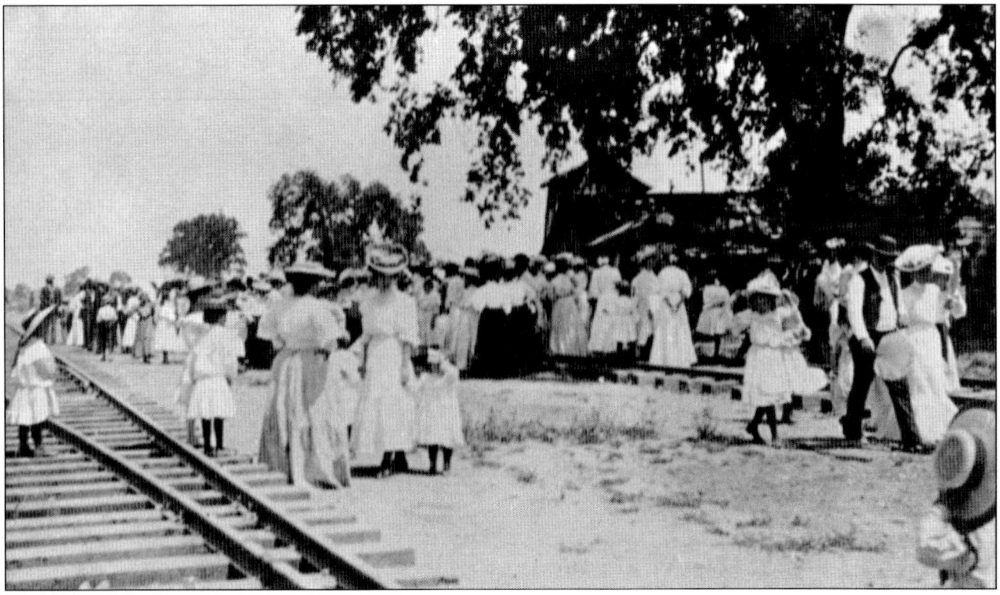

At the intersection of the road from Sacramento to Shasta with the road west from Chico to Newville, A.C. St. John built a store. By 1859, the settlement of St. John was so popular that Charles Singleterry built a hotel. More businesses and schools followed with the rising population of the area. The organizers of the sugar factory looked into increasing the river traffic but were told the river was at its lowest during the harvest months that far north. The natural progression of travel for the population and, primarily, the sugar beet freight, was a railroad. By 1906, the Southern Pacific had built a spur line to the sugar factory in Hamilton City. A line running north from Colusa along the river to Hamilton City was completed in 1913. These pictures depict the arrival of the first passenger train from Willows to Hamilton City. (Both, Hamilton City Community Services District.)

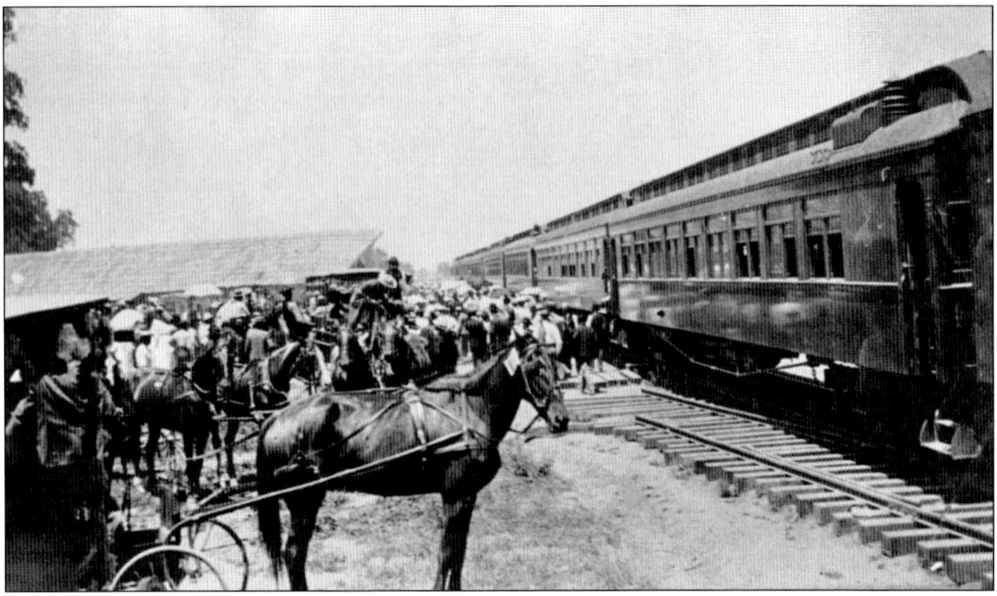

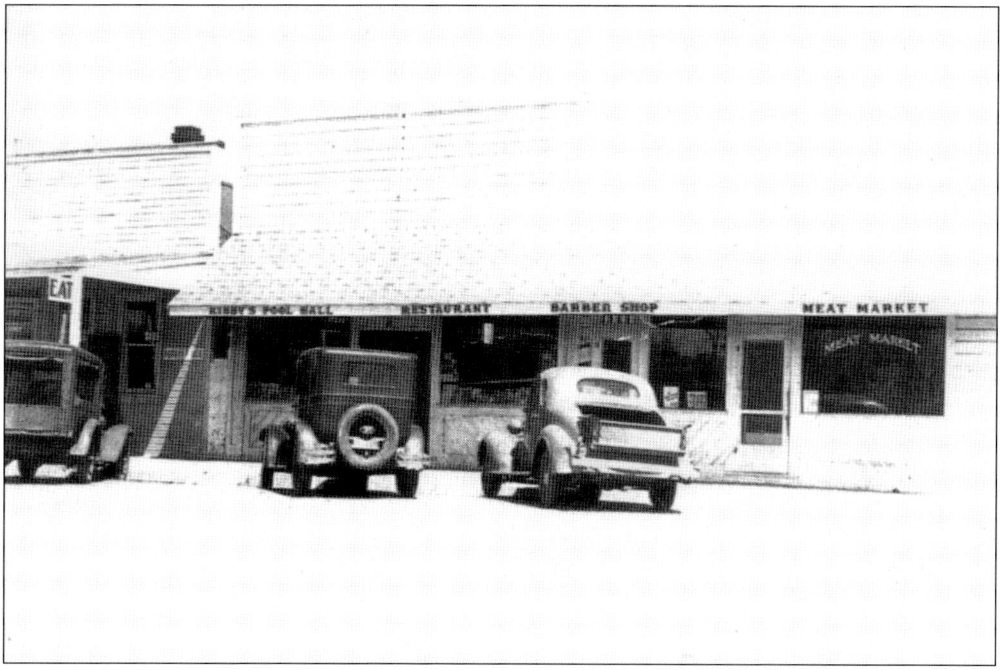

The plans to build the sugar factory involved the laying out of the town. Ernest C. Hamilton, the son of James G. Hamilton, was instrumental in the formation of the factory, the area sugar beet industry, and the railroad right-of-ways, but he handed over the laying out of the town to his father and William and Ralph Burnham. Many of the features suggested in 1906 are still part of the community. The photograph above shows several of the businesses housed in one building along Main Street, including Kibbe's Pool Hall, a restaurant, a barber shop, and a meat market. Main Street in 1908 is shown below. (Both, Hamilton City Community Services District.)

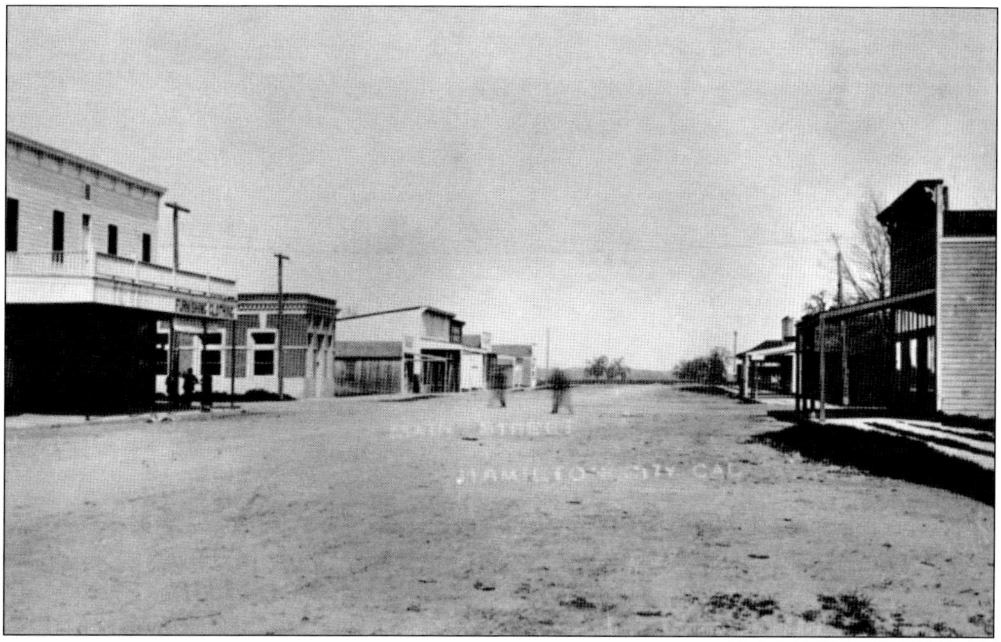

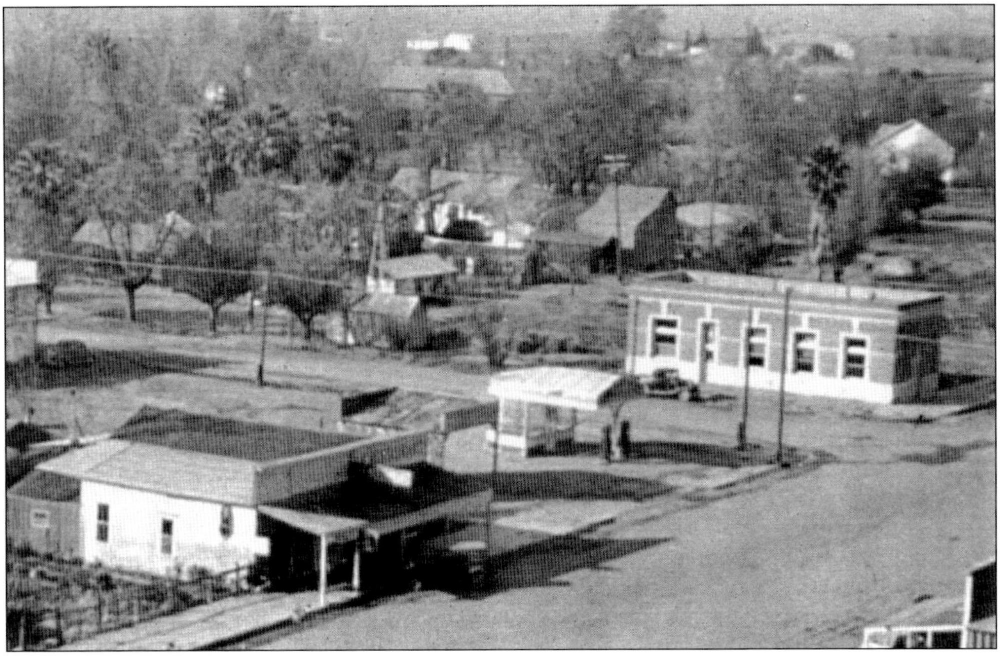

The first post office was established in Hamilton City on May 26, 1906. The building in this photograph still serves as the post office. The gas station across the street belonged to Chet Walker. Bruce Johnson owned the Cantina Bar down the street (at right). A bank, meat market, restaurant, and barbershop were located across the street. (Hamilton City Community Services District.)

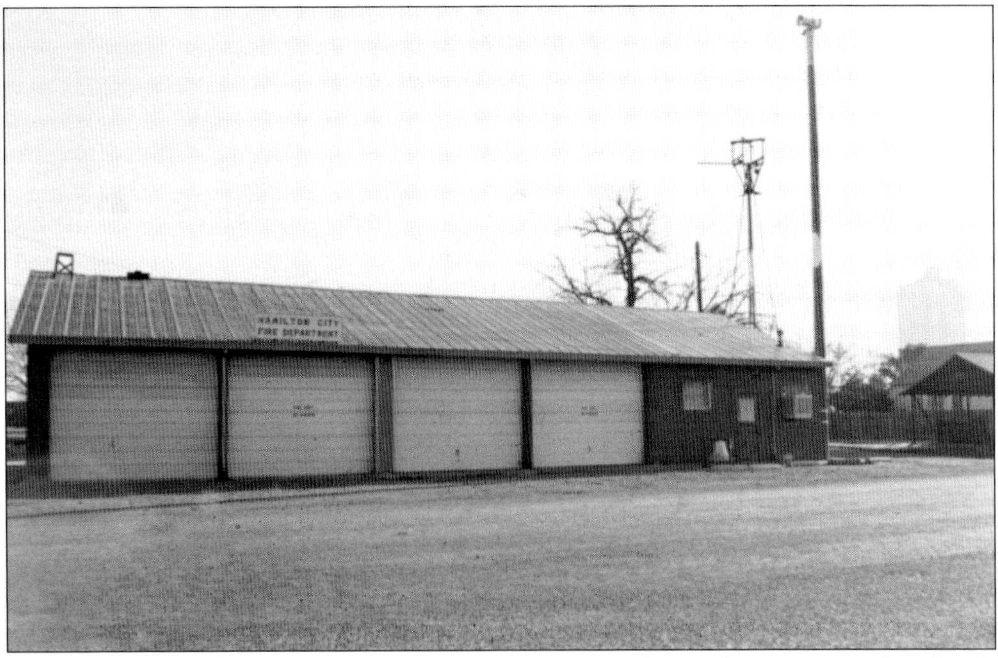

This Hamilton City firehouse was on the corner of Broadway and Second Street in Hamilton City. It was located here from the mid-1940s until the new firehouse was built on First Street. This building is now used to house the First Five program. (Hamilton City Community Services District.)

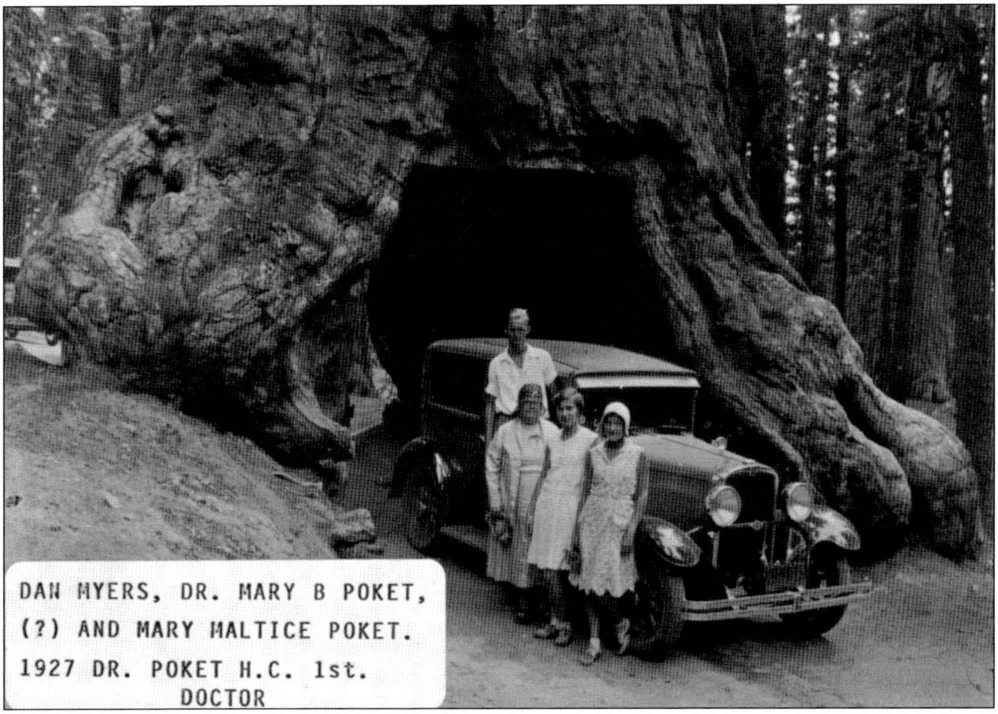

Dr. Mary B. Poket served as a general practitioner in Hamilton City for over 30 years. The young lady at the front of the car, Mary Maltice (Mattis, perhaps) Poket was Dr. Poket's adopted daughter. Dan Myers and an unidentified girl accompany them on a drive through the Wawona Tunnel Tree at the Mariposa Redwood Grove in Yosemite National Park in 1927. The Wawona Tunnel Tree fell in 1969. (Hamilton City Community Services District.)

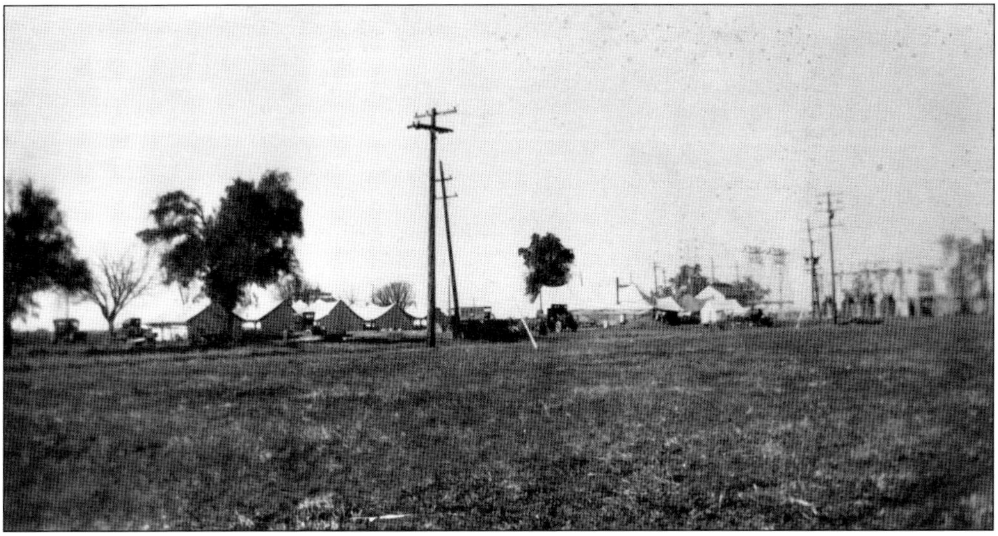

A labor encampment was along Walsh Avenue and what is now Highway 32. The 1910 US Census shows a variety of nationalities boarding here and at the Shotover Inn. They included Canadian, Chinese, East Indian, German, Hungarian, Japanese, Portuguese, Russian, Scottish, and Spanish. These men and women worked at the sugar factory, in local businesses, as farm laborers and as domestic servants. (Hamilton City Community Services District.)

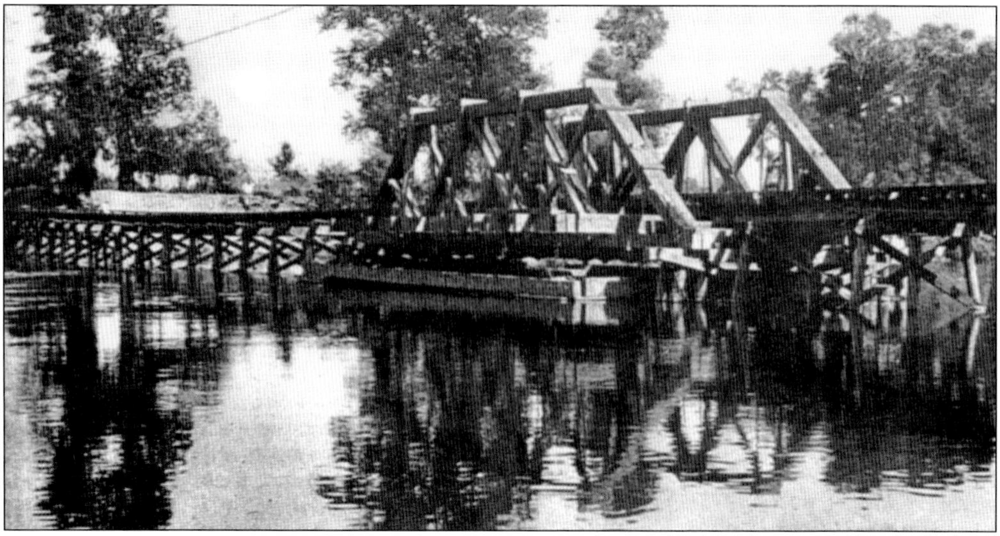

Beginning in 1907, the northern line of the Sacramento Northern Railway ran a passenger-service branch between Chico and Hamilton City. A pontoon bridge was constructed with rails laid on the floating foundation. It crossed the Sacramento River just north of the mouth of Stony Creek. The trolley's terminus in Glenn County was in front of the Shotover Inn at Broadway and Third Street. (Hamilton City Community Services District.)

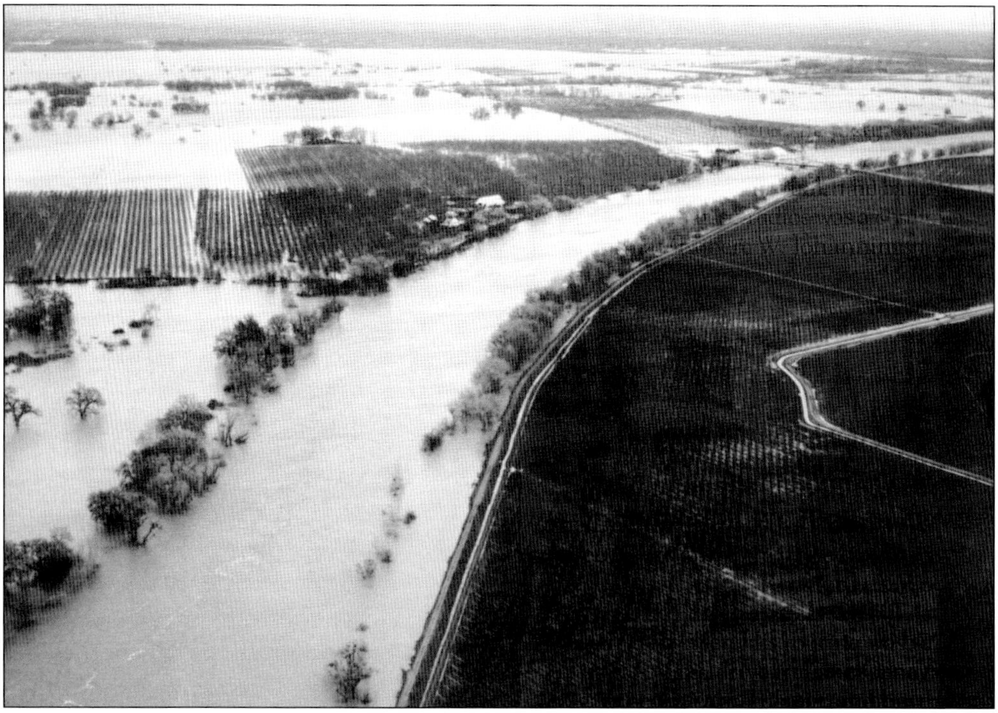

Upon settling on the northern end of Glenn County and the Sacramento River, Ernest C. Hamilton soon learned that levees were a necessity. Flooding created ponds that made excellent breeding areas for mosquitoes carrying malaria. Kerosene oil was put in the ponds to kill the mosquitoes. Hamilton said that the sugar plant had three shifts—one off with malaria, one getting over it, and one working. (Library of Congress.)

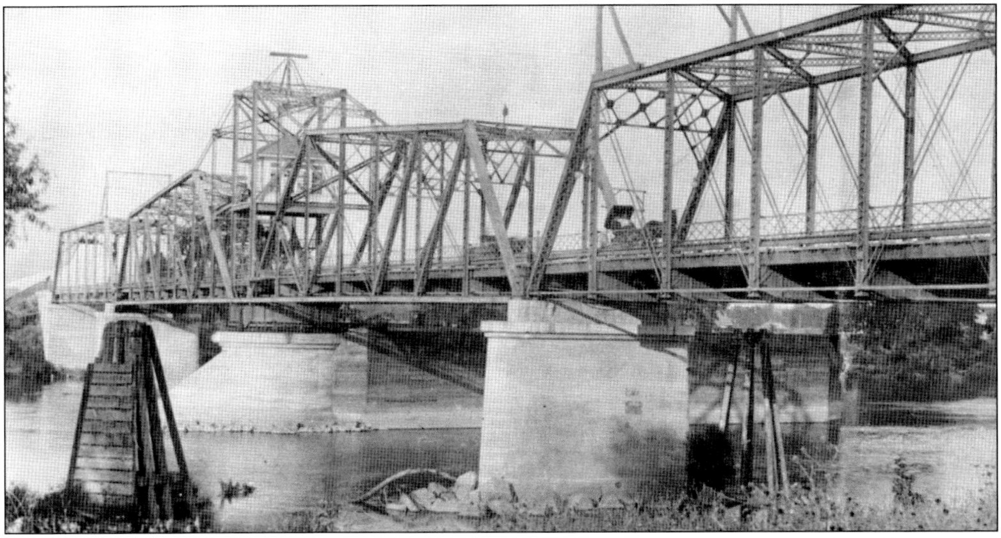

In order to ensure that a permanent bridge would be constructed, Vincenzo Gianella donated 13 acres of land for an approach to the bridge. On June 25, 1908, the first major shipment of materials for the bridge arrived on the river steamer *Dover*. Included in the shipment were 2,000 bags of cement and 200,000 board feet of lumber. After many setbacks, the bridge was accepted on December 8, 1910. The bridge was made of two approach spans, each 133 feet long, and one 311-foot-long swing span. The swing span allowed river craft to pass and was operated electrically. Hiram Crenshaw ran the ferry during the bridge construction and then became the bridge tender. The last operation of the swing span was in 1971. The center pier in the photograph below contains the turntable assembly. (Both, Library of Congress.)

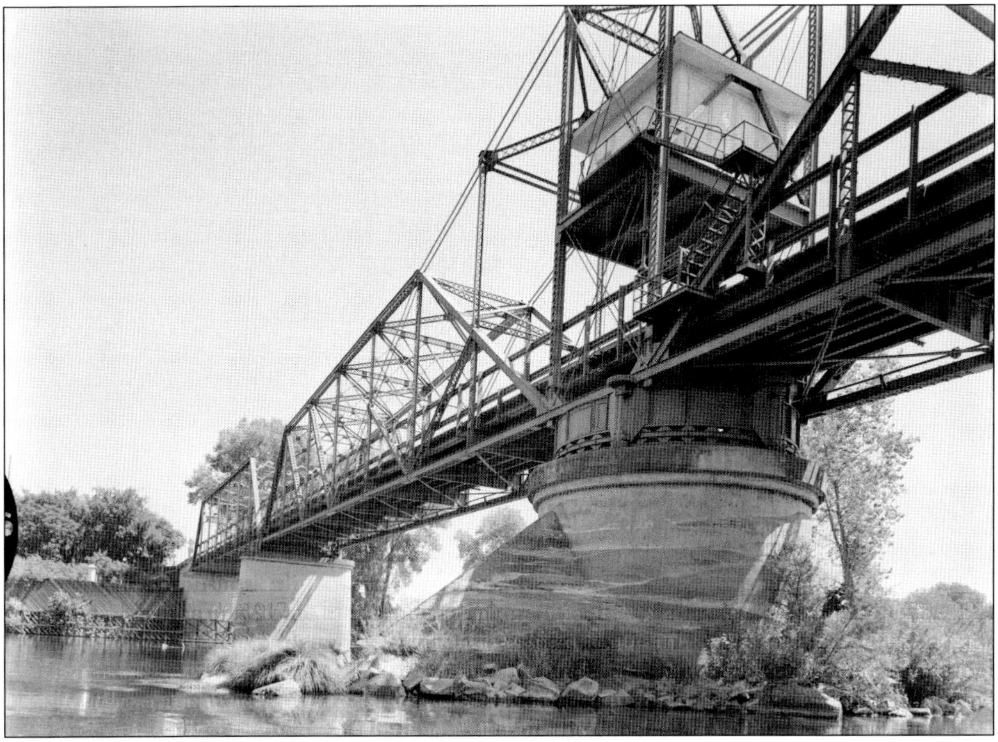

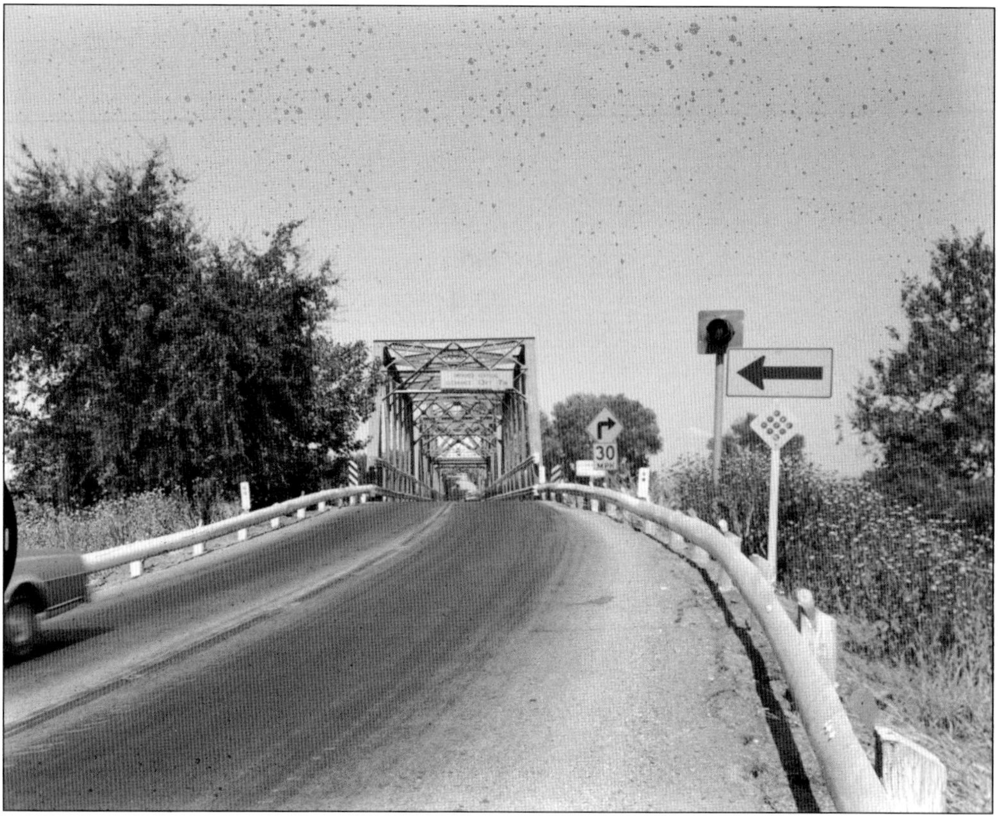

The Gianella Bridge was 19 feet wide. Between 1981 and 1984, it was the site of about 40 accidents, a number of which resulted in injuries or death. As traffic increased on Highway 32 between Glenn and Butte Counties, the need for a new bridge was apparent. A site 250 feet downstream was chosen for a concrete bridge with two 12-foot traffic lanes and eight-foot shoulders. This bridge replaced the swing bridge in 1987. (Library of Congress.)

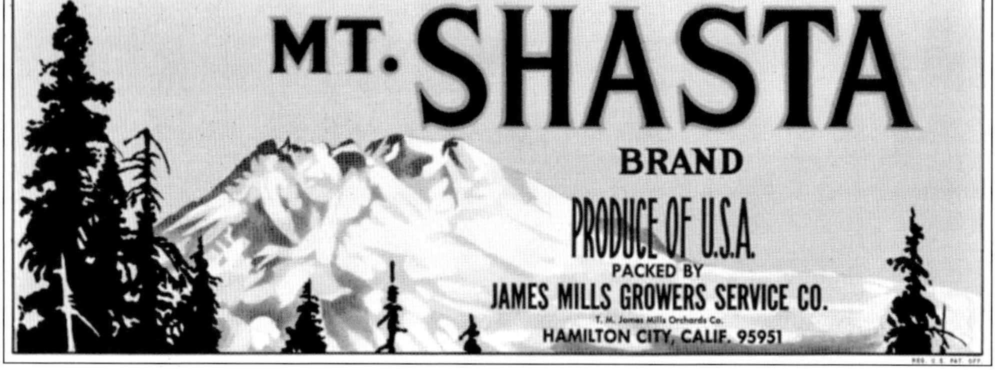

James Mills Orchards Company began in the Hamilton City area in 1912. The company also farmed land at Maxwell, California. The Orland Unit, as it was called, contained oranges, prunes, pears, peaches, apricots, almonds, and olives. This shipping label represents one of the lines of fruit that was marketed and shipped from the northern end of Glenn County. (Author's collection.)

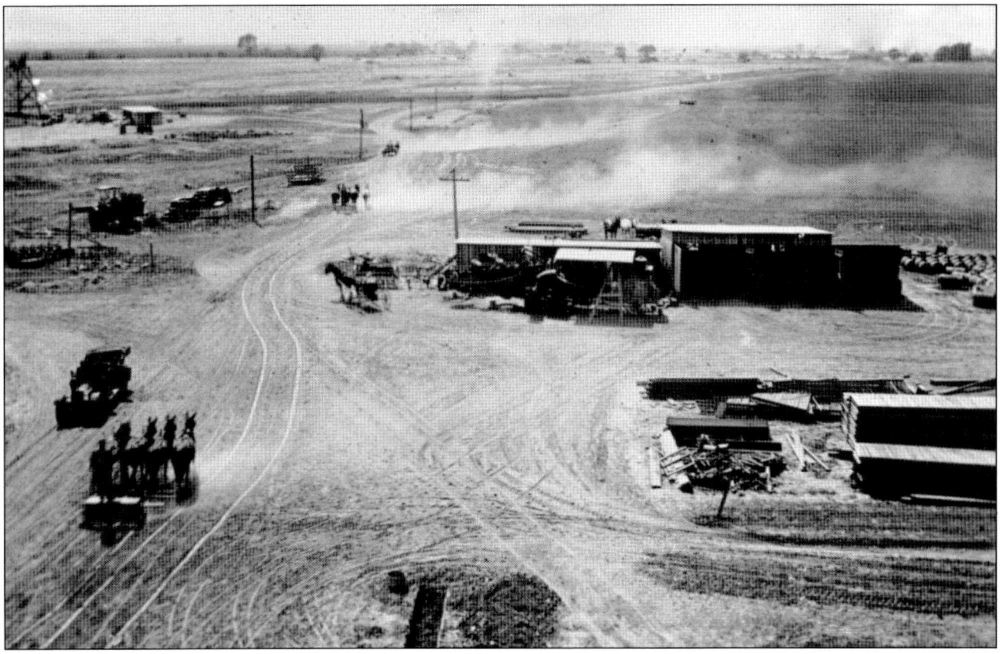

James Mills was an agriculturalist in Southern California before he found his way north to the grain-producing region of northern Glenn County near Hamilton City. Here, he developed what became known as the James Mills Orchards. The property was converted to fruit trees and fitted with an irrigation system. As the soil was conducive to this type of agriculture, all varieties were planted, with the majority of acreage going to oranges. Other deciduous fruits that were grown included prunes, pears, peaches, apricots, almonds, and olives. The orchard facility was very modern and included a dehydrating plant, company store, and office buildings. (Both, Hamilton City Community Services District.)

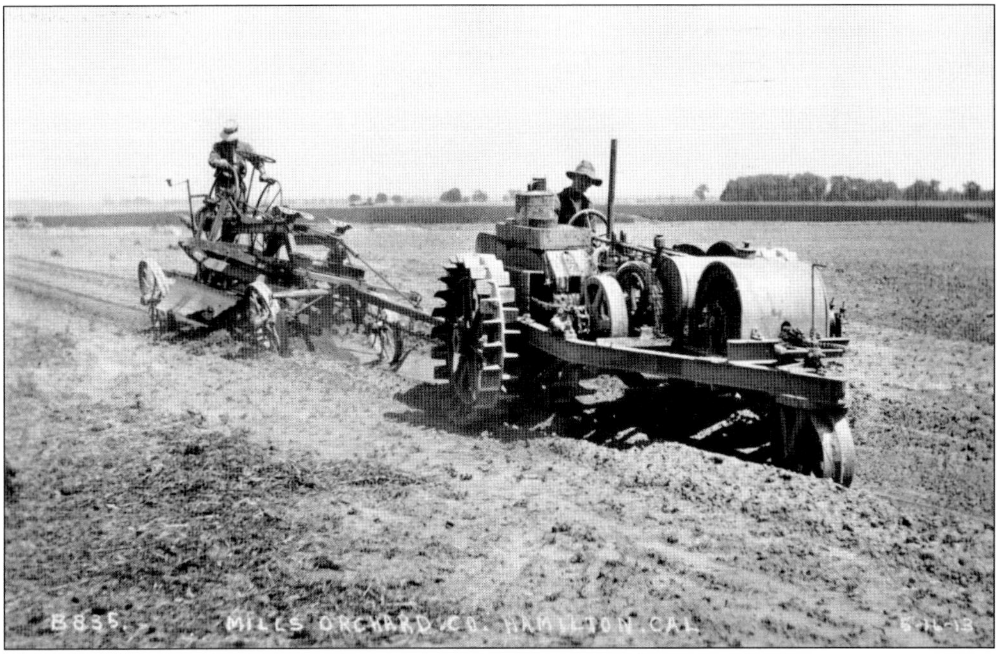

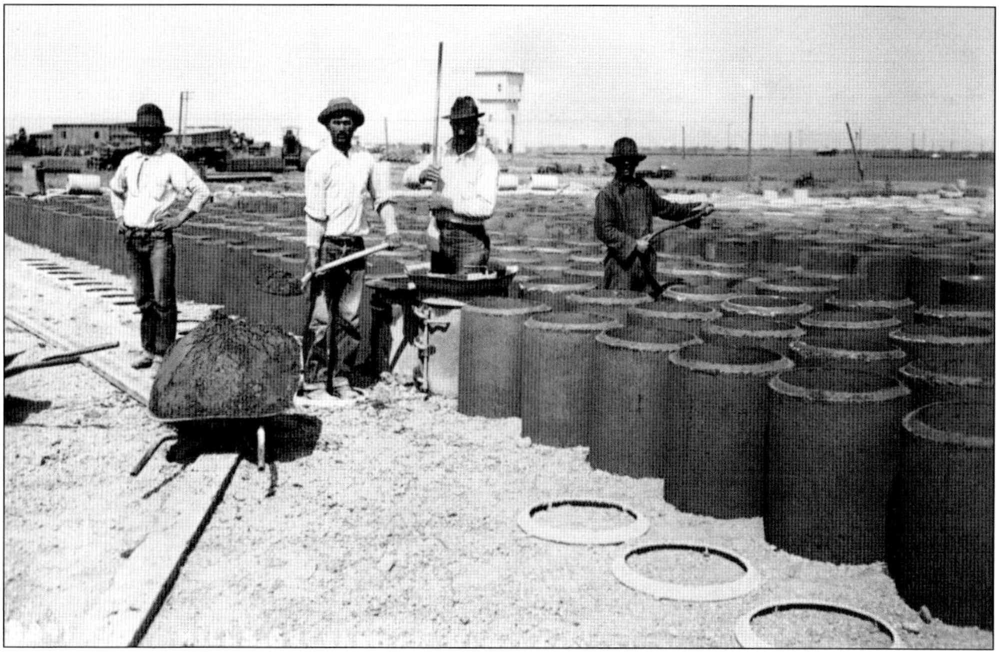

In 1912, James Mills had concrete pipe made and laid in order to carry water to the tops of the rolling hills of his lemon orchards near Maxwell. The water was brought to the surface and then conducted through the contoured ditches to the roots of the trees. Most of the trees were citrus, including lemons and oranges. (Hamilton City Community Services District.)

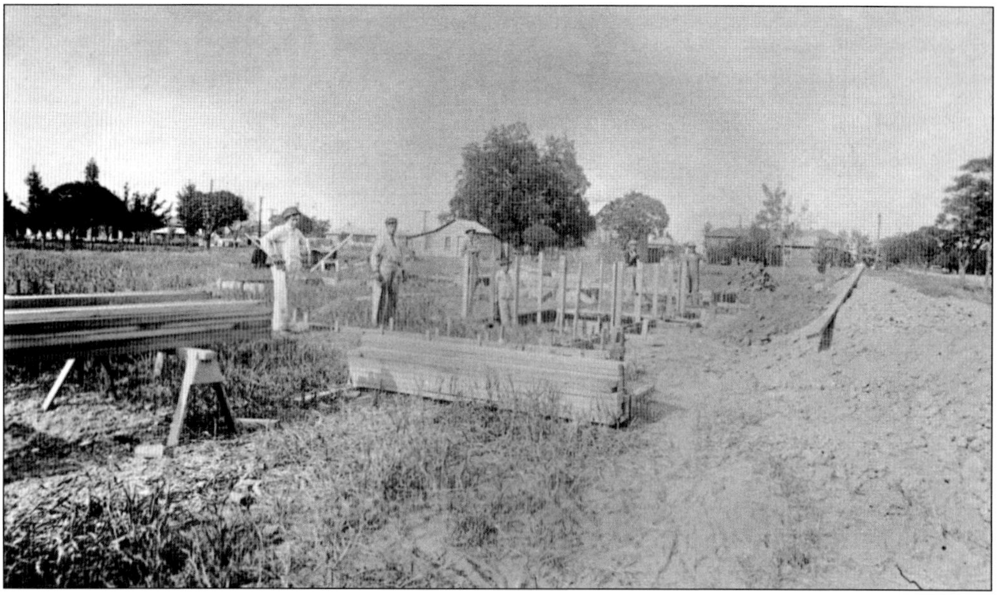

Farmers were reluctant to take their fields out of wheat and barley. They wanted to see how the beets would turn out first. The sugar beet company leased 14,000 acres, put in pumping plants, and built cabins to establish the beet industry. Many of the men who worked for the American Beet Sugar Company had moved to Hamilton City, bought lots, and built houses. This 1906 photograph shows the location on Broadway, between Second Street and Fourth Street. (Hamilton City Community Services District.)

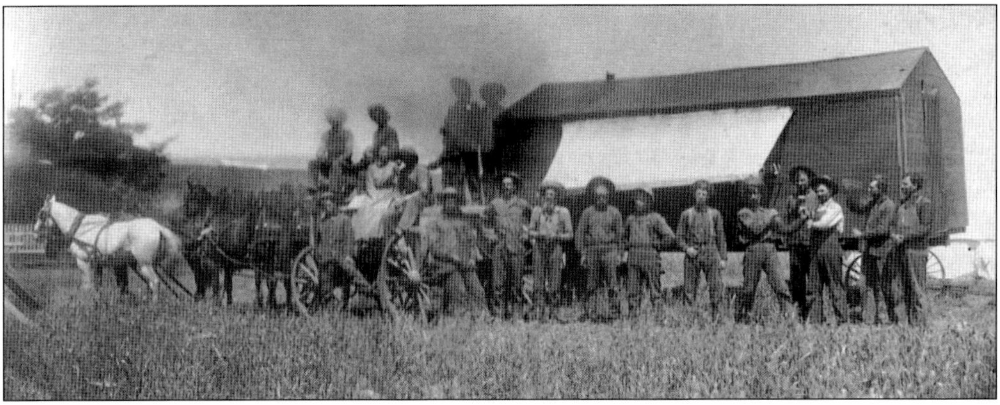

According to Will S. Green, there was not much in the way of stock raising or farming in the territory that comprised Colusa County before 1850. After 1851, there were ranches started for the purpose of supplying the demand for hay and barley to the teamsters heading to the Shasta mines. The crews depicted in these photographs worked the harvests and were mostly transient labor. They were fed and housed in the fields they harvested. Some of the farmers on the assessment rolls in 1851–1852 were Monroe and Williamson, Nelson and McClanahan, R.J. Walsh, Wm. Swift, Reager, and Cleek. (Both, Hamilton City Community Services District.)

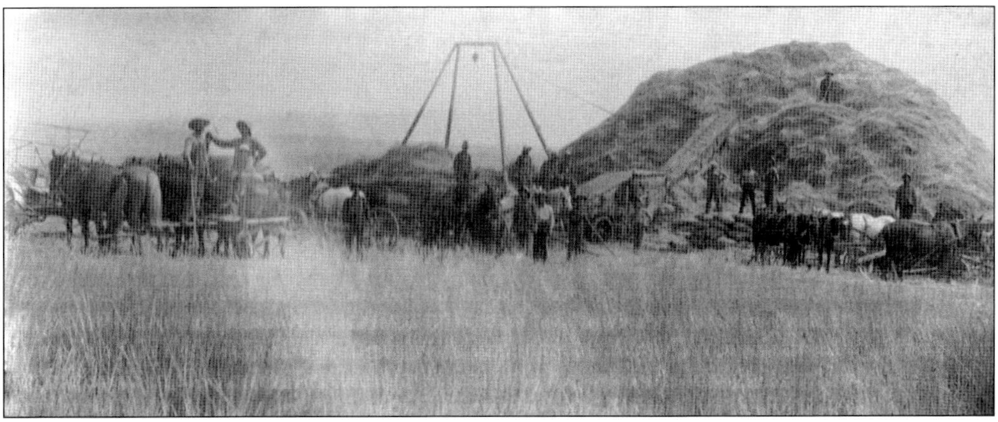

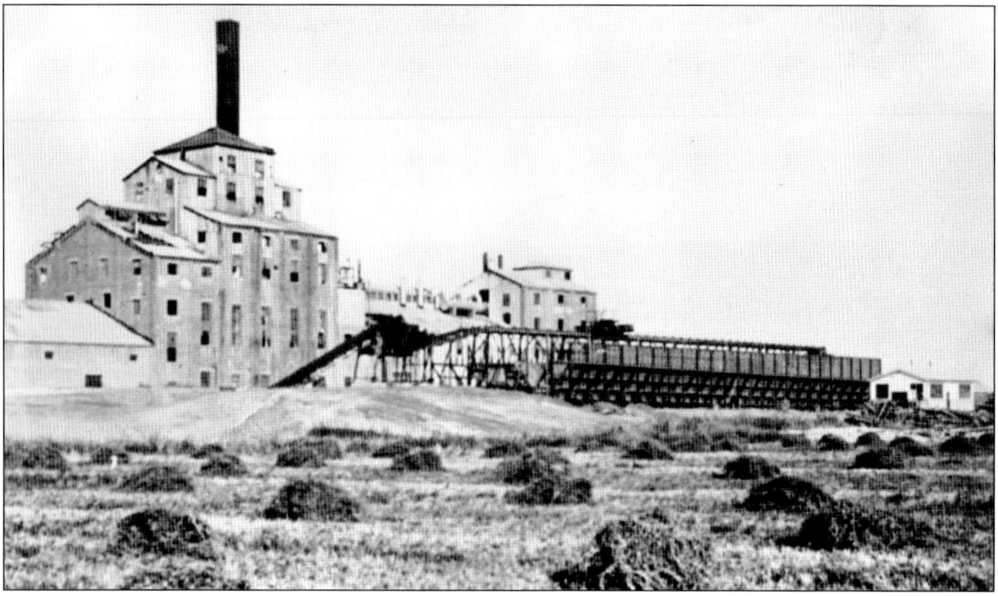

Based on research of the European sugar beet industry that began in 1888, sugar magnates from New York brought the sugar beet industry to America. The locations they chose were Nebraska, Colorado, and Southern California. Based on a chance meeting with some ladies who were looking to purchase land west of Chico, J.G. Hamilton spent several days traveling by horse and buggy and looking over the land being marketed by the St. Louis Trust Company. (Hamilton City Community Services District.)

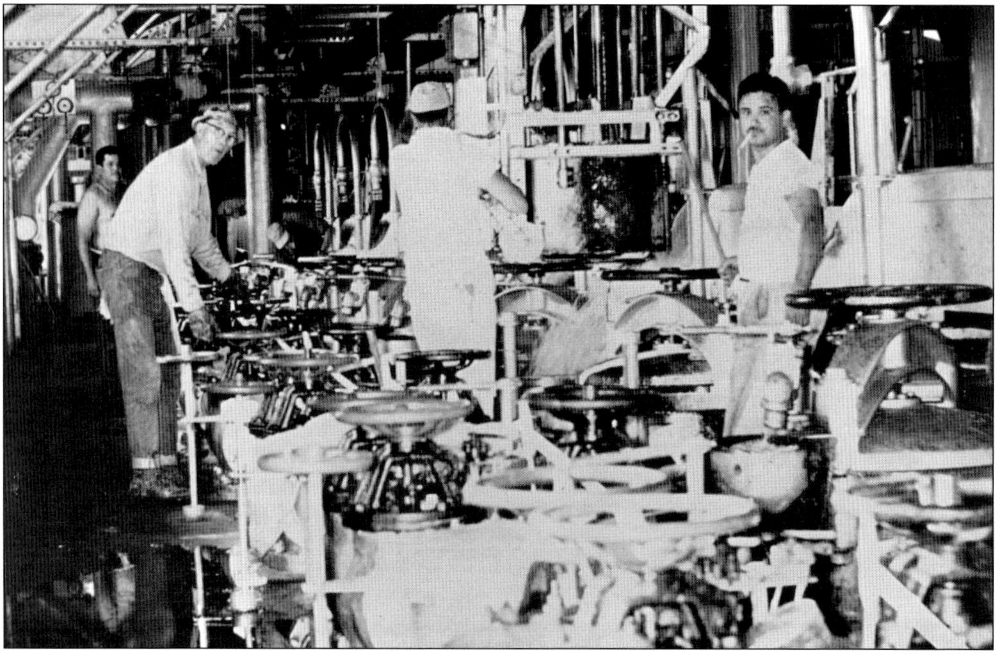

The original boilers and motors were ordered while E.G. Hamilton was in New York designing the factory with Oxnard Construction Company. The equipment was to be shipped to San Francisco. The irrigation plant was to be in operation by May 15, 1906; however, the earthquake and fire in San Francisco destroyed the pumps and motors. (Hamilton City Community Services District.)

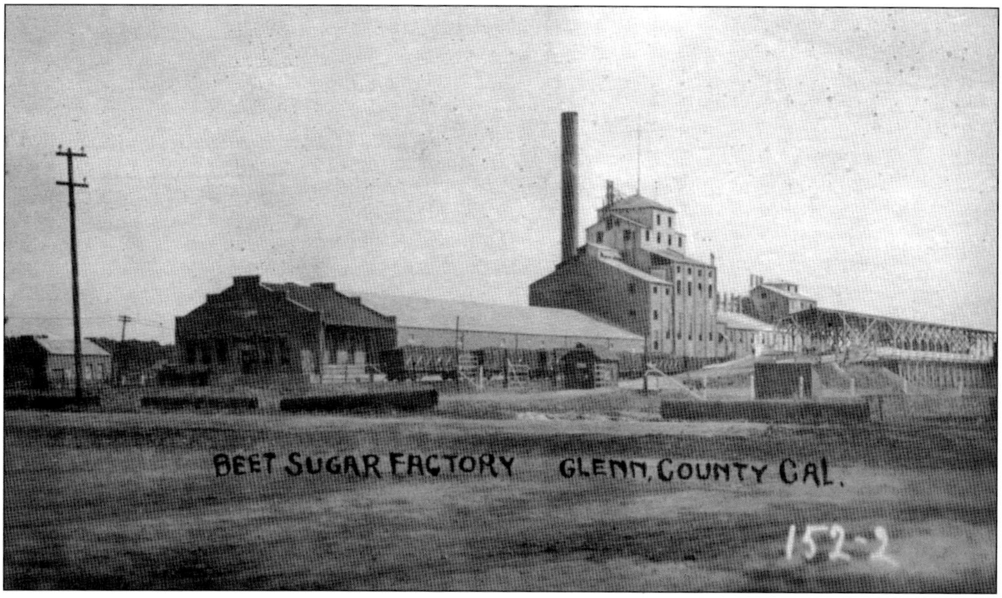

Under the direction of Ernest G. Hamilton, the 600-ton-capacity sugar plant was completed in 1906. Many troubles occurred during the development and operation of the plant, including flooding of the Sacramento River, low water hindering the use of barges, malaria, railroad right-of-way issues, white fly, sugar tariffs, and, finally, the Free Sugar Bill, which closed the factory in 1913. (Hamilton City Community Services District.)

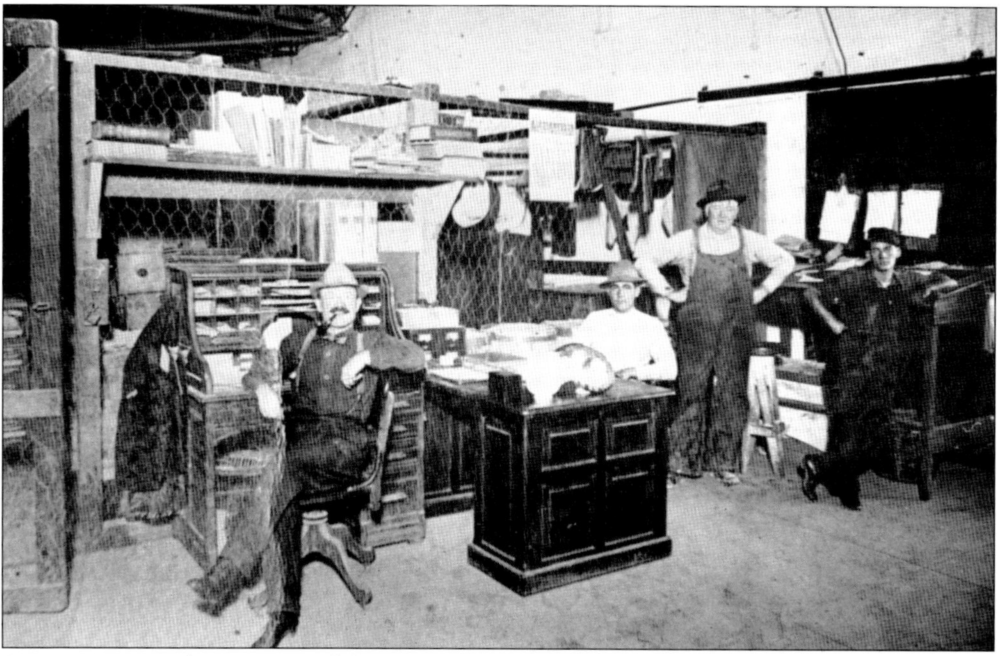

During its 90-year history, many different companies operated the sugar plant at Hamilton City. The plant started as the Alta California Sugar Company and was named the Holly Sugar Corporation when it closed. Whatever the name, the operations of the office staff were as important as the workers in the factory. From left to right are unidentified, Bruce Johnson, unidentified, and Miguel Mendoza. (Hamilton City Community Services District.)

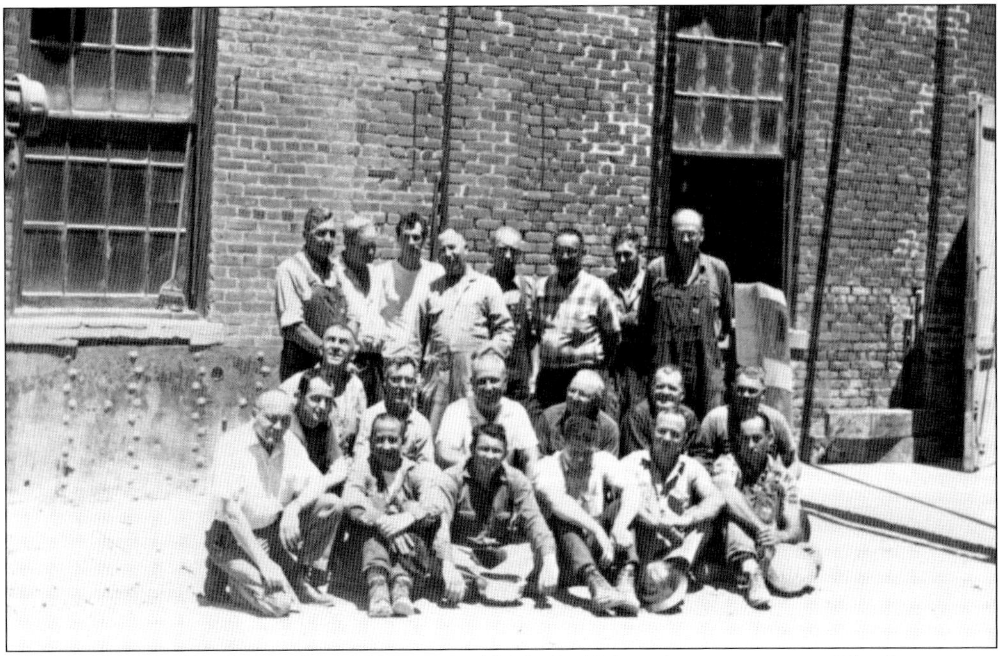

The sugar factory remained closed during World War I. Although it was reopened for the seasons of 1917 and 1918, it was not productive enough to remain open. E.G. Hamilton speculated that the lack of productivity was due to the inability to get beets delivered. With a change in some of the board of directors, the factory again operated for the 1925 season with a similar outcome. Holly Sugar took over the factory in 1936 and increased the capacity of the plant from 600 tons to 1,200 tons. The openings and closings of the plant most affected employees who had settled their families in the area. Holly Sugar offered a stable workplace until 1996. The above photograph has no date or names associated with it. Pictured below, from left to right, are Carolyn Meyer, Mary Lyons, Christy Stott, Melanie Martens, and Loretta Norberry. (Both, Hamilton City Community Services District.)

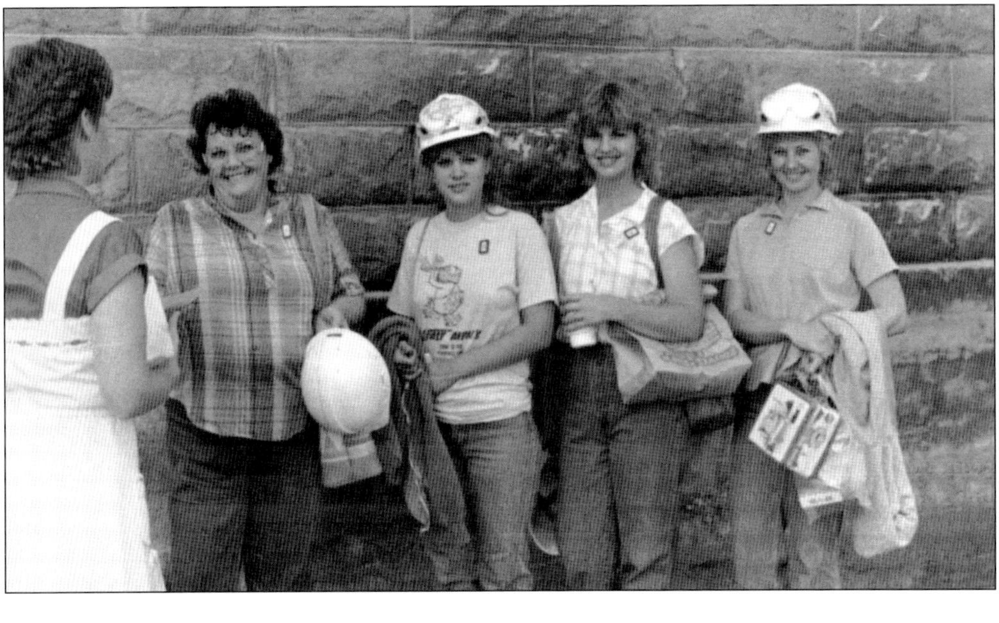

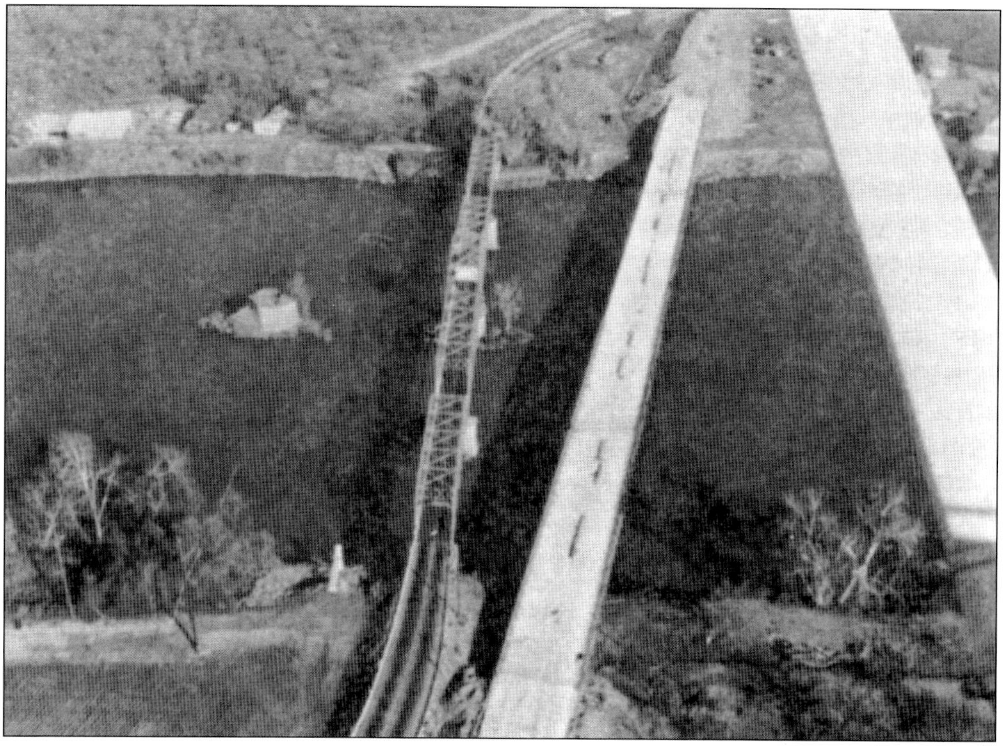

The Gianella Bridge was in use for 76 years before construction began on a concrete bridge. This photograph shows both bridges, old and new, in 1987. The Gianella Bridge, even though it was removed, is listed in the National Register of Historic Places. (*Wagon Wheels*, spring 1987.)

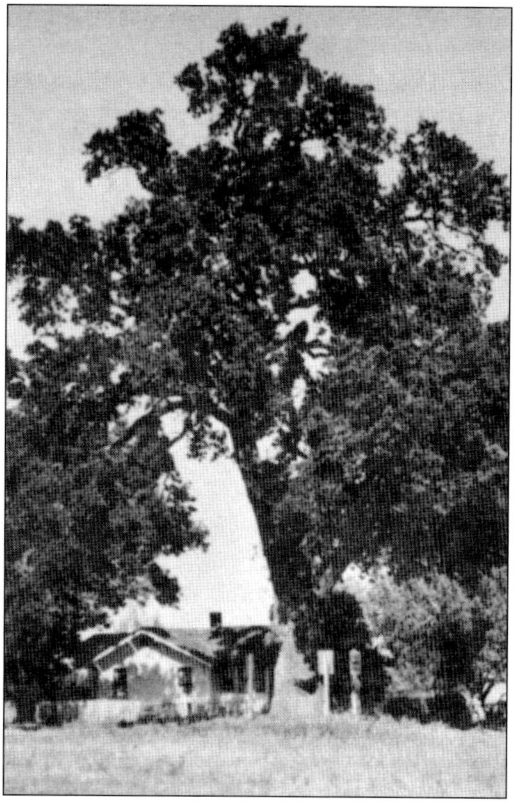

The Witness Tree stands in the middle of the road north of Hamilton City (just south of the diversion dam and west of the Sacramento River). It has been used as a marker to divide Glenn and Tehama Counties since 1891. It is just west of the location of the first framed house in Glenn County, which was erected by Martin A. Reager and Andrew S.C. Cleek in 1850. (*Wagon Wheels,* spring 1985.)

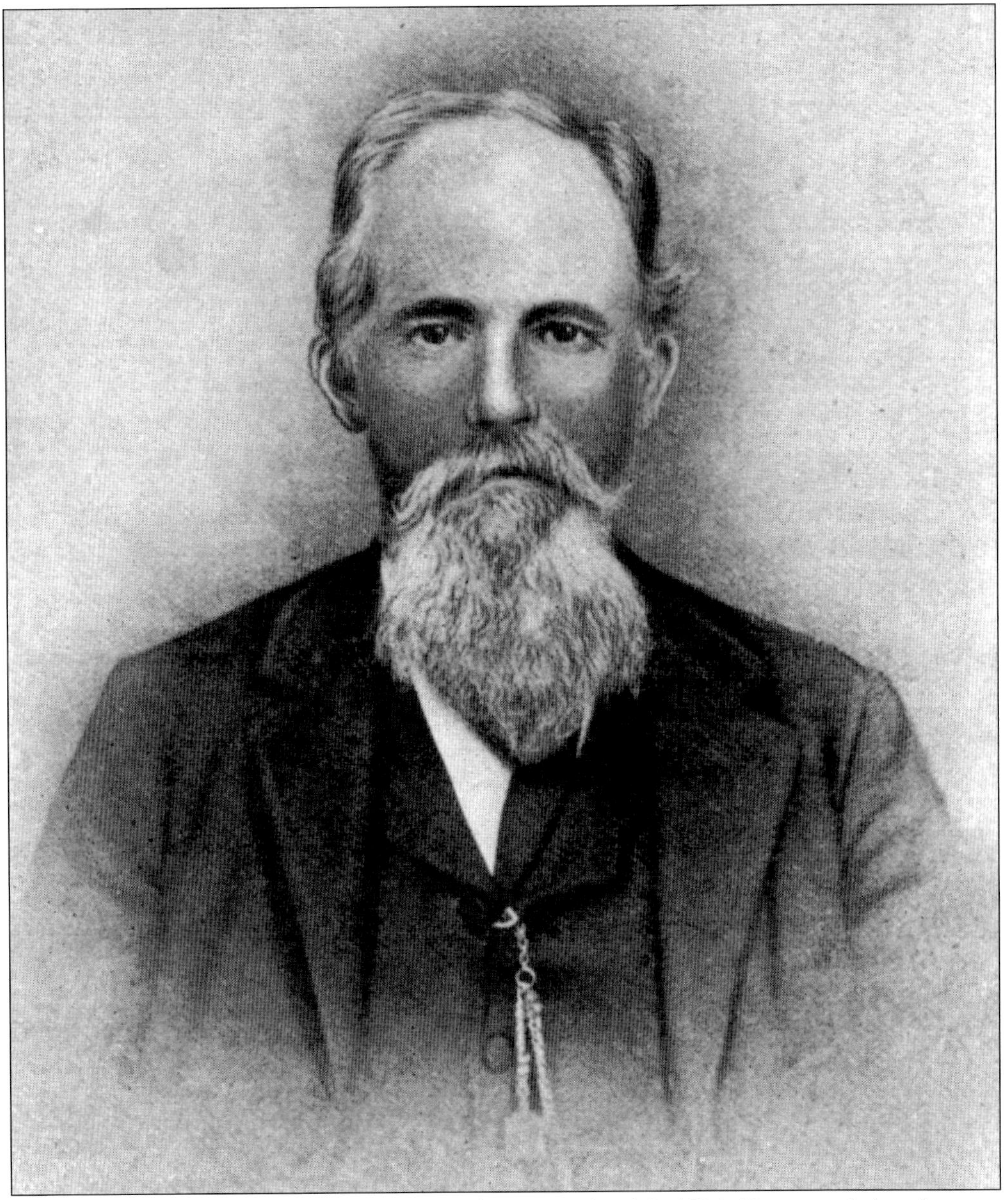

Rufus G. Burrows was born in La Porte, Indiana, on April 8, 1834. He crossed the plains to California with his parents when he was an adolescent. Their wagon train came upon the camp of the Donner party and buried the remaining skeletons of those who had perished there. Burrows married Charlotte T. Hull in Oregon on May 24, 1854. In July 1857, Rufus, Charlotte, and their son Orlando moved back to California. They traded a steer for a claim of 160 acres of land with a small spring five miles southeast of Newville. Over the years, the acreage grew to thousands of acres and was used for farming and stock raising. Burrows was an integral part of the foothill community and made his mark in several ways. He created the Thribble Cross breed of sheep, which is known for its wool and meat quality. He had a fruit orchard that contained one of the largest fig trees in California. He was involved in the Battle of Eagle Peak in the spring of 1862. The Burrows home place was known as Burrows Hollow, and their descendents continue to reside there. (Justus H. Rogers.)

Two

FOOTHILLS

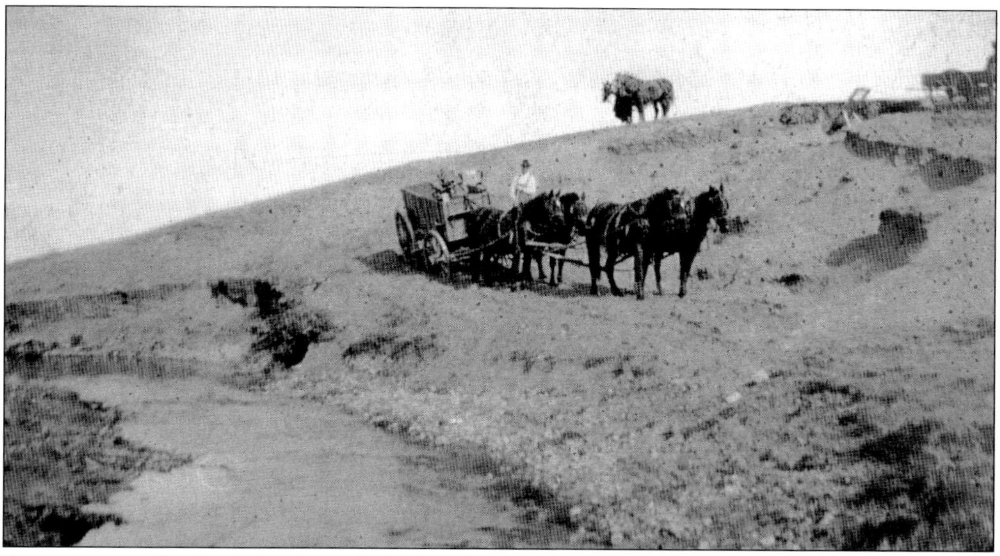

According to Charles D. McComish, "After the river district, the next section of the county to be settled was the foothills, because water could be obtained there more easily than on the plains." Hardy pioneers who enjoyed the open grazing country and its proximity to the mountains settled the area. Prior to the automobile, transportation required a wagon and a team of horses, mules, or oxen. As pictured here, anything from moving a family to hauling freight was done with a team. (Hollis Burrows Spurlock.)

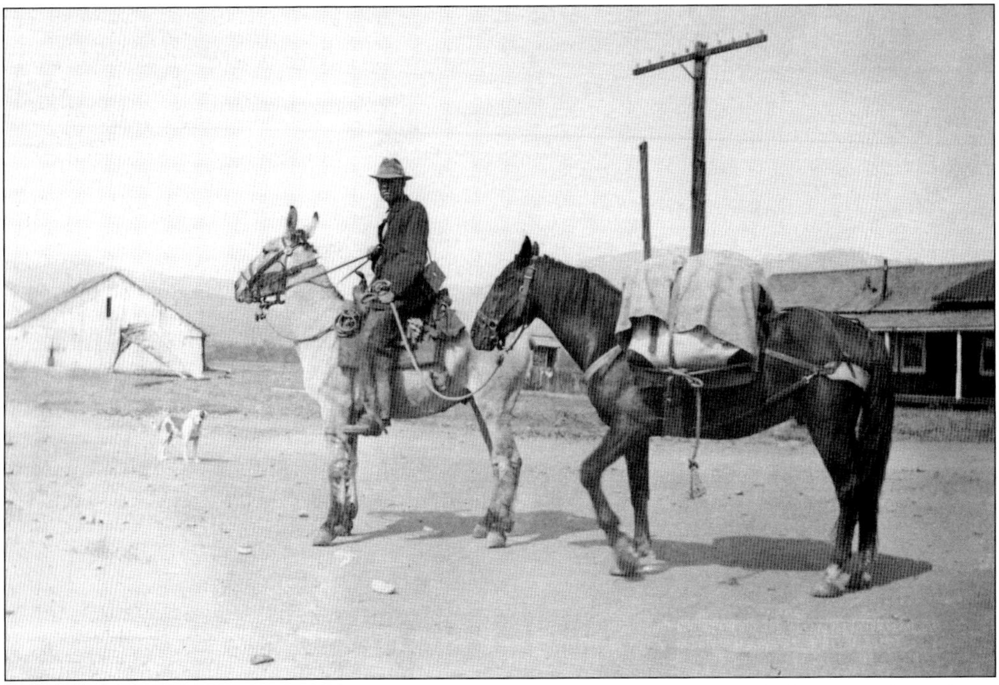

Accounts from the early 1900s show that as long as the weather was good, the ground was firm, and the animals and people were healthy, trips were uneventful. Many individuals traveled with all of their essentials packed onto their animals. Mules were surefooted and horses easy to keep. This mode of transportation would be used well beyond the advent of the automobile. (Robert Wesley Johanningsmeier.)

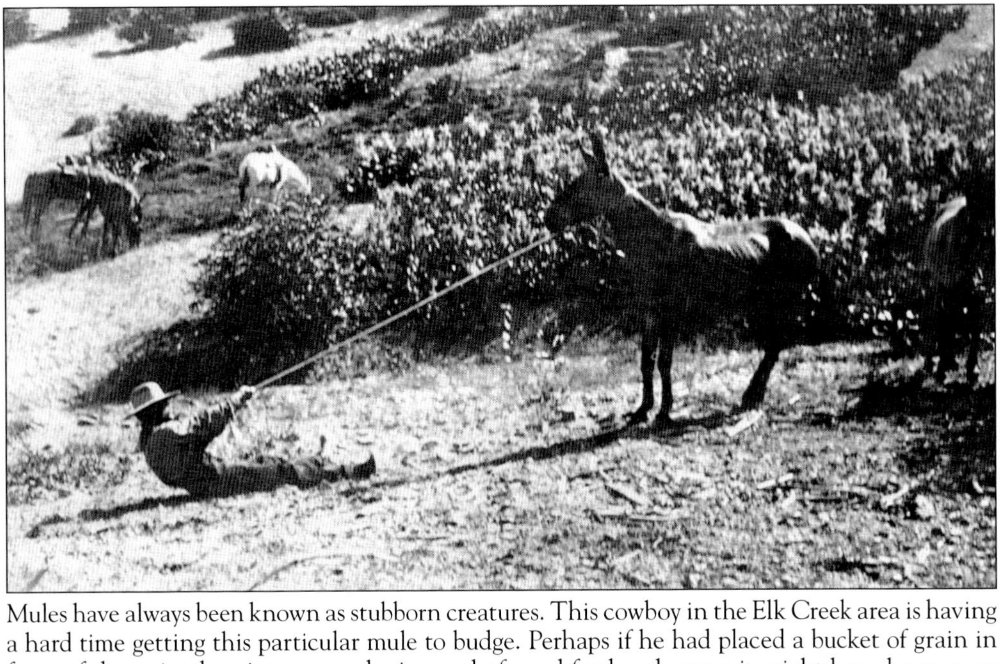

Mules have always been known as stubborn creatures. This cowboy in the Elk Creek area is having a hard time getting this particular mule to budge. Perhaps if he had placed a bucket of grain in front of the animal, as it seems to be in need of good feed and water, it might have been more inclined to move. (Hollis Burrows Spurlock.)

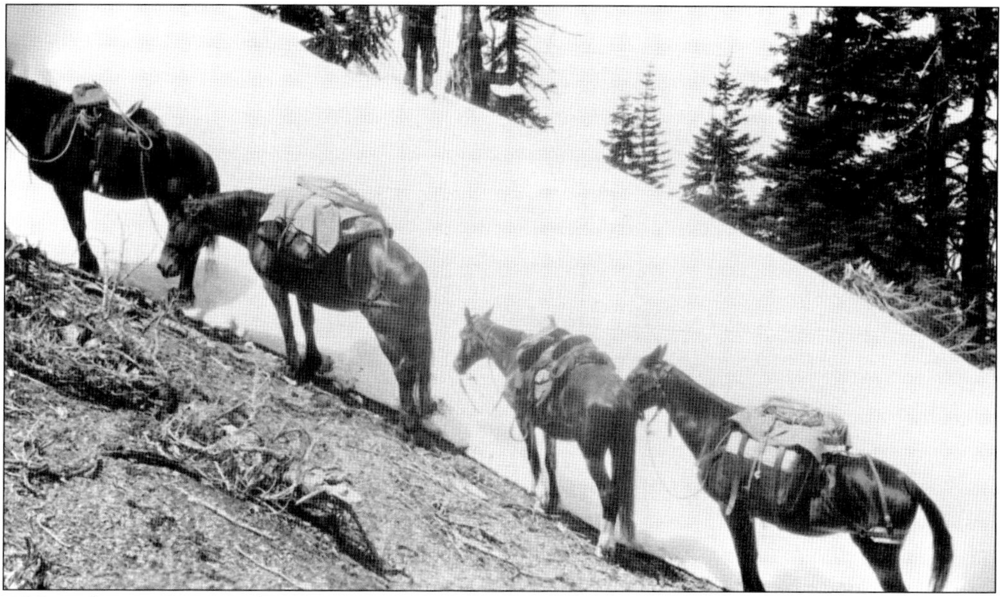

Although passage over the mountains by wagon was made fairly easily in the summer months, the snowmelt may not have occurred until June or July. Ritta Tanson Millsaps related that if they took too long to cross the mountain, they had to camp along the road wherever night overtook them. (Hollis Burrows Spurlock.)

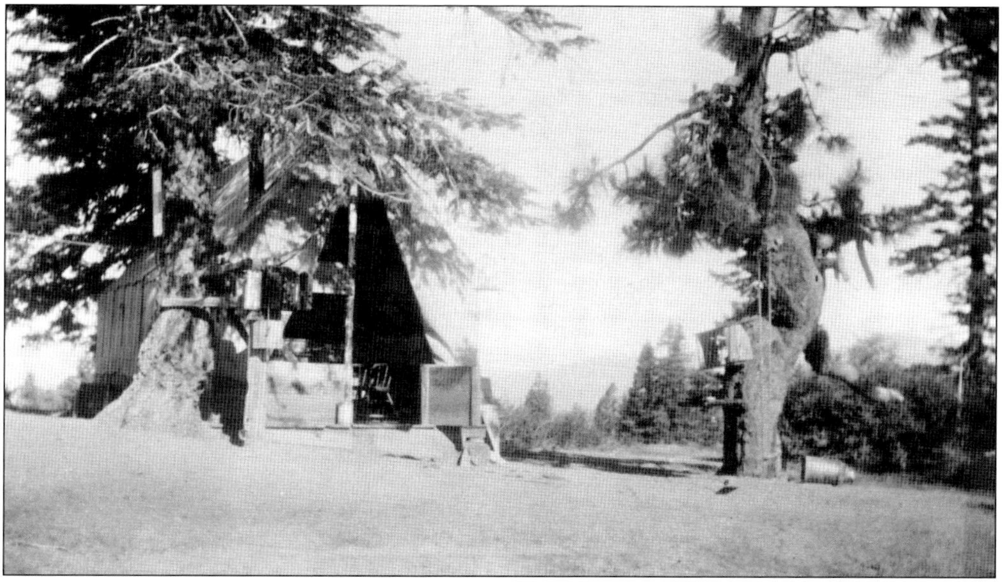

Whenever a camp was set up, such as this one on Bald Mountain in the Coast Range, it was made sure that there was water nearby. The valley heat and dryness made a lot of the valley residents flee into the mountains during the summer months. The purpose of this exodus may have been to take the sheep into better pastures or just to get away from the heat. Either way, a family that had retreated to the mountains may have had accommodations similar to these. (Hollis Burrows Spurlock.)

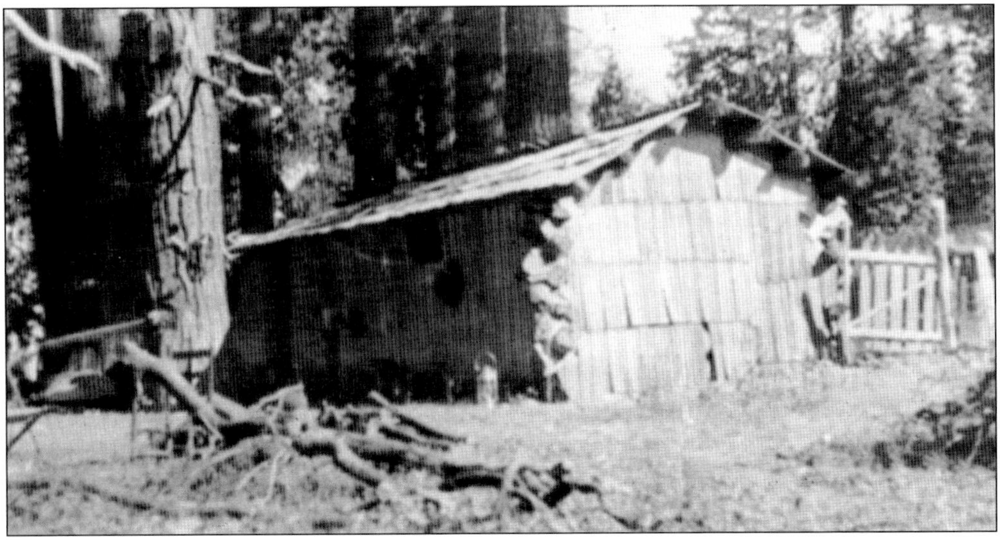

The Butler family were known as pioneer stock raisers in the Elk Creek area. They first raised sheep and then cattle. During the summer season, the stock was moved to summer range on Pinto Ridge (near Black Butte in the Coast Mountains). In 1895, Mr. Butler and his cousin John Shields built the cabin shown in this 1913 photograph. The Butler family occupied the cabin during the summer months until 1914. (*Wagon Wheels*, September 1971.)

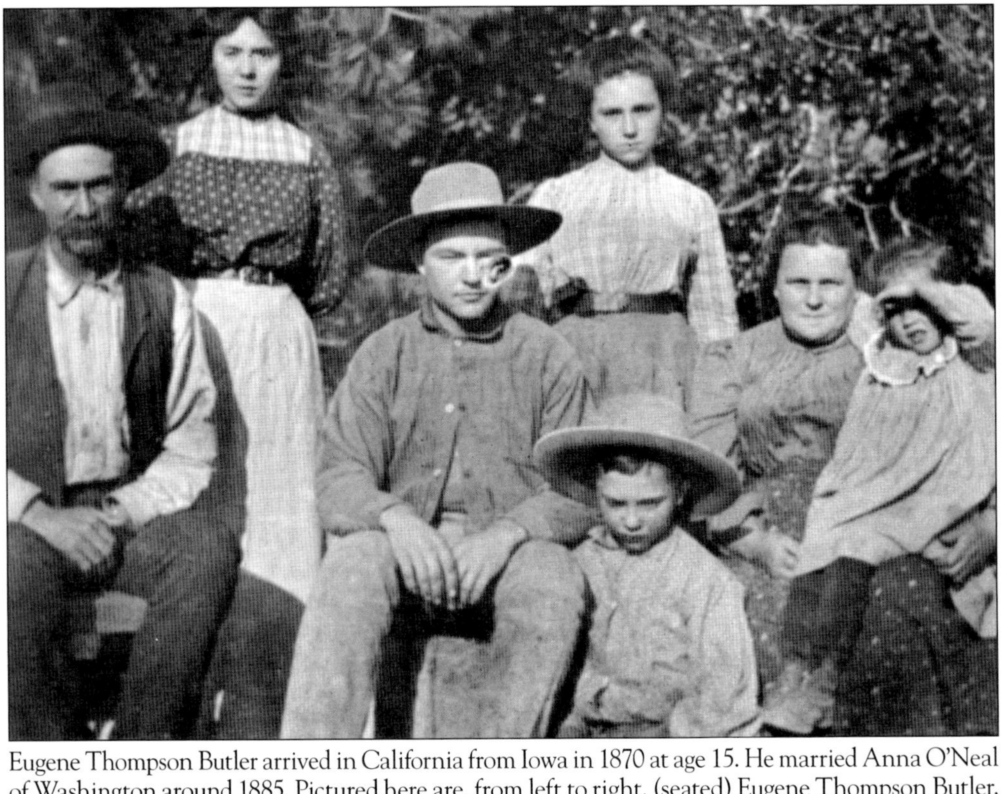

Eugene Thompson Butler arrived in California from Iowa in 1870 at age 15. He married Anna O'Neal of Washington around 1885. Pictured here are, from left to right, (seated) Eugene Thompson Butler, Charles Butler, Albert Hugh Butler, Anna O'Neal Butler, and Hazel Etta Butler (White); (standing) Alma Butler (Warmack) and Bessie Butler (Haskell). (*Wagon Wheels*, September 1971.)

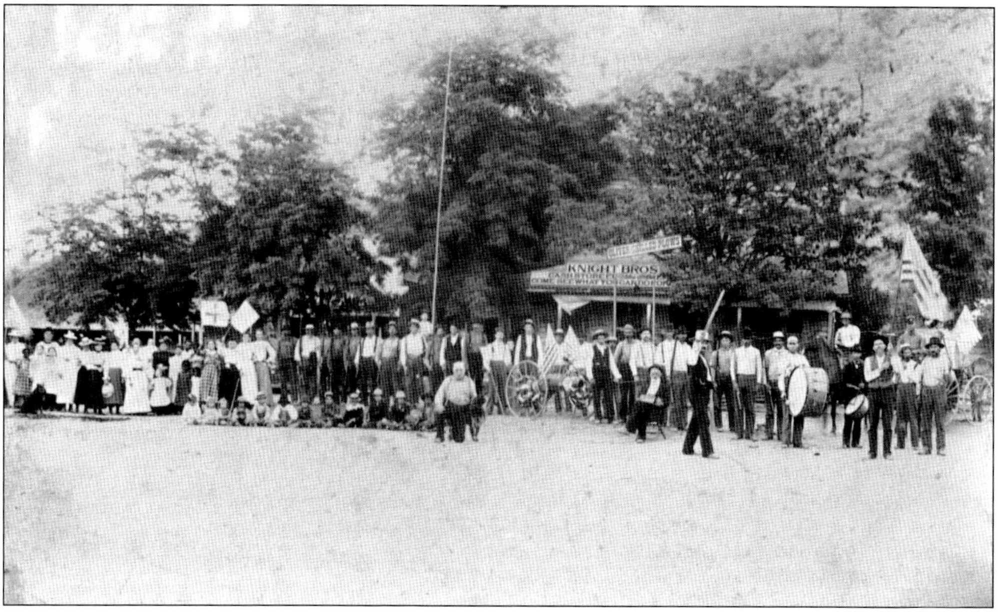

Any Fourth of July was a cause for great celebration. The citizens of Elk Creek pictured here in front of the Knight Bros. store are ready for the festivities. A cannon is decorated with flags, riflemen stand ready, drummers are prepared for their march, children are seated patiently, and the women are gathered (probably with a celebratory feast prepared for after the festivities). All are waiting for the sword to be dropped by the unidentified leader in the front of the crowd. (Hollis Burrows Spurlock.)

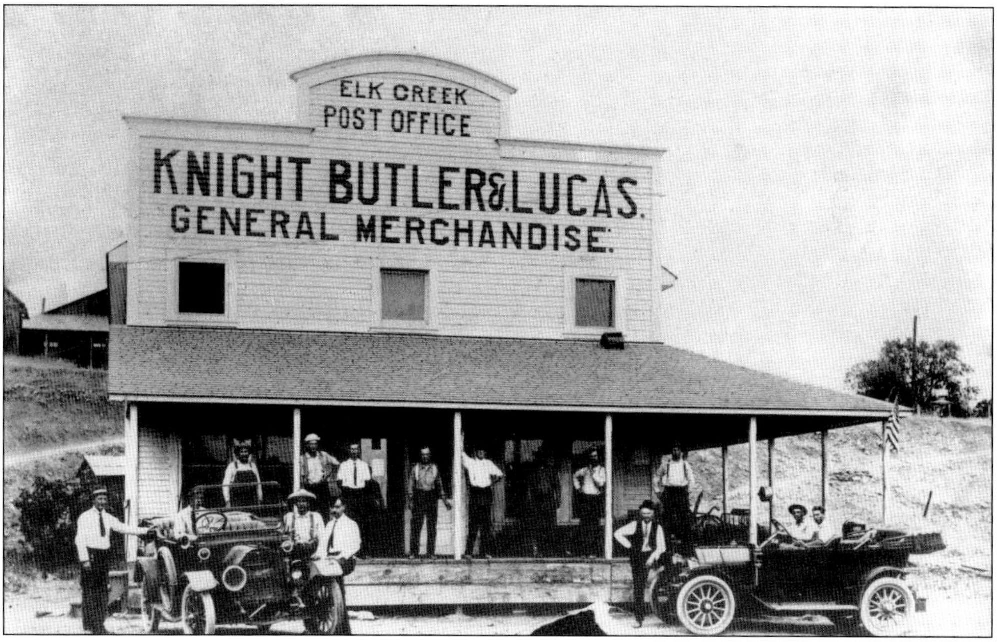

In 1913, Henry D. Knight, Charles A. Butler, and James LeRoy Lucas became partners in the Knight, Butler, and Lucas General Merchandise store in Elk Creek. Prior to this, a store in Elk Creek was operated by H.D. Knight (1902), J.W. Houston (1880), and M.M. Feder (1869). The men in front of the store are unidentified. (Hollis Burrows Spurlock.)

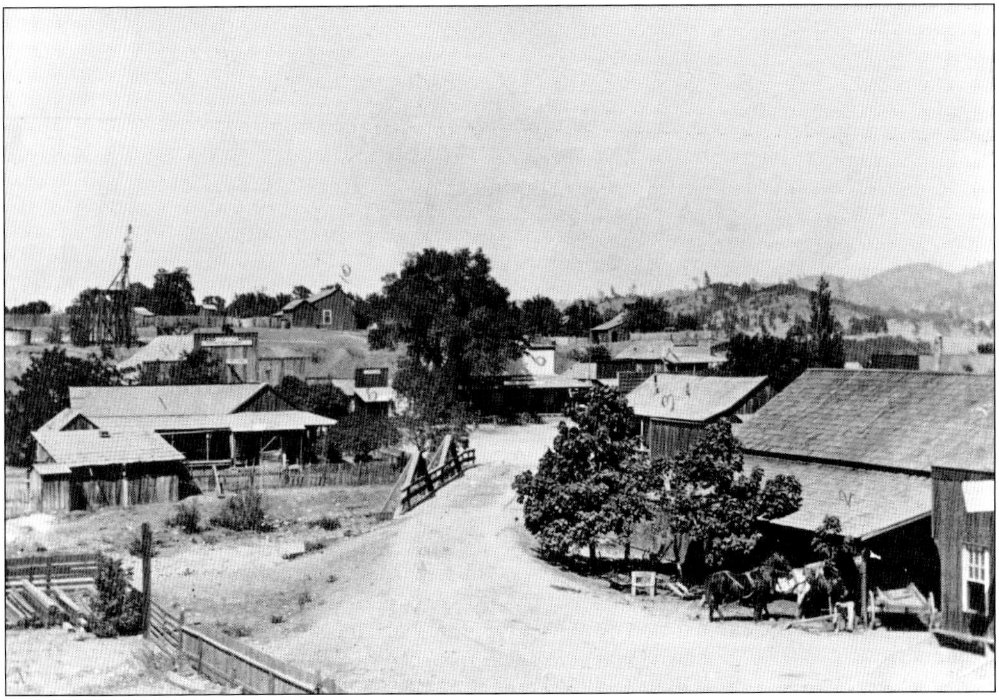

Will S. Green described Elk Creek as "situated on a little stream, by the same name, near its junction with Stony Creek." By the time he was writing in 1880, it had been a trading point for a number of years; M.M. Feder kept a store here in 1869. This pre-1900 photograph shows a millinery, blacksmith shop, livery stable, harness shop, lumber store, general merchandise store, and several homes. (Hollis Burrows Spurlock.)

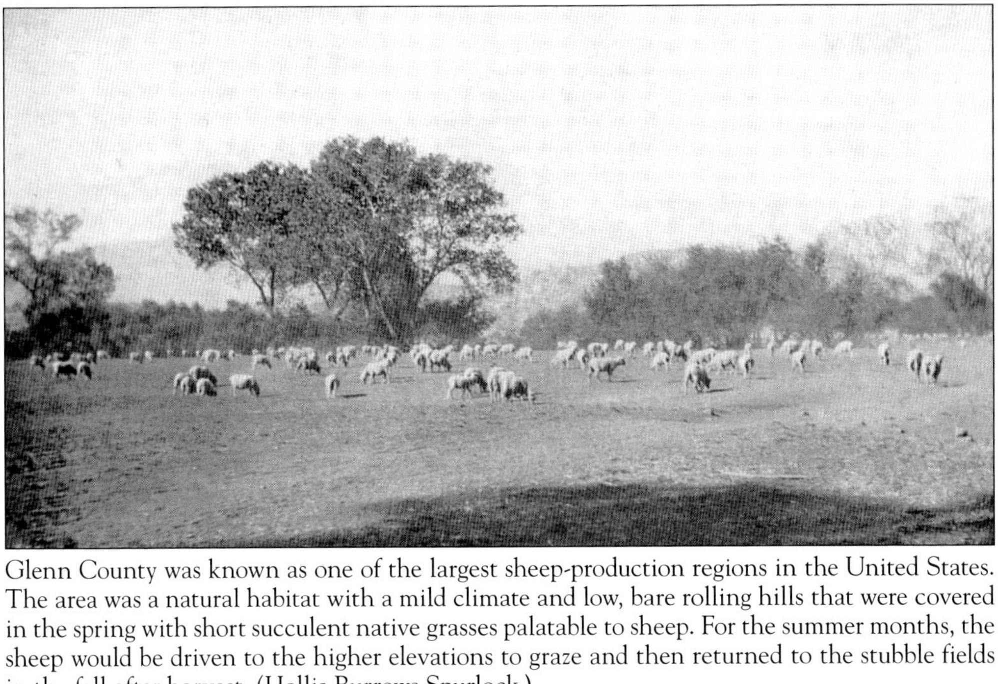

Glenn County was known as one of the largest sheep-production regions in the United States. The area was a natural habitat with a mild climate and low, bare rolling hills that were covered in the spring with short succulent native grasses palatable to sheep. For the summer months, the sheep would be driven to the higher elevations to graze and then returned to the stubble fields in the fall after harvest. (Hollis Burrows Spurlock.)

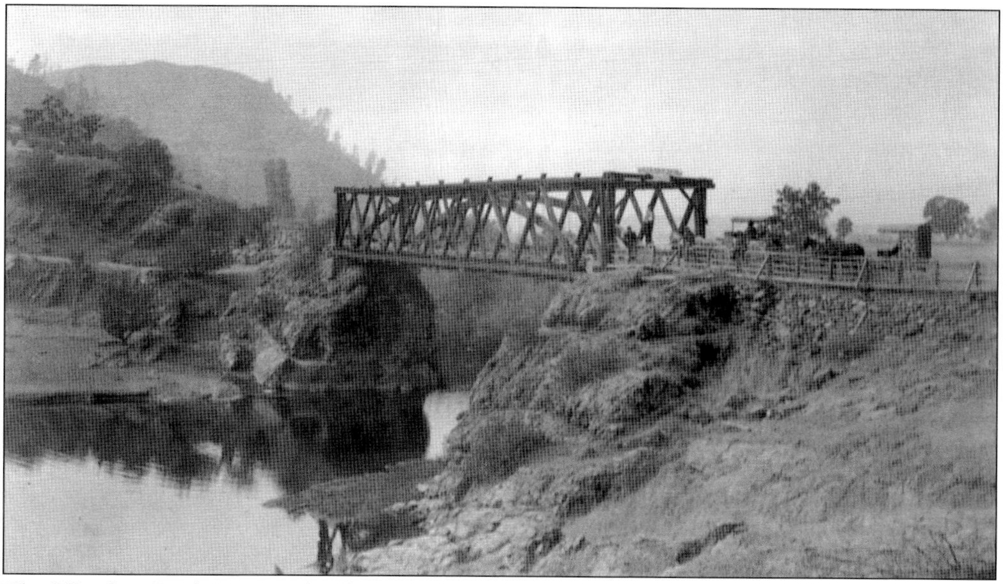

The Winslow Bridge, a wooden bridge built in 1873, was the first bridge to span Stony Creek. Because there was no flood control, this was the only place where the creek could be crossed safely during high water. The approaches to the bridge were formed by natural abutments. It was replaced with a steel bridge in 1895 and then a cement bridge in 1920. (Orland Historical and Cultural Society.)

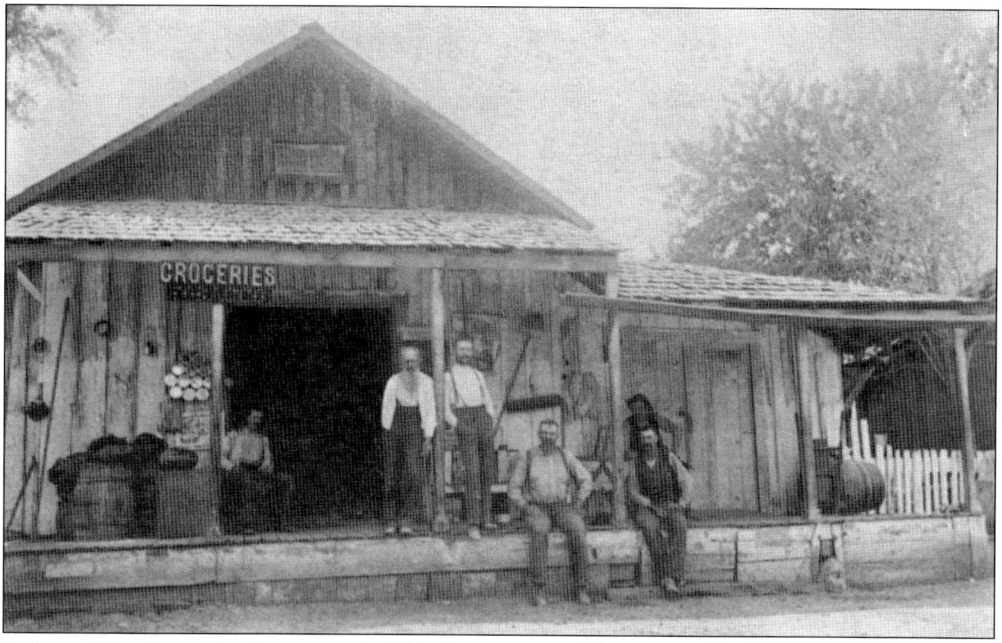

Jackson Van Scyoc built a store in Winslow, pictured here in 1890, and it was operated by O.O. Laraway. The town of Winslow was first known as Bridgeport, but upon filing for a post office, it was found that there was already another town with that name. Winslow was located a mile east and south of Elk Creek. Pictured from left to right are Arthur Anderson, O.O. Laraway, George Laraway, Jackson Van Scyoc, Franklin Van Scyoc, and Benton Van Scyoc. (*Wagon Wheels*, February 1961.)

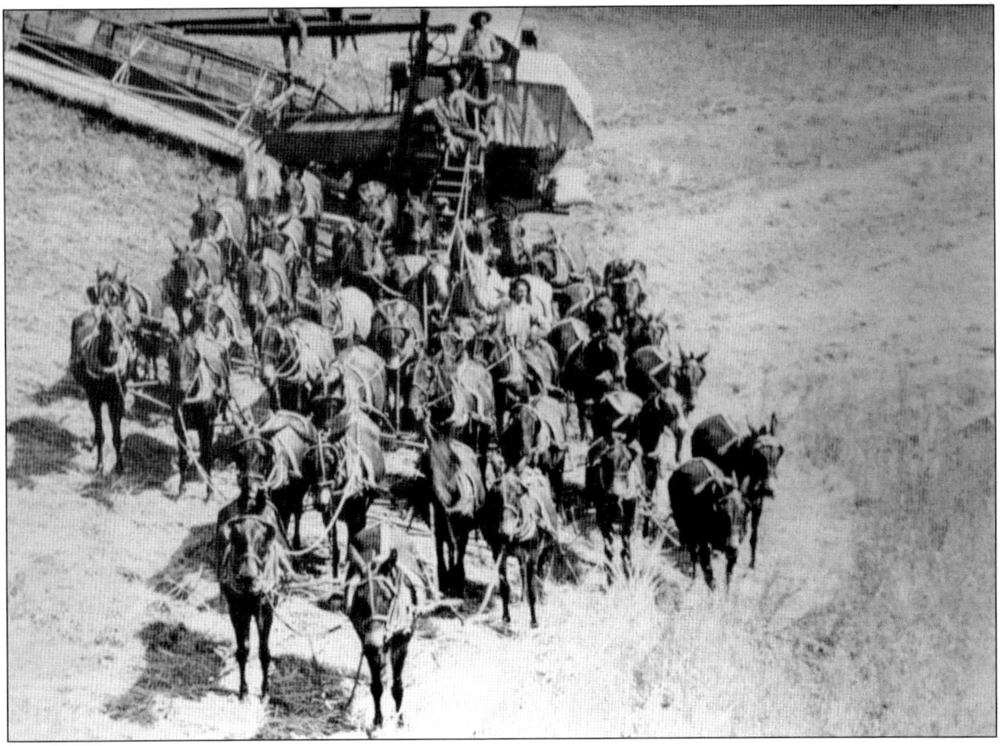

In 1856, John Flood established the Flood Ranch when he took up a claim of 160 acres in the Newville area. There, he built the first house and blacksmith shop in the district. He married Mary Williams on September 6, 1860. They were involved in raising dairy cattle, mules, wheat, and barley. This hillside harvest scene was photographed in 1902. Fred Cushman owned the harvester pictured, which was powered by 42 mules. (Orland Historical and Cultural Society.)

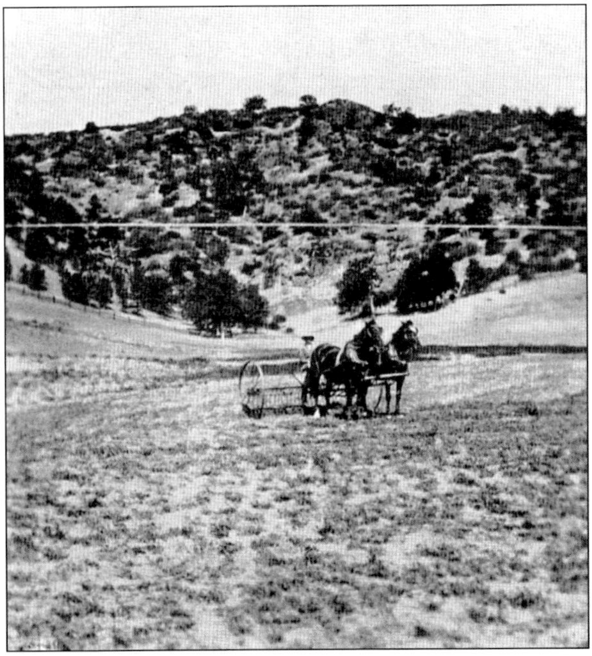

In Ritta Tanson Millsap's "Early Days in Elk Creek," she relates an incident that occurred around 1908 while driving a hay rake like the one in this photograph: "I put my foot on the trigger that dumped the hay, I fell off down behind the mules and rolled around and around in the hay but kept crawling toward the outside . . . My father saw me about that time and came to help me." (Hollis Burrows Spurlock.)

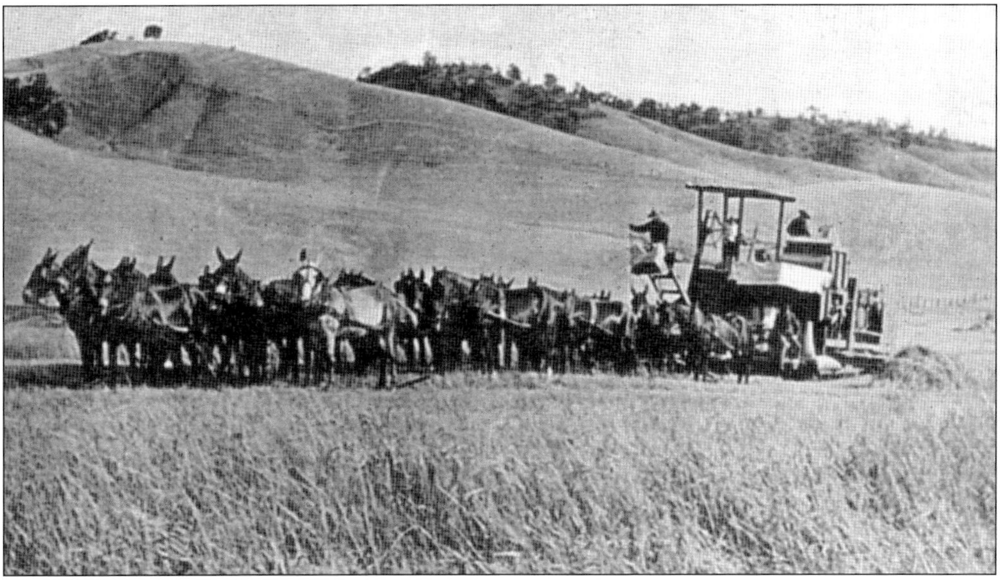

The Fred Cushman Ranch was very active in the early 1900s. The harvest crew would work at all the local ranches until the end of the season. Once the wheat was harvested, it would be hauled to a mill in the valley to be ground into white flour. These trips also included taking other fresh farm products, such as butter and eggs, and exchanging them for material, coffee, sugar, and tea. (Hollis Burrows Spurlock.)

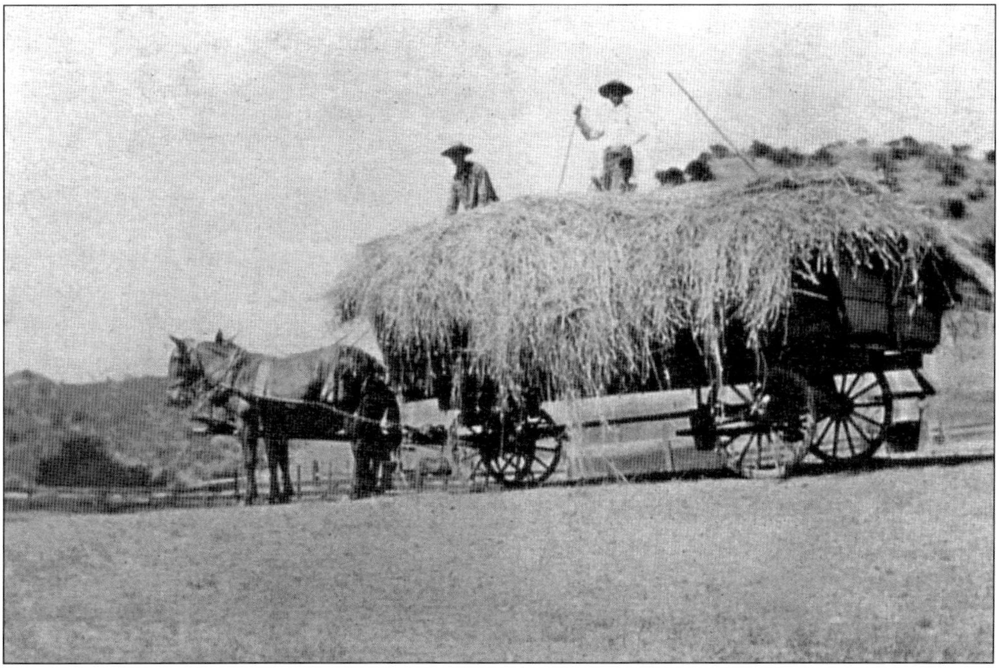

The harvesting of hay, either in barley or oats, was essential for keeping livestock fed during the harsh winter months. The foothill ranches, like the Cushman Ranch shown here, built huge barns to hold the loose hay. It would be loaded onto the wagons and then unloaded by hand. It was not until the early 1900s that mechanization made its way to the foothill ranches. (Hollis Burrows Spurlock.)

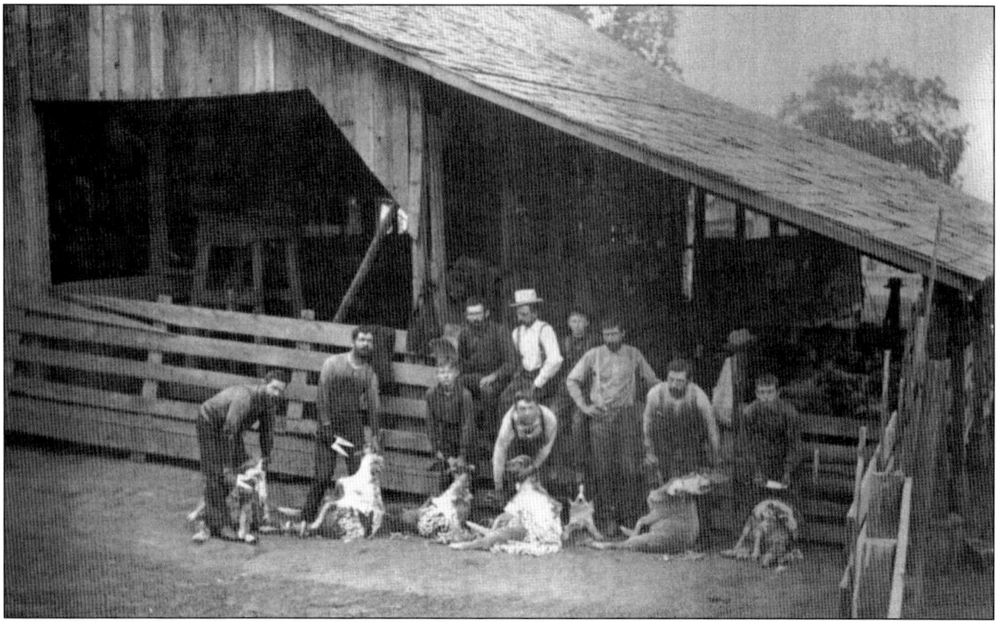

The removal of the wool from the sheep served dual purposes. The wool was a by-product that was sold as fiber, most of the time for a profit, and it kept the sheep cool in the warm summer months. Expert sheep shearers removed the wool by hand blade shearing. Men would travel from ranch to ranch shearing sheep as their primary occupation. Although machine shearing had been introduced by 1888, it required electricity, which many of the foothill ranches did not have until much later. Sheep shearing continues to be a skill that is utilized and valued today. Pictured here in the spring of 1906 are shearers in the Newville area (above) and a pen of white-faced ewes and lambs on the Bailey Ranch (below). (Both, Hollis Burrows Spurlock.)

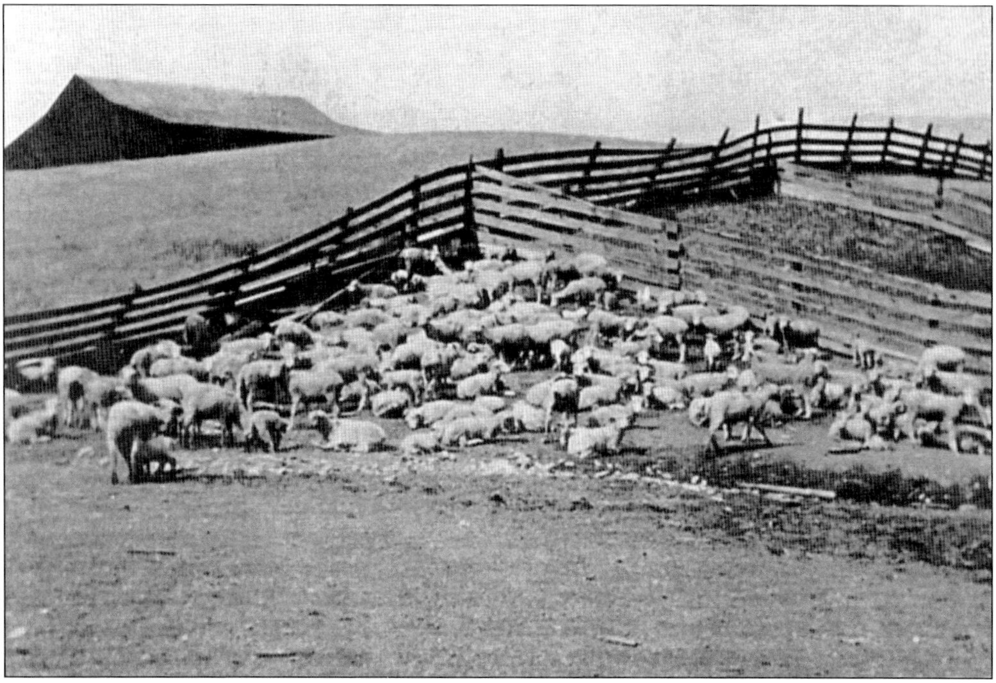

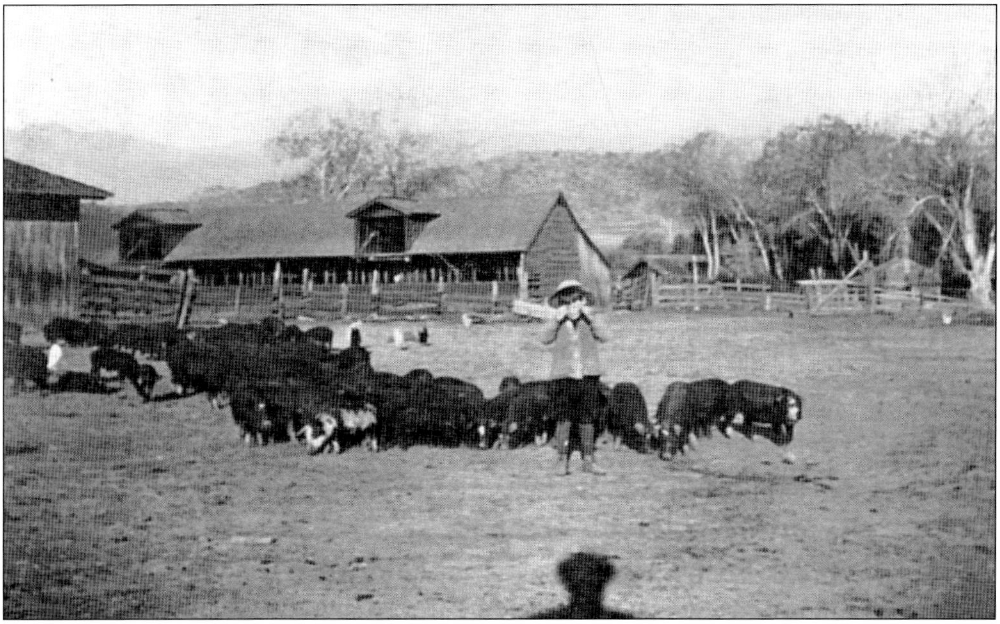

The Jim Cushman Ranch was diversified in that it raised not only sheep, but also hogs, grain, and hay crops. This photograph gives an insight into the farmyard of an early 20th-century foothill ranch in Glenn County. The young man posing for the photograph seems as comfortable with the hogs as they are with him. (Hollis Burrows Spurlock.)

Every ranch and farm had chickens. They were raised for eggs, meat, and feathers. Although chicken feathers were used to make pillows and bedding, the down from a goose or a duck was preferable. The feathers would be washed and dried before use. Two unidentified women are feeding chickens at the Ruff Ranch near Newville. (Hollis Burrows Spurlock.)

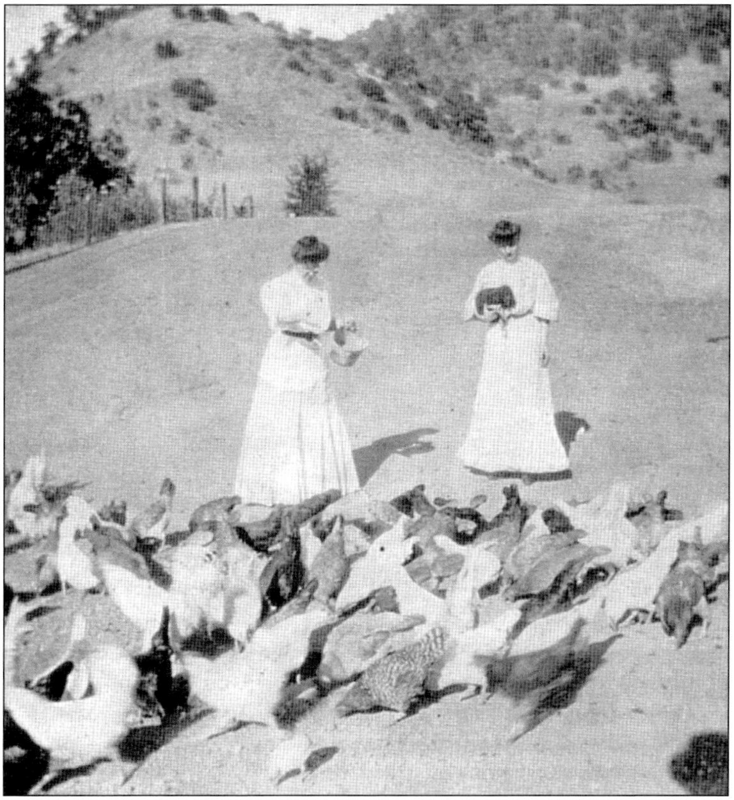

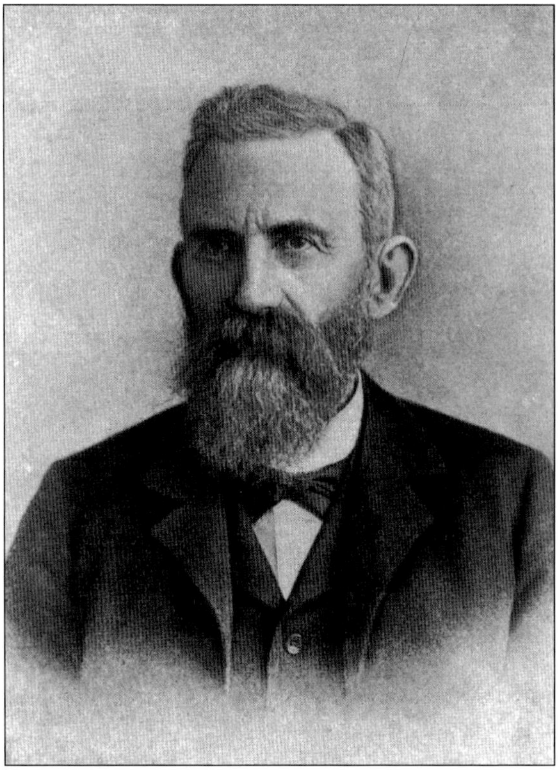

Irving Woodbridge Brownell was born in New Bedford, Massachusetts, on October 10, 1826. He drove a team of oxen from Illinois to California, arriving in Weaverville on August 27, 1849. In August 1859, he purchased 80 acres and a flock of sheep on Stony Creek. He married Lois R. Smith in September 1861. They raised their family in the Stony Creek Valley, where they continued to acquire acreage, sheep, and cattle. They became an integral part of the foothills, where their descendents still reside. (Justus H. Rogers.)

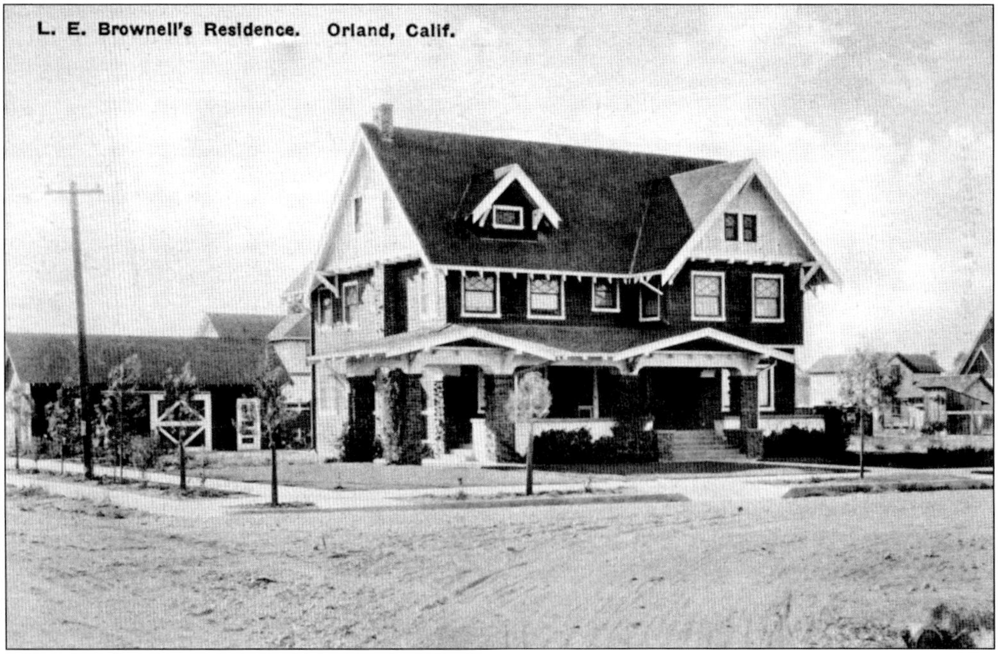

The Louis Elmer Brownell house is located on the corner of A and Yolo Streets in Orland. L.E. Brownell was the son of I.W. and Lois Brownell, pioneers of the foothills and Coast Range of Glenn County. Many of the ranchers in the foothills had houses in town. In the 1920s, Brownell and his wife, Helen, boarded three high school teachers. (Author's collection.)

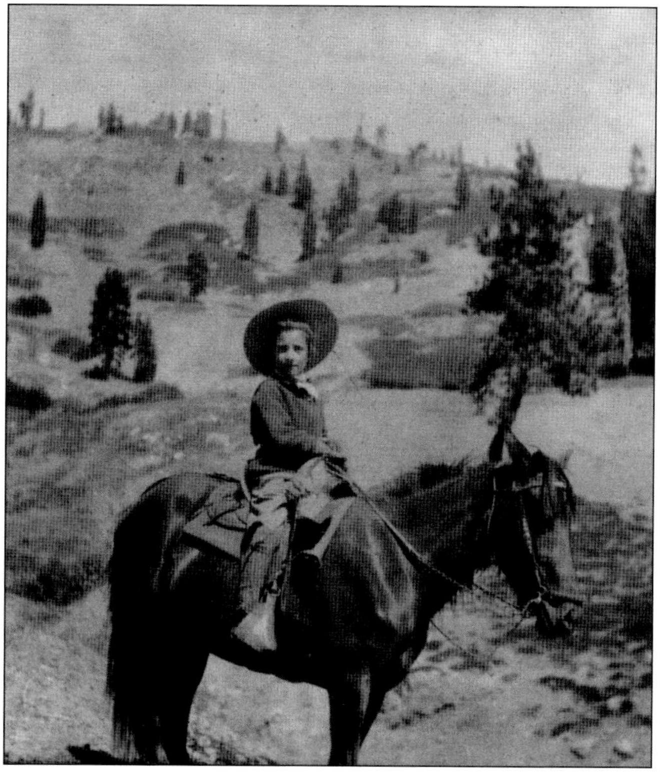

Phebe Brownell was born in November 1897 to Roscoe and Laura Brownell. The granddaughter of I.W. Brownell, she inherited the Brownell property upon the death of all of her grandfather's sons. Phebe, an avid horsewoman, is seen here in 1906 on Bonnie. (Orland Historical and Cultural Society.)

Three unidentified men are stacking hay on the Brownell Ranch near what is now the south end of Black Butte Lake. The horse carriage team, Jack and Polly, are seen at left carrying Irving Woodbridge Brownell. (Orland Historical and Cultural Society.)

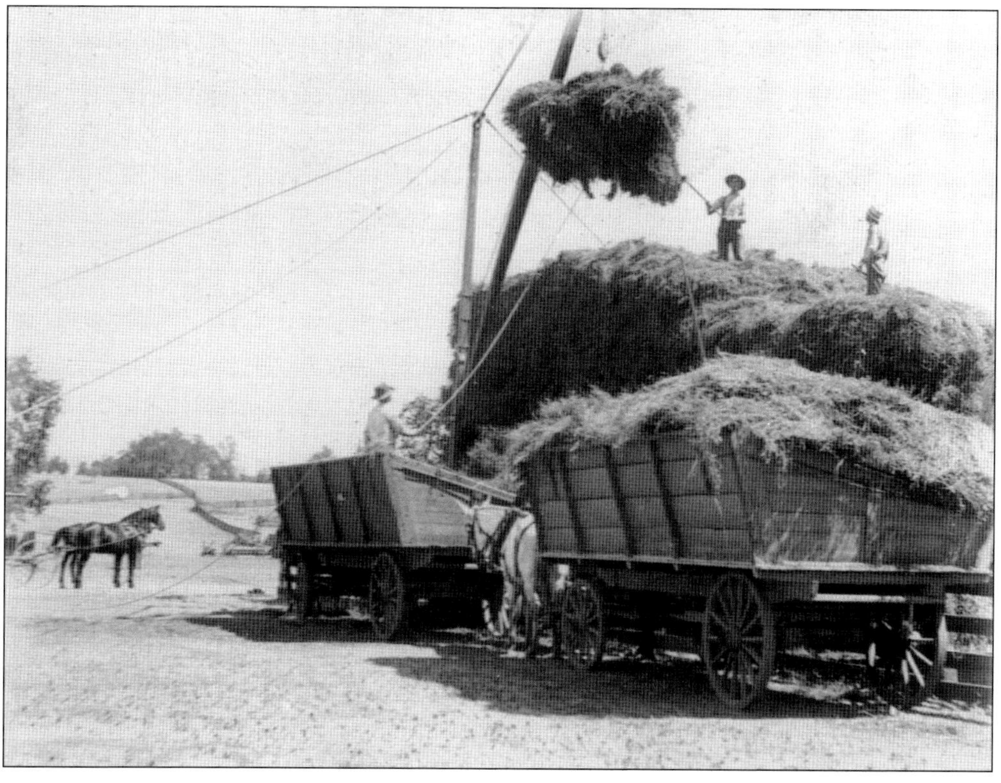

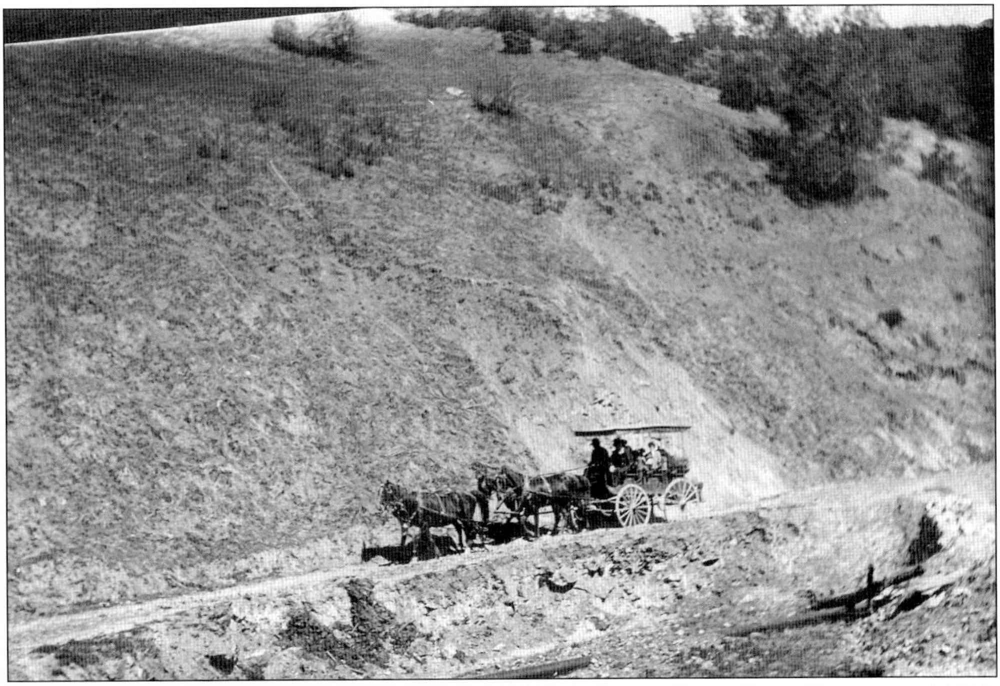

This surrey is carrying people across the newly graded road to see Stony Gorge Dam around 1928. Even though automobiles were available, horses were still the preferred mode of transportation because they were more reliable. (Orland Historical and Cultural Society.)

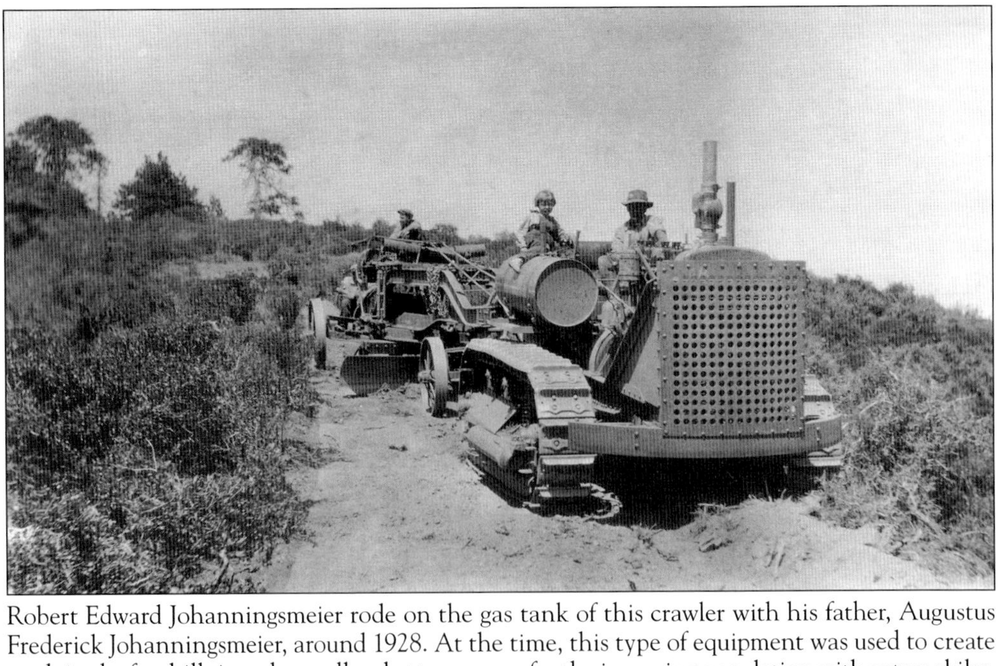

Robert Edward Johanningsmeier rode on the gas tank of this crawler with his father, Augustus Frederick Johanningsmeier, around 1928. At the time, this type of equipment was used to create roads in the foothills in order to allow better passage for the incoming population with automobiles. The roads remained dirt for many years and became difficult to traverse in the winter months. (Robert Wesley Johanningsmeier.)

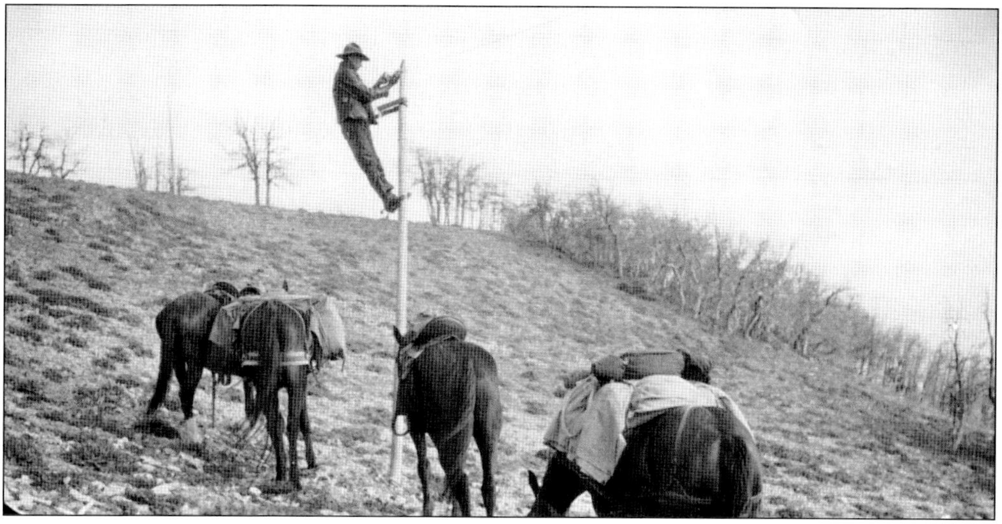

The rising population also meant progress. In 1878, the first successful long-distance telephone line in the world was built along the San Juan Ridge (about 100 miles west of the Glenn County foothills). This lineman had all the tools he needed for the job as well as his bedroll and grub for many miles of work. (Hollis Burrows Spurlock.)

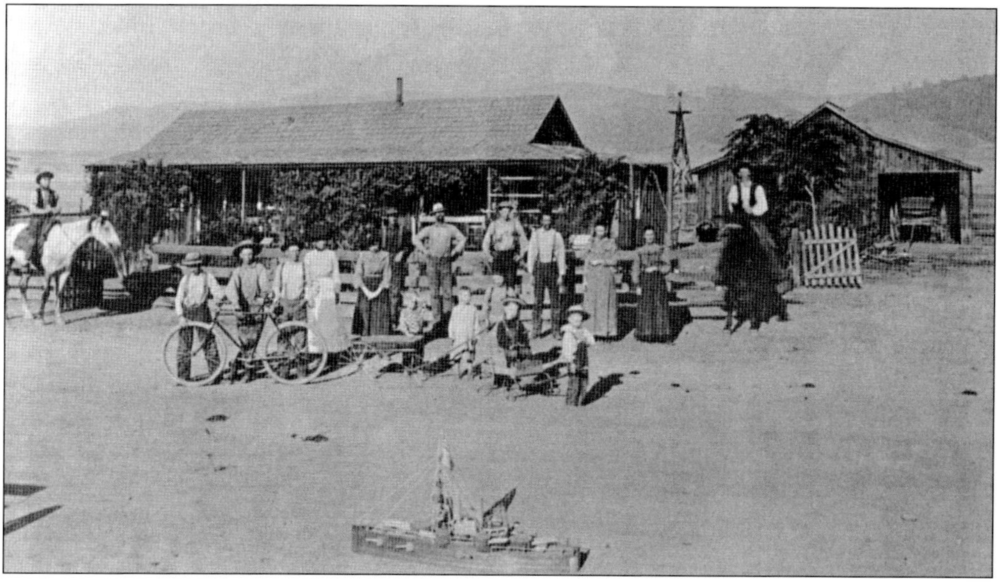

This photograph almost looks like a kids' parade was taking place at the home of Jim Roden in Chrome. Jim and his brother Walter owned and operated a blacksmith shop. G.W. Millsap owned the store and was postmaster. J.C. Cooper drove the stage from Chrome to Elk Creek twice a week. The men mentioned are standing near the fence. The children belonged to Millsap, Cooper, Roden, and Grundy. The ship was built by Andy Roden and was a replica of a Spanish-American War ship. (Hollis Burrows Spurlock.)

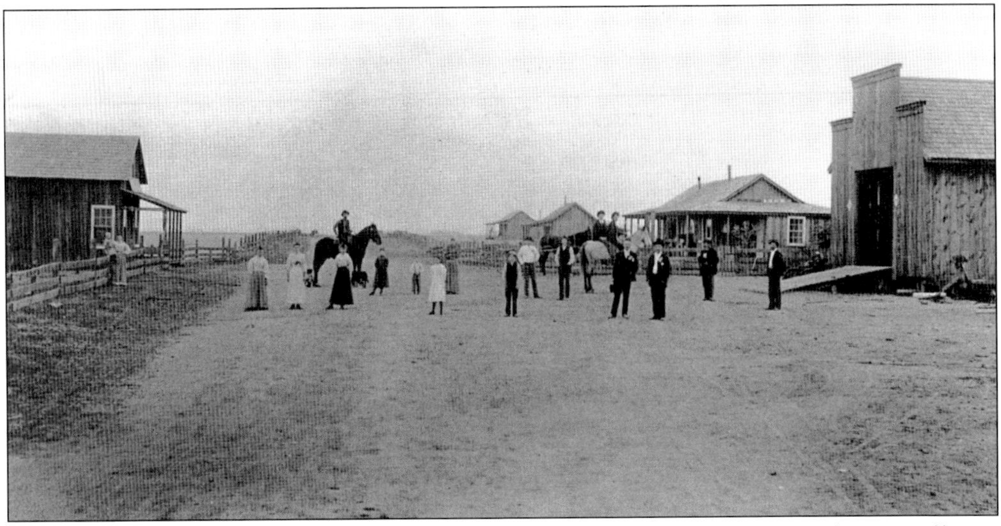

The foothill town of Chrome had 10 buildings in 1899. From left to right are the post office, a home, the Hooper store, the Jim Roden house, and the blacksmith shop. The remaining buildings not seen here were homes. Eva Armstrong Cooper Bywater's memories of Chrome were published in the December 1965 issue of *Wagon Wheels*. Pictured here from left to right are Mary Hooper and her granddaughter Josie Hooper, Minnie Floyd, Maude Millsap, Old George Millsap (on horse), Hattie Roden, Pedro Roden, Dillie Grundy, Becky Roden, Andy Roden, George Cooper, John Hull, Lewis Cooper and Oscar Millsap (both on horse), Alcie Hooper, unidentified, Bert Hull, and Jim Roden. (Hollis Burrows Spurlock.)

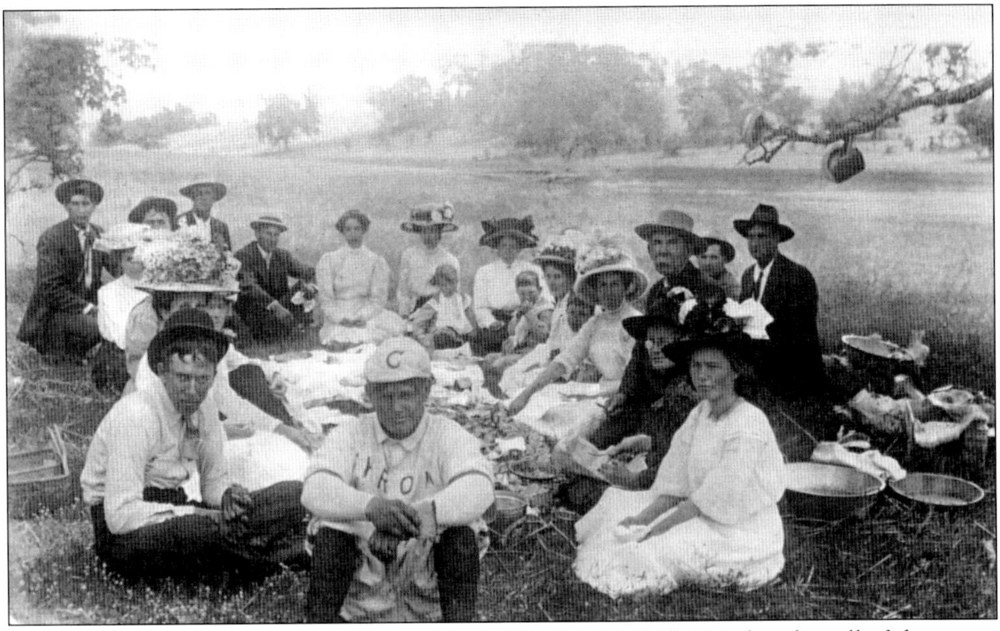

Baseball has always been the great American pastime. Town ball was played in all of the towns in Glenn County, foothill and valley alike. In the Chrome area, it gave the Niesen, Hull, and Drew families an opportunity to dress in their finery and picnic together. This meal was served from tin cans and baskets on tin plates. The children wore napkins to keep their town clothes from getting soiled. (Hollis Burrows Spurlock.)

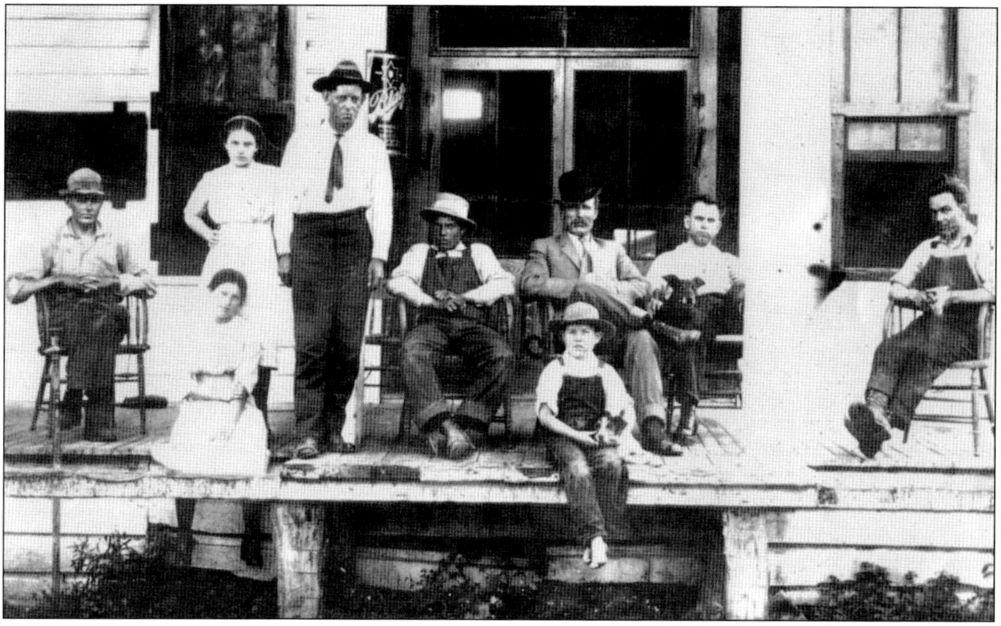

Up the Stony Creek Valley six miles to the north is Newville. Sheltered on every side by hills, it was a half-mile from the northern boundary of the county. Because stockmen, including Kendrick, Bedford, and Millsaps, began settling in the area in the 1850s, the town was a natural consequence. Lee Dobkins's saloon is pictured here in 1917. From left to right are (first row) two unidentified children; (second row) unidentified, Ida Dobkins, Henry Miller, Harry Lee, Bill Brunk, and two unidentified. (Hollis Burrows Spurlock.)

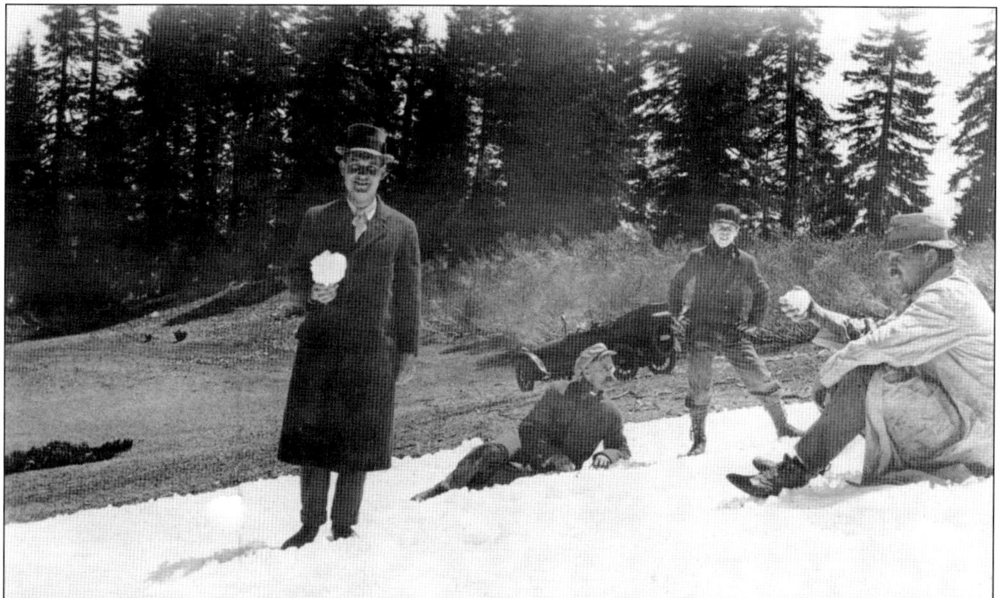

The sale of a Studebaker was the ultimate result of this trip to Government Flat at the summit of the Coast Range on July 4, 1917. From left to right are Earl Hazelton, H.M. Keene, Don Keene, and H.E. Johnson. Johnson, the Orland Studebaker dealer, demonstrated the vehicle's capabilities on this trip. (Orland Historical and Cultural Society.)

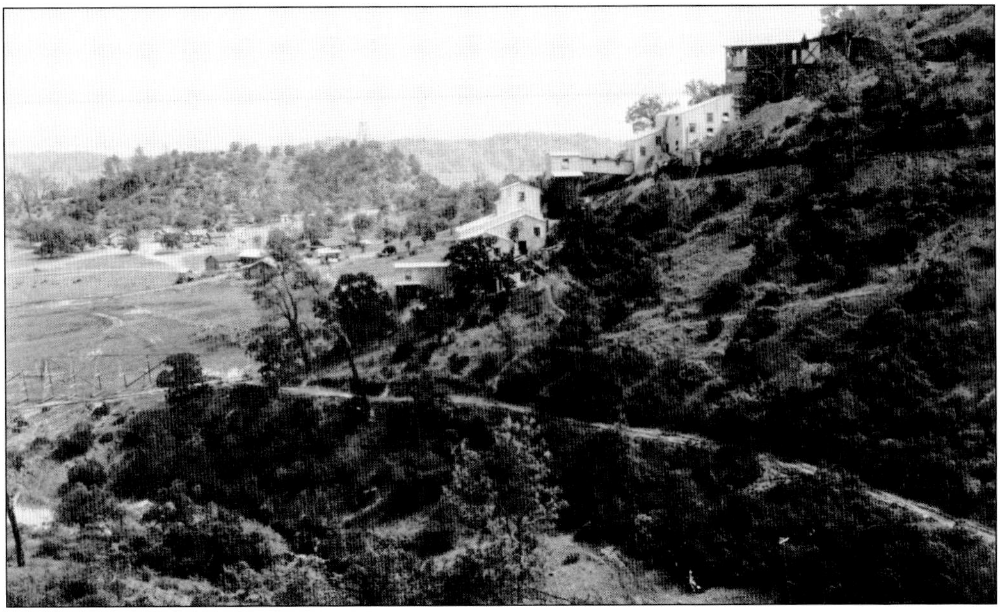

According to the California State Mining Bureau Bulletin No. 76, chromite was first mined in Glenn County by J.R. Whitlock and F. Oakes during the early 1890s. By 1894, 3,000 tons had been shipped by way of the railroad at Fruto. The mines were opened sporadically from 1916 to 1918 during World War I. In 1921, Glenn County was recognized as the 43rd most important mineral-producing county in California, mainly due to the presence of sand and gravel. The Grey Eagle mine, operated by the Rustless Mining Company, was one of the first commercially successful chromite mines in the country. It produced 30,800 long tons of concentrates before the mine was exhausted in 1944. The Grey Eagle mine produced most of the chromite from Northern California during World War II. It was the only mine that had been worked on a large scale since 1918. The Glenn County production in 1942, 1943, and 1944 came entirely from the Grey Eagle mine. (Both, Hollis Burrows Spurlock.)

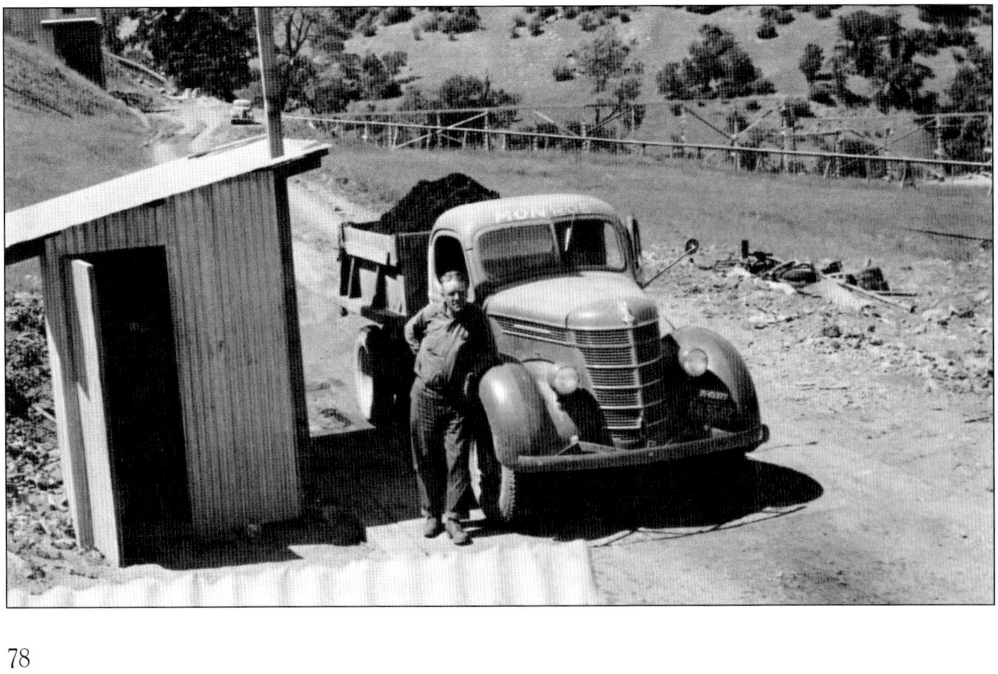

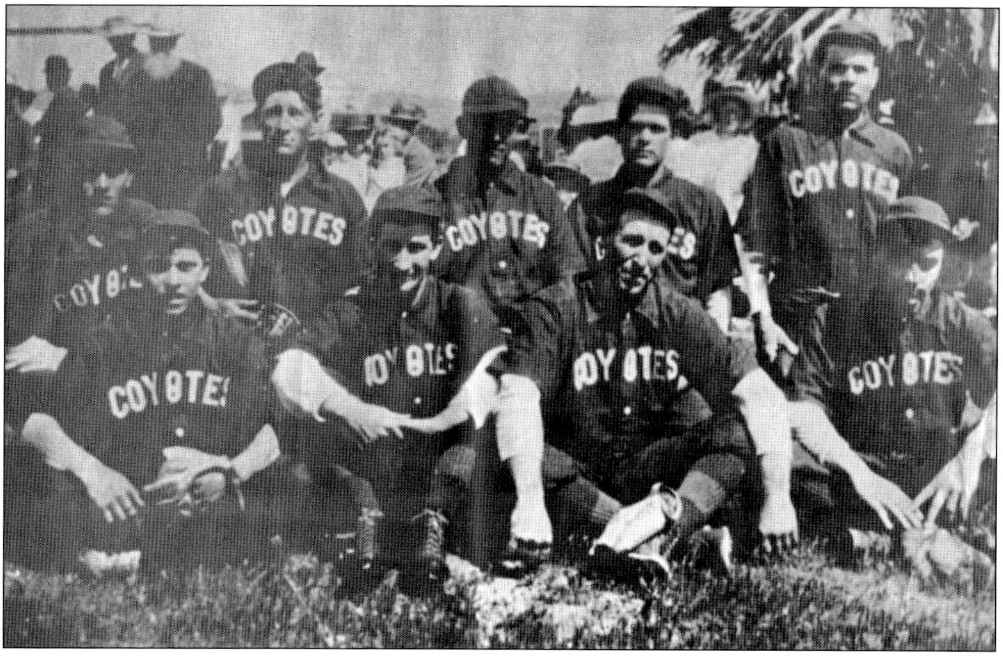

In September 1869, the Cincinnati Red Stockings barnstormed their way through California. The extremely popular team played in San Francisco and Sacramento, handily beating the home teams as they had done on their entire West Coast adventure. This brief tour ignited a passion for baseball in urban and rural areas alike. Baseball was played at picnics and other informal gatherings throughout the late 1800s. As the standardization of the game continued, creating the essential elements of the modern game, rural areas continued to play "baseball in the olden time." These newspaper images depict a matchup between the Stonyford Tigers and the Elk Creek Coyotes at Stonyford in 1910. (Both, Hollis Burrows Spurlock.)

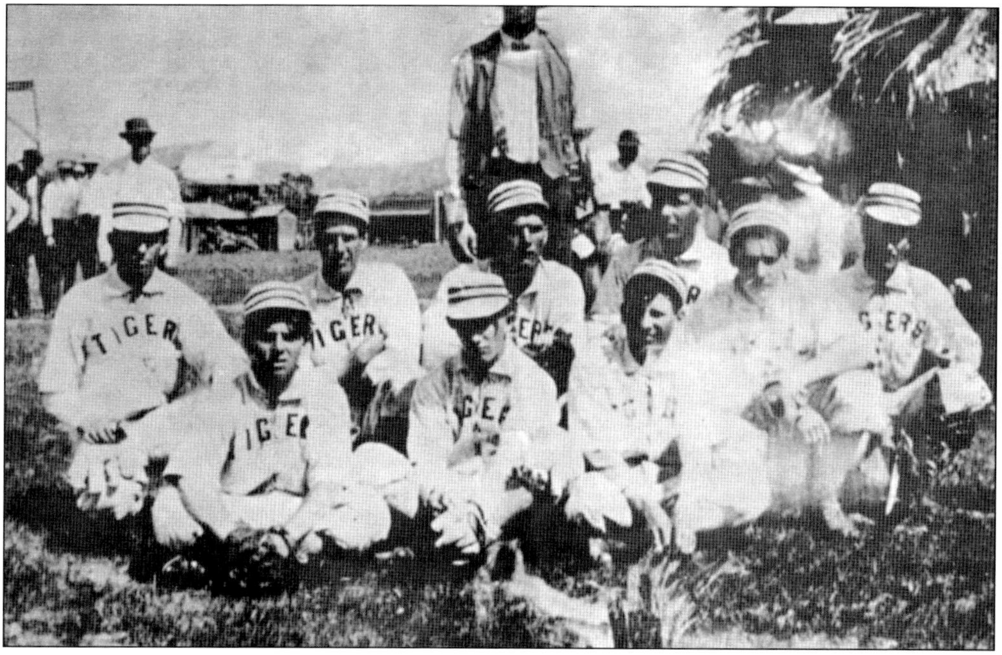

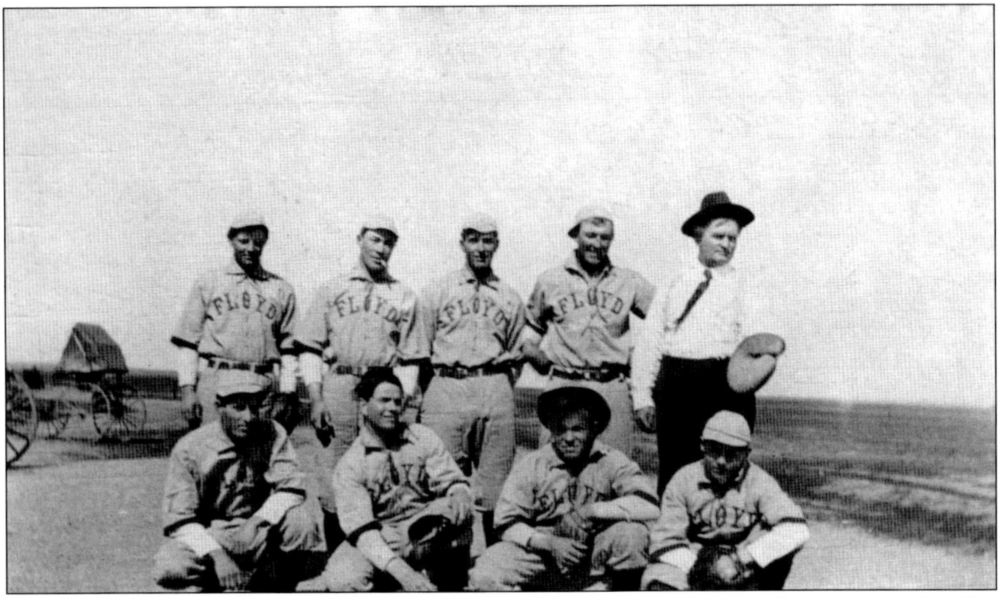

The earliest documented use of a glove by any baseball player was by a catcher on June 28, 1870. According to the *Encyclopedia of Baseball Catchers*, a sportswriter for the *Cincinnati Commercial* reported that Doug Allison of the Cincinnati Red Stockings had "caught in a pair of buckskin mittens, to protect his hands." A.G. Spaulding, a pitcher and founder of the Spaulding sports equipment company, saw his first mitt used by New Haven first baseman Charles C. Waite in 1875. Spaulding created a mitt for sale alongside the first baseball. The manager of the Floyd baseball team pictured here is wearing a catcher's mitt that dates from 1905 to 1920. (Orland Historical and Cultural Society).

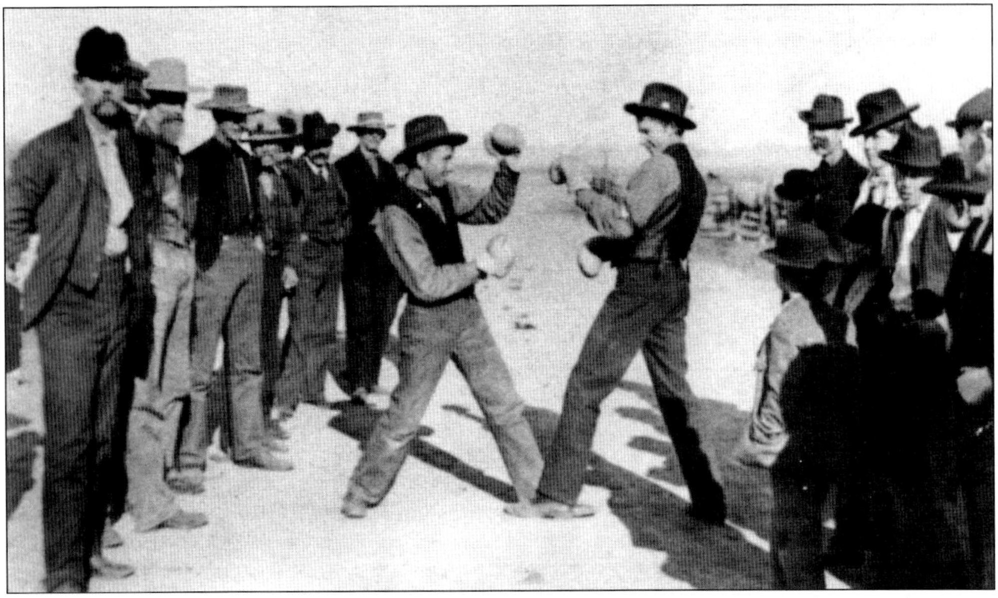

Boxers have protected their hands in one way or another since the beginning of the sport; however, padded gloves did not become part of the rules until the early 1900s. Here two young men from Chrome are cutting up at a community gathering. These gatherings were frequently held in the foothill towns. (Hollis Burrows Spurlock.)

Three

VALLEY

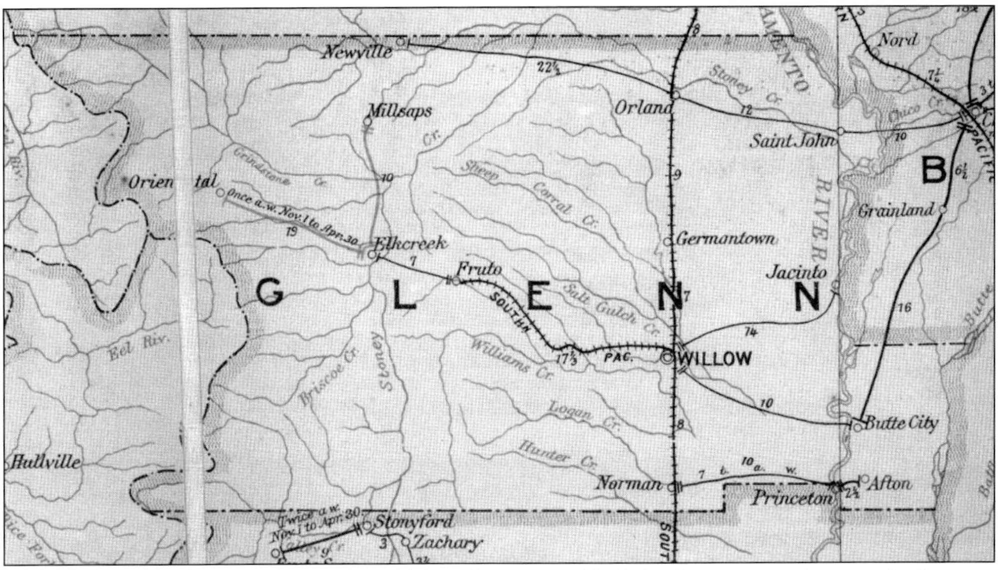

This map shows the postal routes in Glenn County in 1901. Each town on the map had a post office, and the numbers in between indicate the distance between post offices. Also indicated is the mail delivery schedule. Many towns in Glenn County have come and gone, and this map shows some of each. The history is rich because of the significance of all the settlers in towns present or past. (David Rumsey Map Collection.)

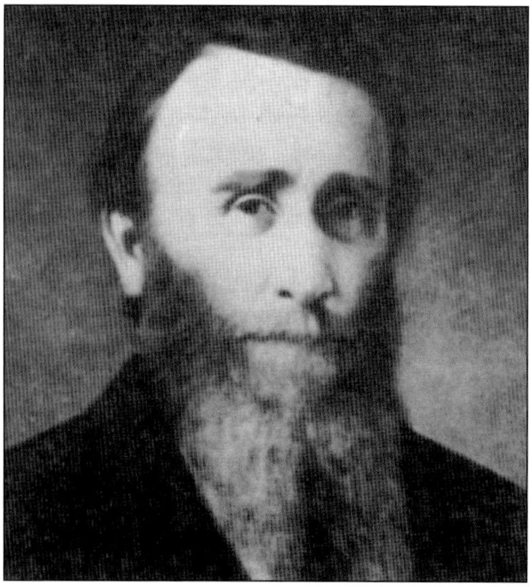

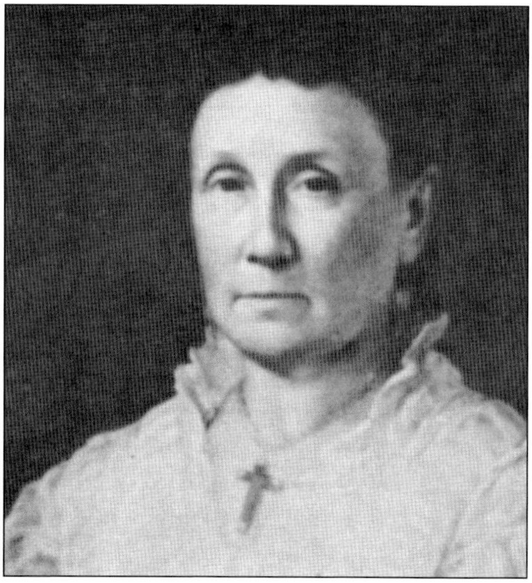

The name Glenn County was derived from the contributions of Dr. Hugh James Glenn and Nancy Harrison Abernathy Glenn, who are pictured here. The Glenn ranch covered over 55,000 acres with the Sacramento River as an eastern border. Jacinto, where a Grange hall remains, was the location of the headquarters of the ranch. Wheat was a contributing factor to the wealth of the Glenn family. The Glenn estate financially backed the proposal for creating and naming the county. (*Wagon Wheels*, fall 1984.)

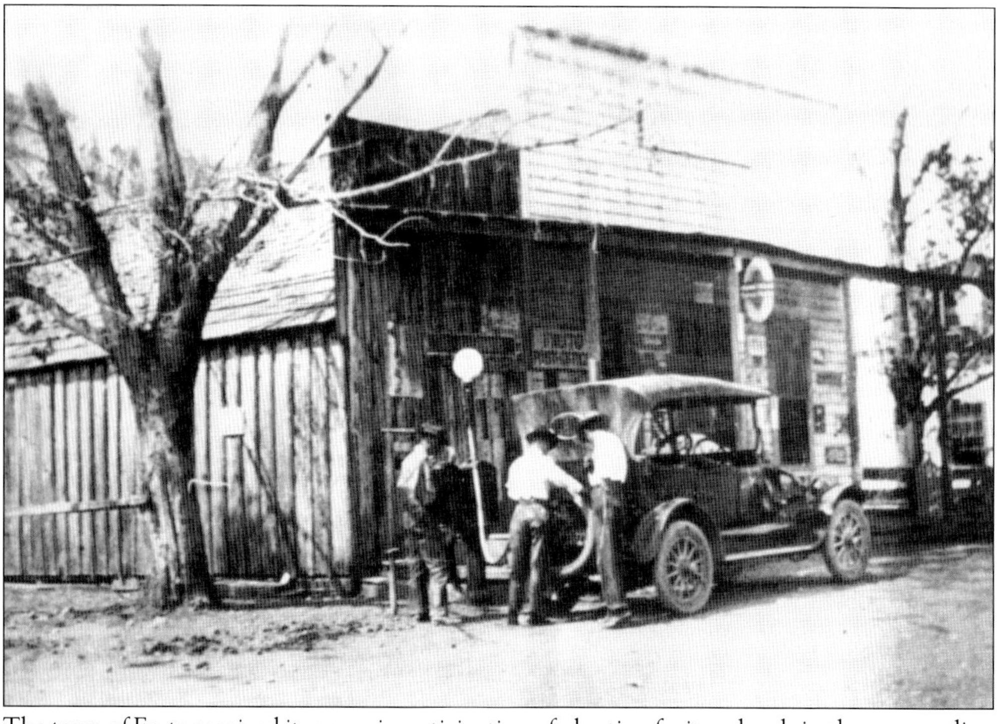

The town of Fruto received its name in anticipation of planting fruit orchards in the surrounding area. It lies 16 miles west of Willows. A town was mapped out on paper with streets named after trees and letters. The trees that were planted could not survive the long, hot summers. Over time, the settlement of Fruto mostly disappeared. (Hollis Burrows Spurlock.)

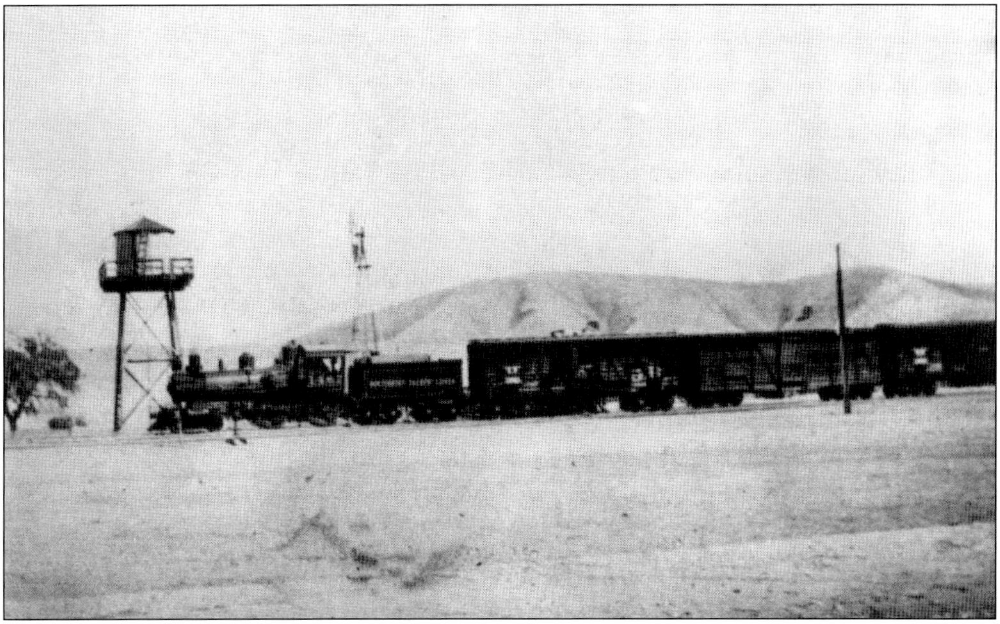

The Westside & Mendocino Railroad Company laid 16 miles of track with Fruto as the terminus. The next leg of the track would climb over the mountain to Elk Creek, but it was never finished. For over 30 years, Fruto had daily train service from Willows. The trains carried grain, livestock, logs, chromite ore, and seasonal fruits. (Hollis Burrows Spurlock.)

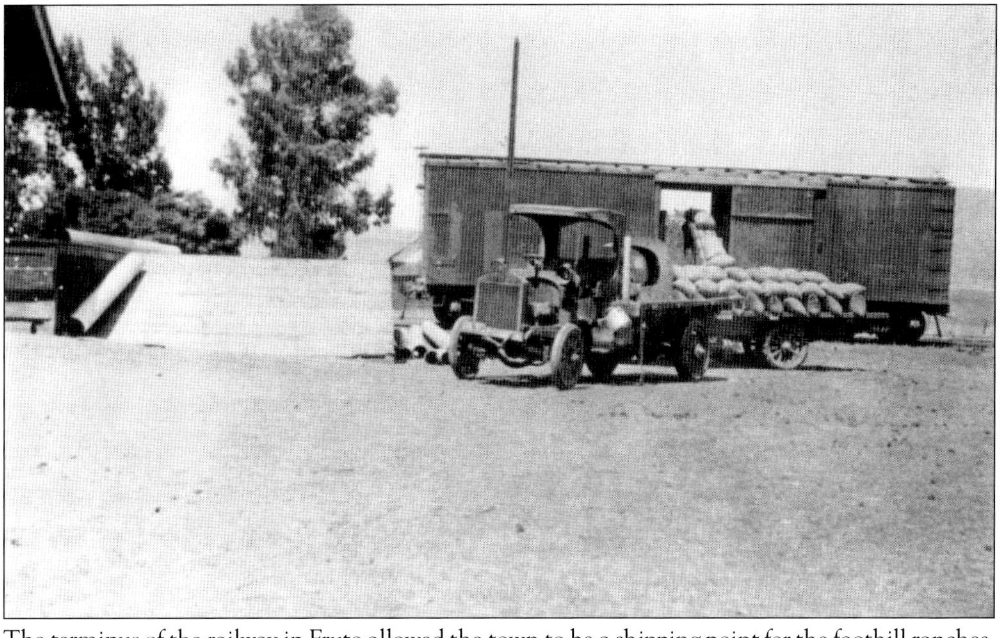

The terminus of the railway in Fruto allowed the town to be a shipping point for the foothill ranches. The ranchers would load their sacked wheat, fresh produce, or livestock in a freight wagon or truck and haul it to the railroad. This permitted the ranchers to have a closer shipping point than the previous stop in Monroeville. There was a warehouse for grain and hay, corrals and loading platforms for livestock, and even a small park beside the depot. (Hollis Burrows Spurlock.)

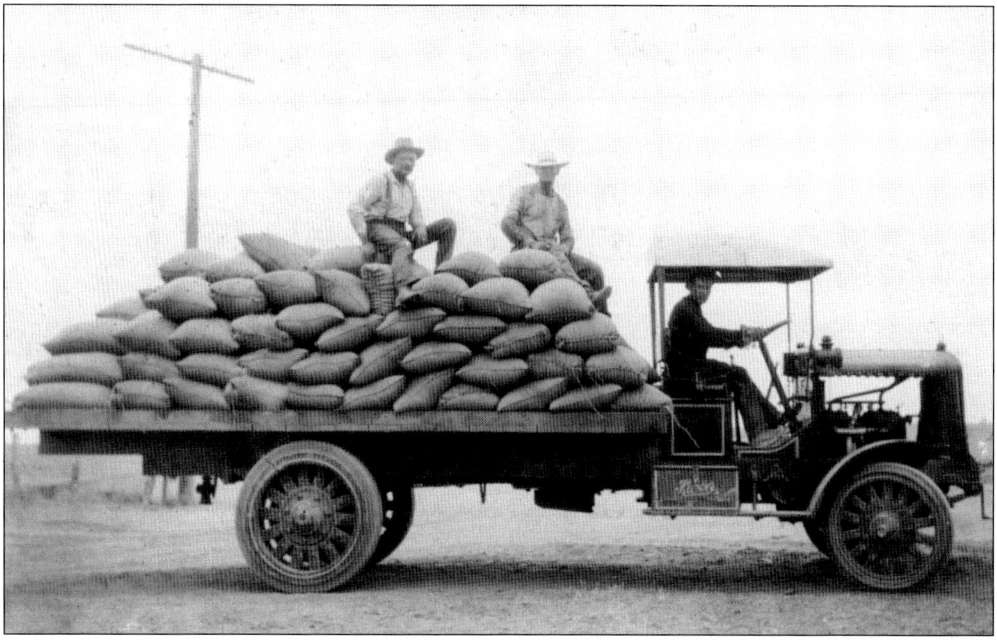

Wheat and barley were harvested and sacked in the field each summer. This load of grain was being transported to the train station. The crop would be sold in Sacramento or San Francisco and often shipped to Europe. This 1917 photograph shows, from left to right, Ed Rehse, Bill Behnke, and unidentified; it was probably taken east of Germantown (currently Artois). (Orland Historical and Cultural Society.)

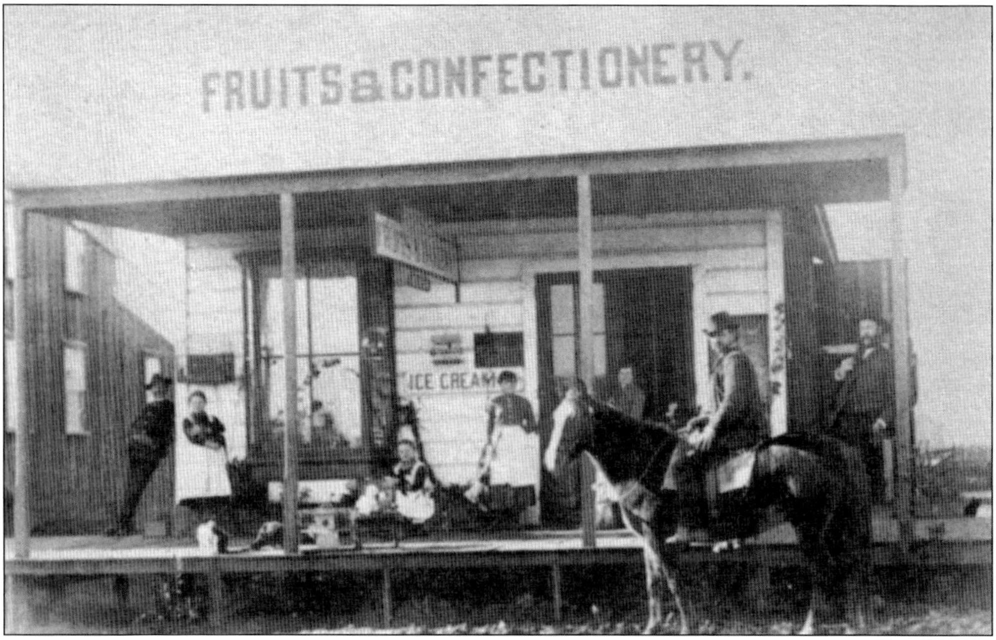

The first house built on Tehama Street in Willows was owned by Constable and Mrs. George Potts, who was known for her delicious bread. From left to right are Cora Potts (Wickes), Maud Potts (Lightner), Eva Ogle, Mrs. George Potts (at door), John Stormer, George Potts (on horse), and unidentified. (*Wagon Wheels*, February 1961.)

On February 17, 1894, the laying of the cornerstone for the first Glenn County Courthouse was celebrated with a parade led by Silvey's Cornet Band followed by Company G of the National Guard. In this c. 1909 photograph, the home of Sheriff Jack Bailey and the jail are to the right of the courthouse. The dome atop the structure as well as the statues on either side of it have long since been removed. (*Wagon Wheels*, September 1976.)

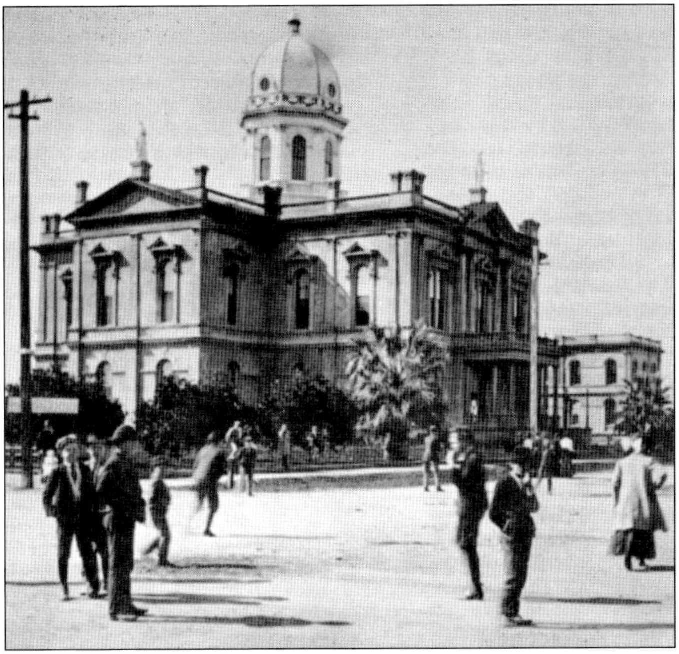

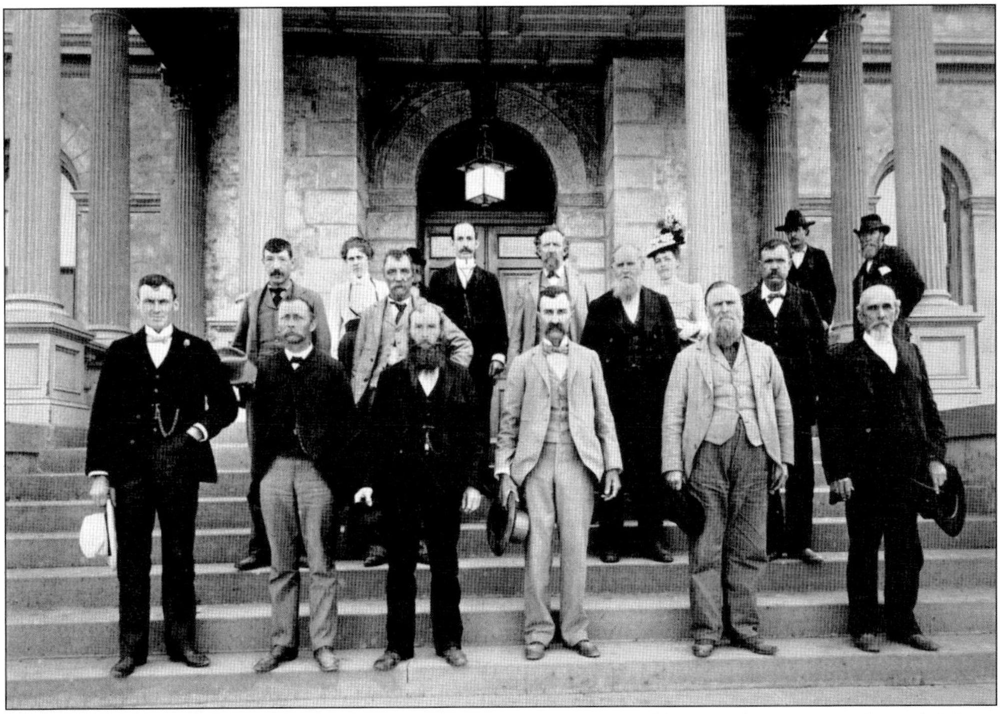

The jury for the "Murdock Note Case," pictured here, remained hung after a six-week trial. Their vote was split six to six. Six believed that a promissory note written to Mary Helen Murdock for $100,000 by her father-in-law for the support of her two children was a forgery. Six believed that Samuel Murdock wrote the note in support of the children to be paid when they came of age. The trial was very sensational in the spring of 1899 and was eventually settled for $90,000. (Laura Blevins.)

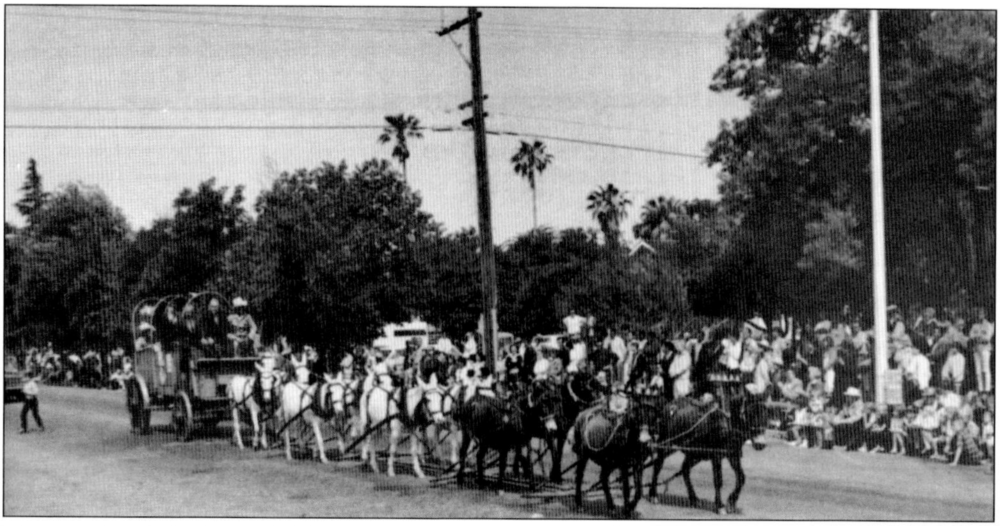

The first Lamb Derby in 1934 was organized to celebrate the sheep industry in Glenn County. The three-day event begins with a parade and the crowning of the Lamb Derby Queen. Past events have included sheep shearing competitions, wool displays, a Saturday night dance, and a lamb barbeque. The Glenn County Board of Supervisors rode in this mule drawn wagon, which was driven by Joe Lema of Redding, in the 1969 parade. From left to right are an unidentified muleskinner, C.E. Polzin (unseen), William C. Reimers, John Fiack, and Ralph Colbert. (*Wagon Wheels*, September 1970.)

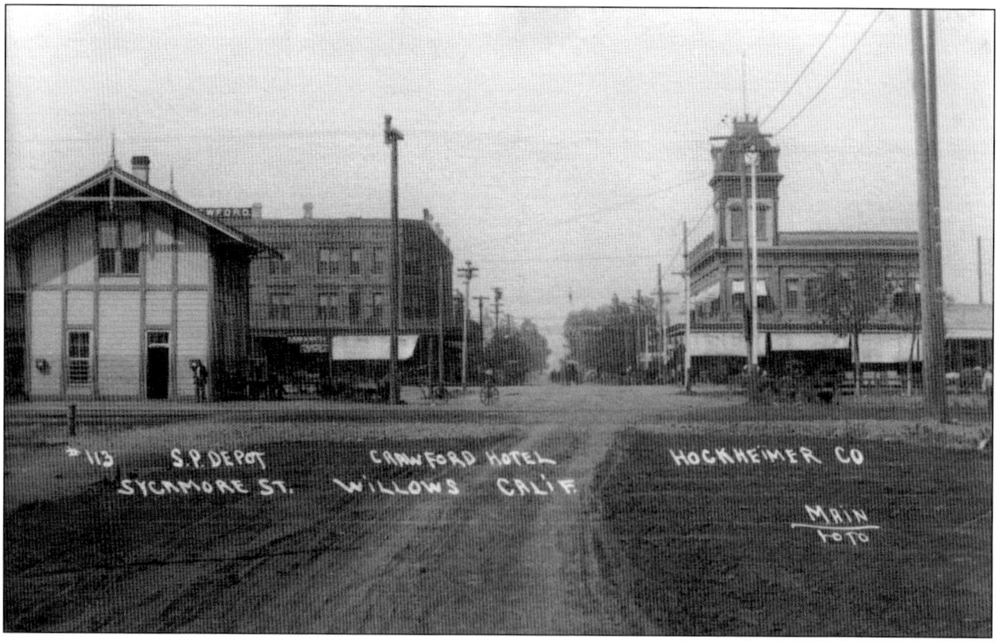

The town of Willows was founded near a pond surrounded by willow trees, but it took its current shape when the railroad came up the valley in 1878. Daniel Zumwalt deeded ground to Charles Crocker upon the agreement that Zumwalt would receive proceeds from the sale of lots. In this 1910 photograph, the Southern Pacific Depot building is on the left on Sycamore Street. The Crawford Hotel was west of the depot across Tehama Street. The Hochheimer Store was just across from the Crawford Hotel. (Orland Historical and Cultural Society.)

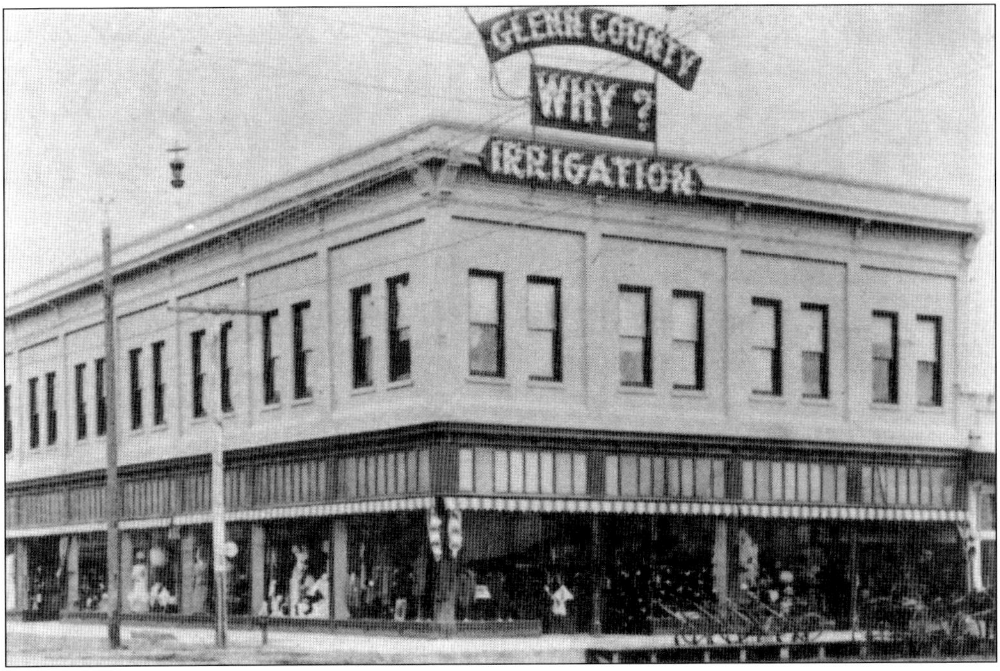

Moses Hochheimer and William Johnson opened the first general store in Willows in June 1876. It was described as a small building built on the most convenient ground, which happened to be on space reserved for the railroad tracks. The town continued to grow, with over 32 substantial buildings going up within a few months. The Hochheimer store moved to the northwest corner of Tehama and Sycamore Streets, where it remained and was rebuilt after fires in 1882, 1885, and 1920. It ceased operations in Willows in 1922. (*Wagon Wheels*, fall 1982.)

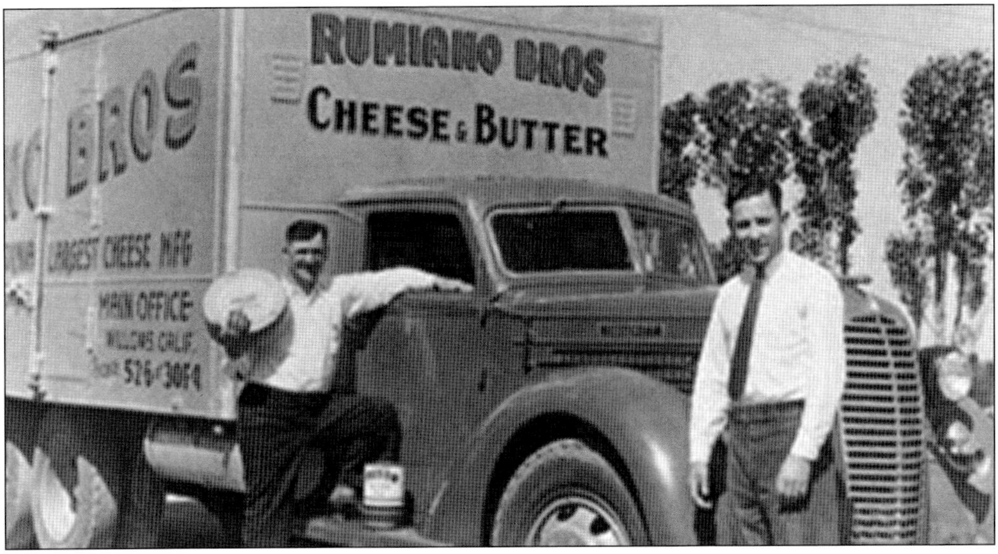

In 1910, brothers John, Fred, and Richard Rumiano emigrated from Italy to the United States. Nine years later, they were in Willows operating a dairy. They soon were producing more milk than could be used efficiently, so they started making cheese. In 1921, the Rumiano Cheese Company was begun. The national and state highway system allowed them to expand their cheese making facilities to eight factories throughout California by the mid-1930s. (Owen Rumiano.)

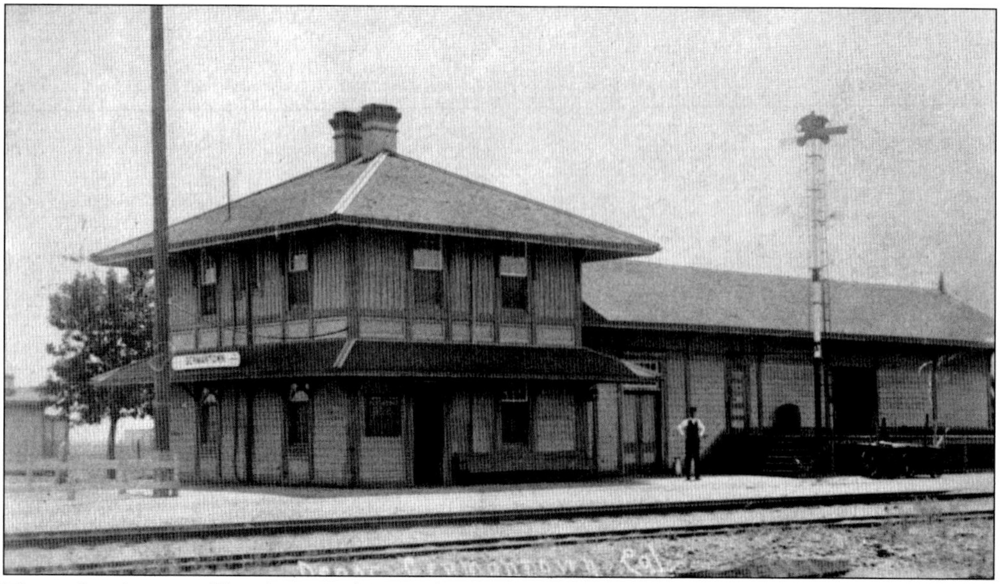

The railroads created brochures to lure settlers to California. They were circulated throughout the United States and Europe. An arduous trip by ship from Germany to New York and then around the Horn or through Panama was the mode of transportation chosen by many who eventually settled in Germantown. By 1869, the transcontinental railroad brought more settlers to California and, more specifically, the railroad headed north from Willows and reached Germantown in 1882. The depot pictured is from prior to World War I, when the town was renamed Artois. (Laura Blevins.)

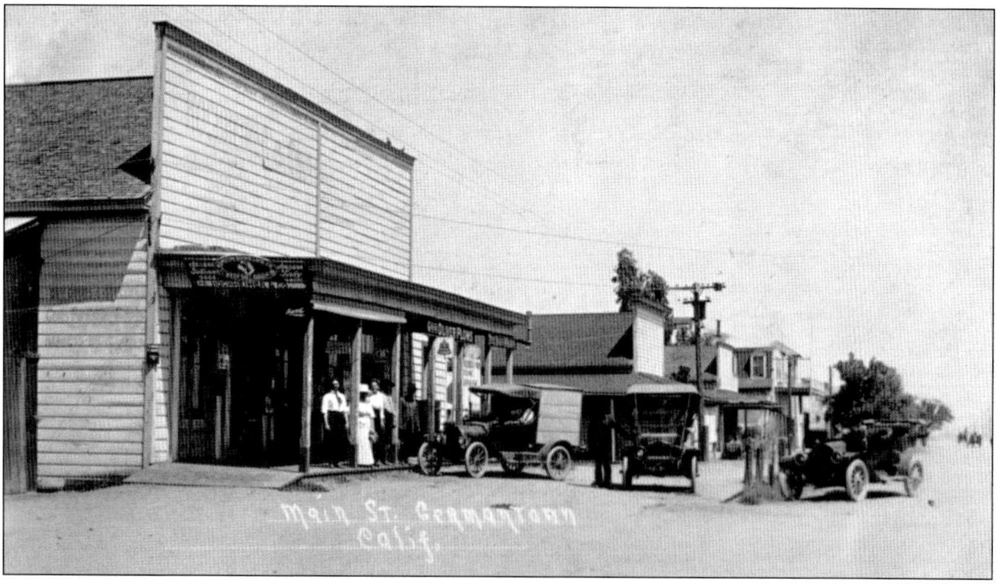

The Hochheimer and Company general merchandise store did so well in Willows that it expanded to Germantown in April 1890. The company had previously established a large grain warehouse there, and this seemed the logical next step. The store had been operated by Eppinger and Co. in 1877. Although it was only one story and one room, it carried all of the goods needed by the people of the area. As evidenced by the signs in this photograph, the store carried dry goods, groceries, shoes, Butterick patterns, and Oliver plows, and had a telephone. (Laura Blevins.)

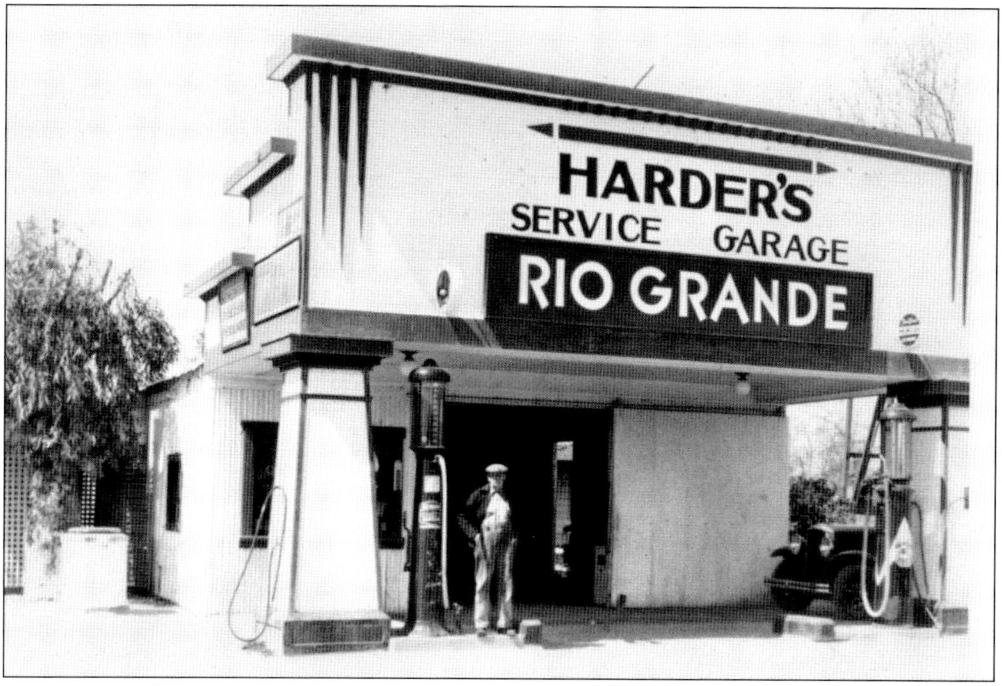

Beginning in the 1920s, gravity-flow visible gas pumps were used as automobiles became popular. The clear glass cylinder would hold 10 gallons. The pump was manual and, by pulling it back and forth, gas from an underground tank would fill the cylinder. The gas would then flow by gravity down the hose and into the car. The Harder family came to what was known as Rixville in the early 1870s. Due to the large settlement of German immigrants in the area, Rixville was known primarily as Germantown. (Laura Blevins.)

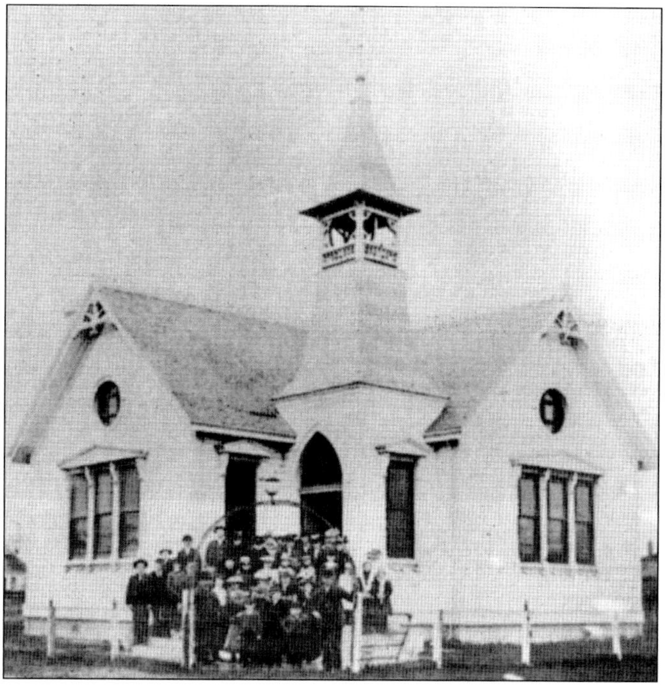

Most of the Germantown settlers were Lutheran. John Henry Gattch, who came from Hamburg, Holstein, in 1885 with his wife and six children, is credited with founding the church. According to church records, it was founded in 1889. The records were kept in German until 1920, and German services were conducted until around 1942. The men officially ran the church until 1950, when women were allowed to vote. (Laura Blevins.)

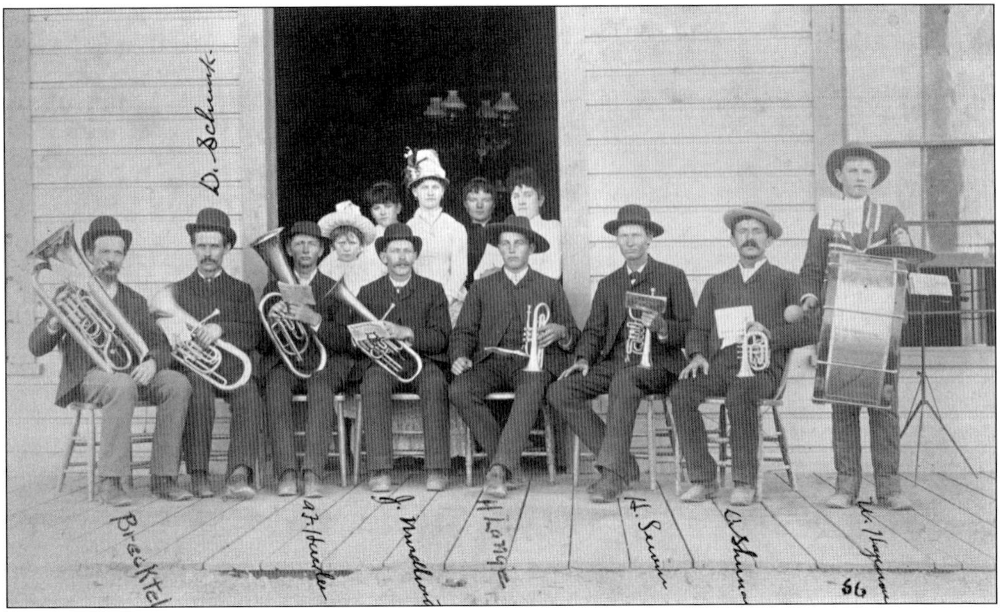

Through the years, Germantown touted many different bands, including a cornet band, brass band, and a quartet for dance music. The Germantown Brass Band played for important occasions, including the Orland irrigation scheme and the passage of the Glenn County Bill in Sacramento. Shown here from left to right are ? Brecktel, D. Schwenk, A.F. Harder, H. Lange, H. Sievers, D. Schumann, and W. Hagemann. This photograph probably dates from the late 1890s. (Laura Blevins.)

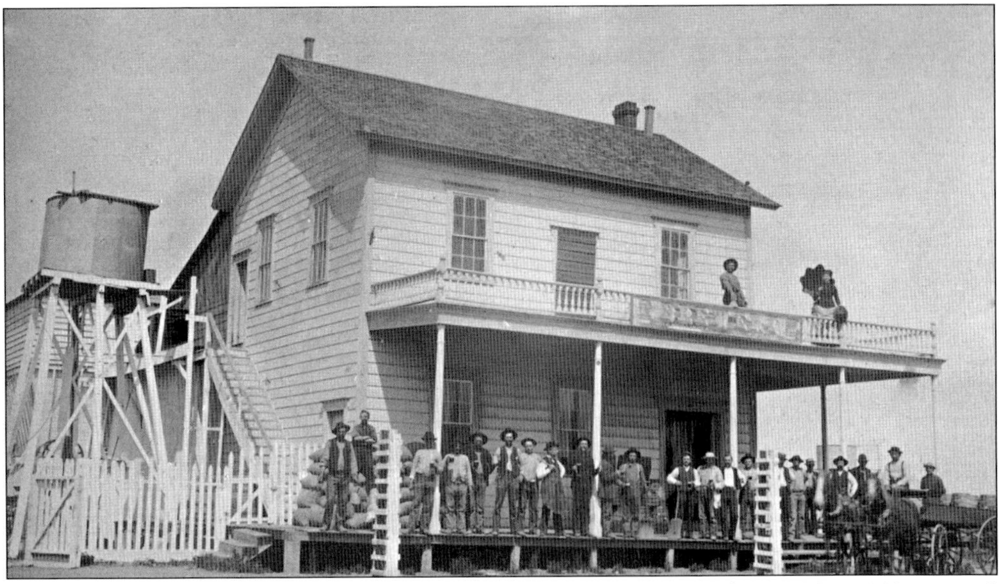

Various business directories of the area show a brewery in Germantown from 1878 to 1889, pictured here in 1886. On November 7, 1889, a fire destroyed the brewery, a saloon, the dwelling of John Beeck, the saddle shop, and the undertaking rooms of David Schwenk. The proprietors of the brewery were H.C. Stillinger and Co. (1878), P. Matzen and Co. (1880), Bachman and Probst (1886), and Charles W. Robbins (1889). (Laura Blevins.)

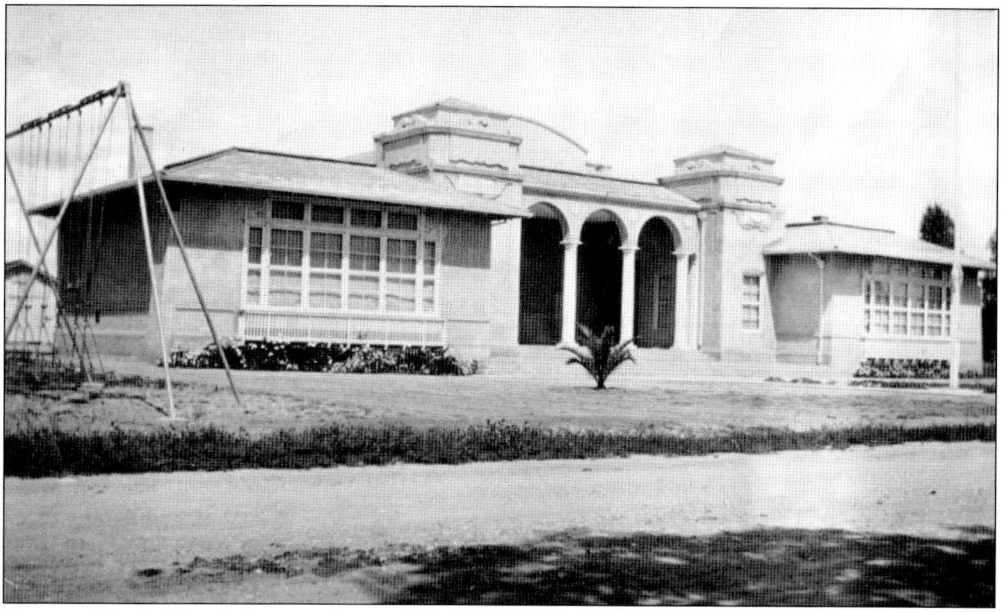

During World War I, the town's name changed to Artois. However, the school retained the name of German until 1968. Pictured here was the second German School, built in 1919–1920. It consisted of two classrooms and an auditorium and showed an enrollment of 51 pupils. The last class to attend the school was in 1980. (Laura Blevins.)

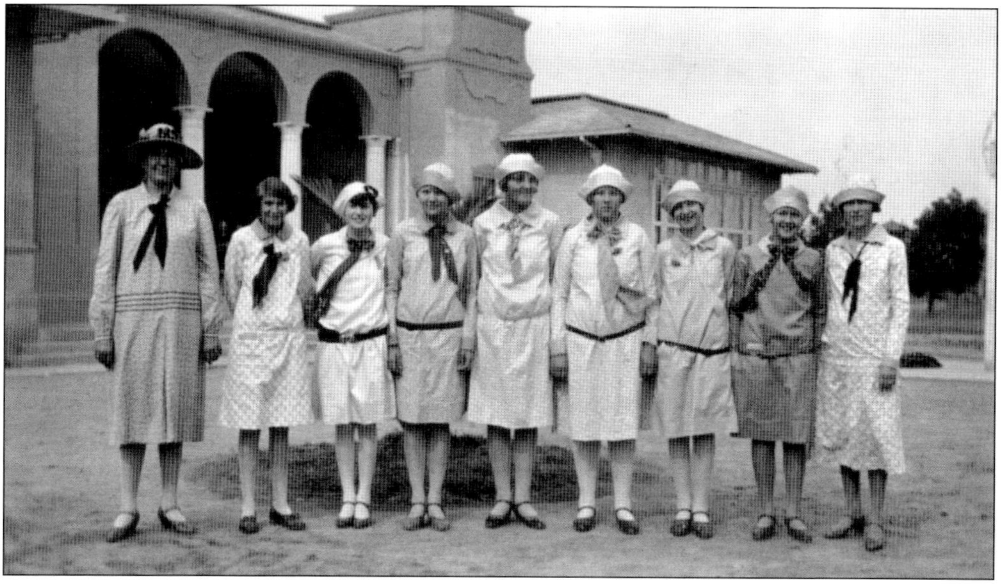

The small schools in Glenn County were often the site of town gatherings and community events. These young ladies took a sewing class in 1927 at the German School in Artois. From left to right are an unidentified sewing teacher, Delia Blunck, Rita Olsen, Minnie Blunck, Margaret von Bargen, Nellie Reimers (Campbell), Erna Lovett, Helen Peterich, and Ruth Pritchell (Harder). (Laura Blevins.)

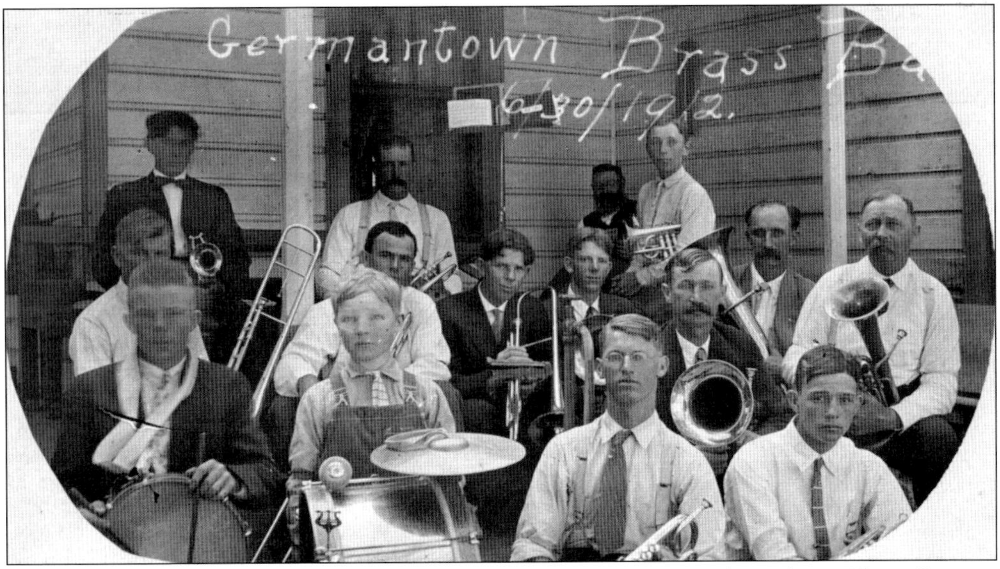

The Germantown Brass Band continued to play for important events throughout Glenn County. This 1912 version of the band consisted of Earl Bearden, Henry Runge, Johannes Mordhorst, Herbert Runge, Herman Breuss, Clarence Hurlburt, Harry Sunbury, Walter Sunbury, Julius Moelk, Judge Harder, Raymond Sunbury, Waldo Runge, Arthur Holtorf, Melvin Hurlburt, and Ed Runge. (Laura Blevins.)

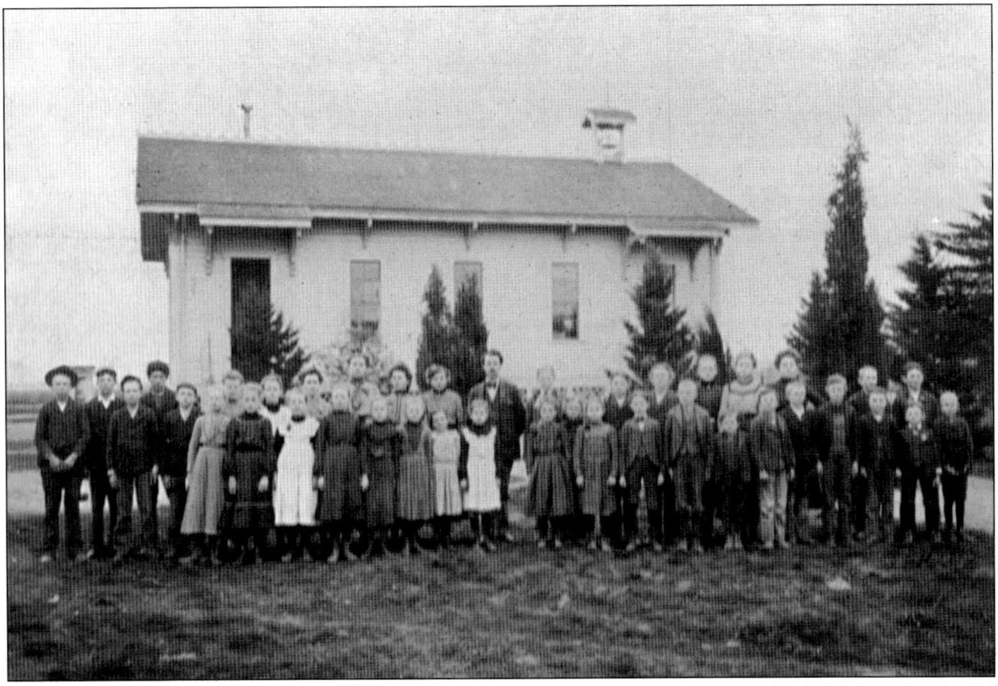

The German School site was recorded on September 10, 1877. It is said that the land was purchased for $400 in gold coin. The school enrolled 27 pupils its first year. Those identified in this 1905 photograph are Curt Mordhorst (first row, 15th from left), Harry F. Harder (first row, second from right), Alma Hinz (second row, sixth from left), Emma Peterich (second row, eighth from left), and Arthur Jansen (second row, far right). (Laura Blevins.)

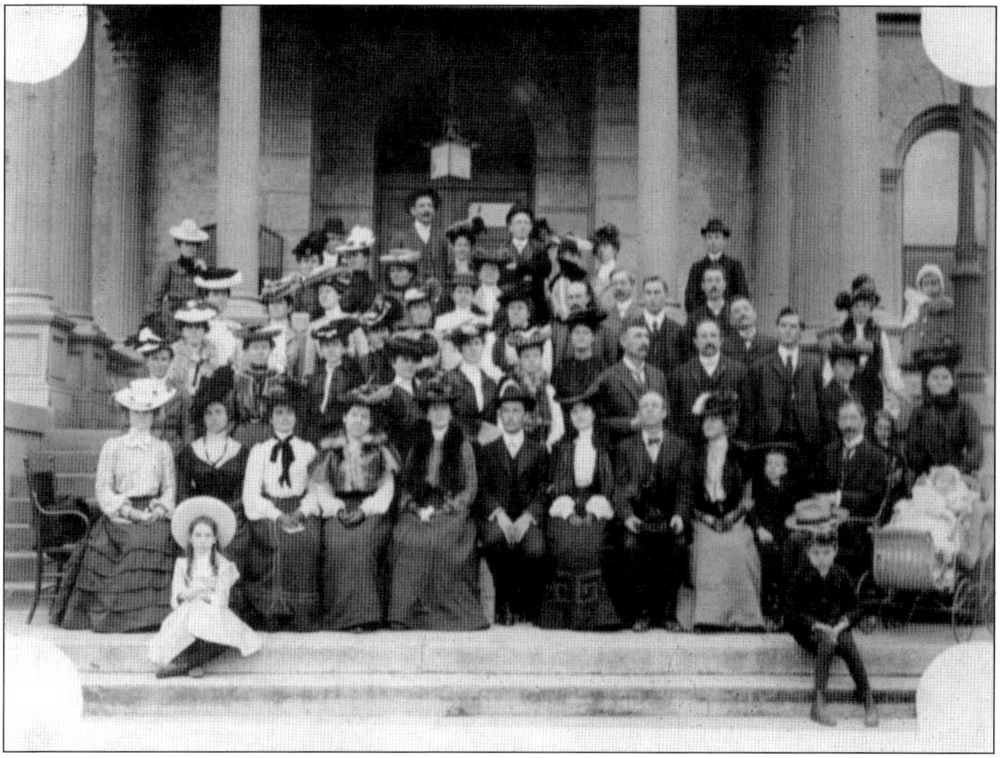

A conference was held at the Glenn County High School (GCHS) in Willows for all Glenn County teachers in 1902. GCHS had two instructors, F.N. Miller (pictured here) and Adrienne Cerf. The Glenn County Board of Education in 1902 was J.E. Wylie, president; Frank S. Reager, secretary; C.J. Lathrop; S.M. Cheney; and H.G. Rawlins. All appear to be present. (Orland Historical and Cultural Society.)

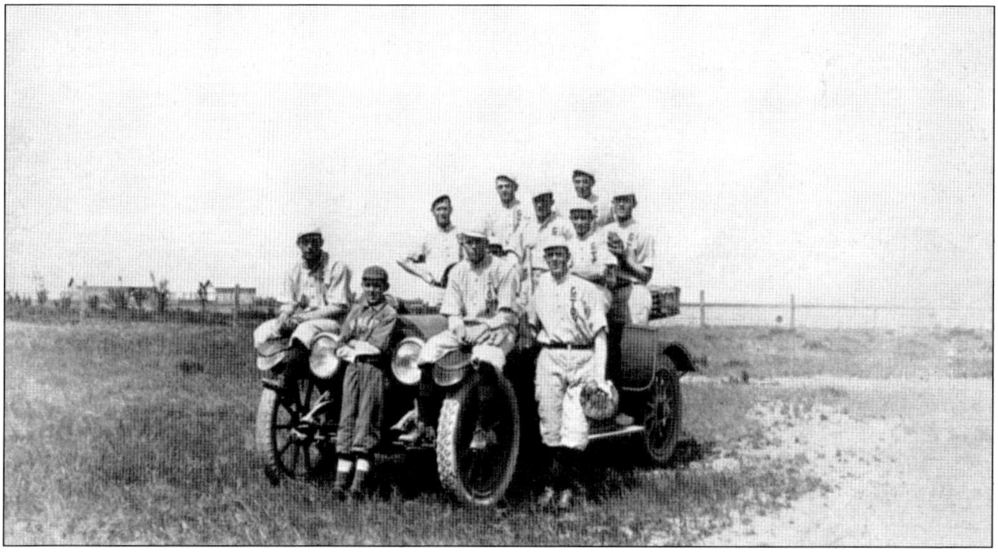

The Germantown baseball team pictured here around 1915 included Ol Fronmeldt, Harry Harder, D. Herbert Runge, Raymond Sunbury, Otto Mordhorst, Leverene Gunn, Walter Sunbury, Arthur Jansen, Ric Rawlins, D. Carl Duhr, and John Rehse in front of the car. (Laura Blevins.)

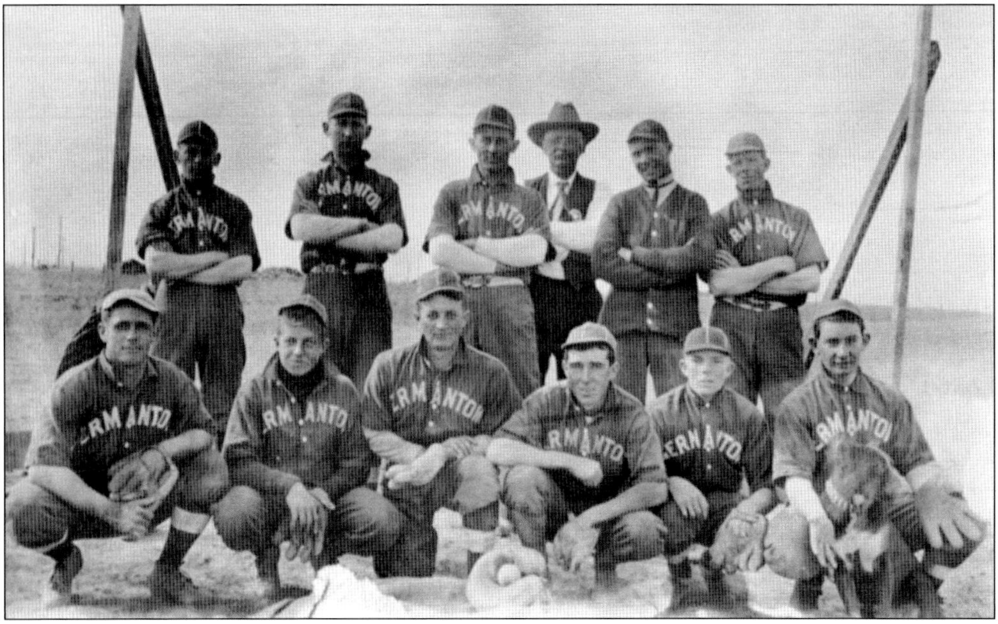

Many of the towns in Glenn County had baseball teams in the early 1900s. They would travel, usually by train, to the surrounding towns up and down the Sacramento Valley to compete. The athletic rivalry between towns was fierce. Any large celebration, such as the Lamb Derby, Glenn County Fair, or the Fourth of July, would host a ball game. The identified Germantown players pictured here are Ray Sunbury (first row, far right), Harry Harder (second row, far left), Arthur Jansen (second row, third from left), and Walt Sunbury (second row, far right). (Laura Blevins.)

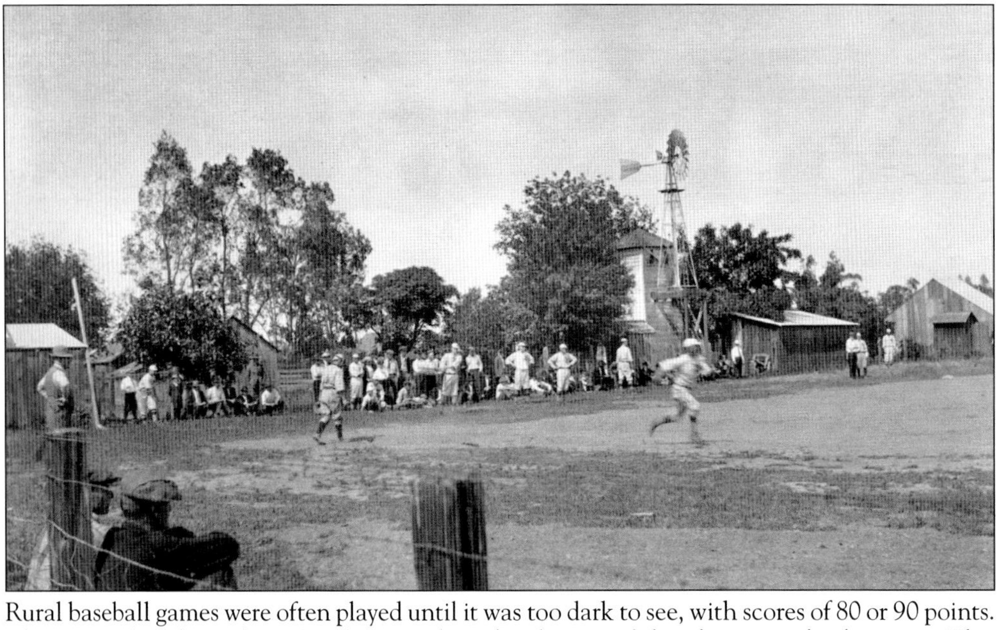

Rural baseball games were often played until it was too dark to see, with scores of 80 or 90 points. They were played mostly on Sundays, much to the chagrin of churchgoers and pub owners. This Germantown player has just made it to base in a baseball field carved out of pasture behind people's homes. (Laura Blevins.)

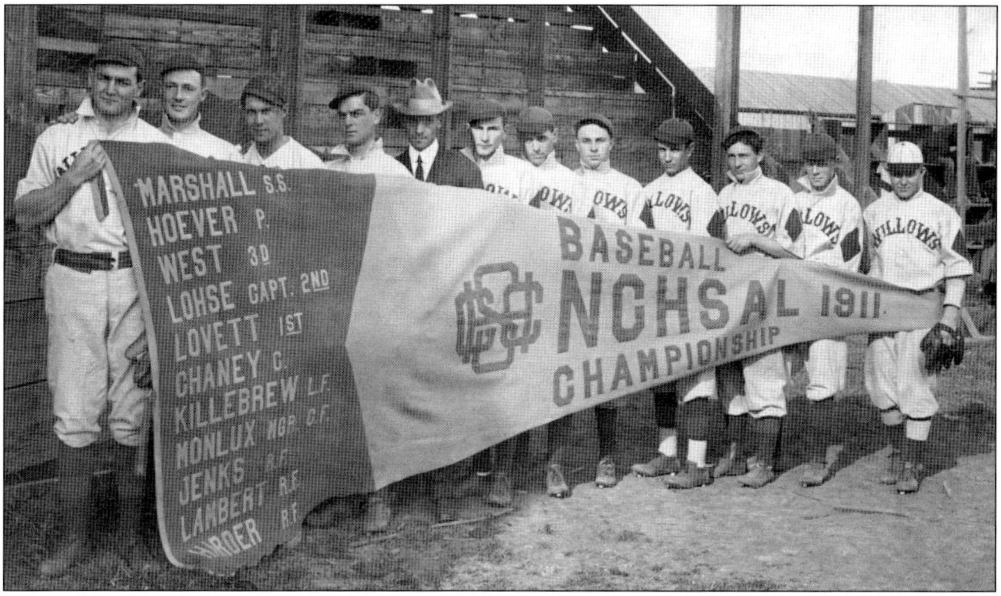

The Willows were the baseball champions for the 1911 season. The banner lists the players as Marshall, shortstop; Hoever, pitcher; West, third base; Lohse, captain and second base; Lovett, first base; Chaney, catcher; Killebrew, left field; Monlux, manager and center field; Jenks, right field; Lambert, right field; and Harder, right field. (Laura Blevins.)

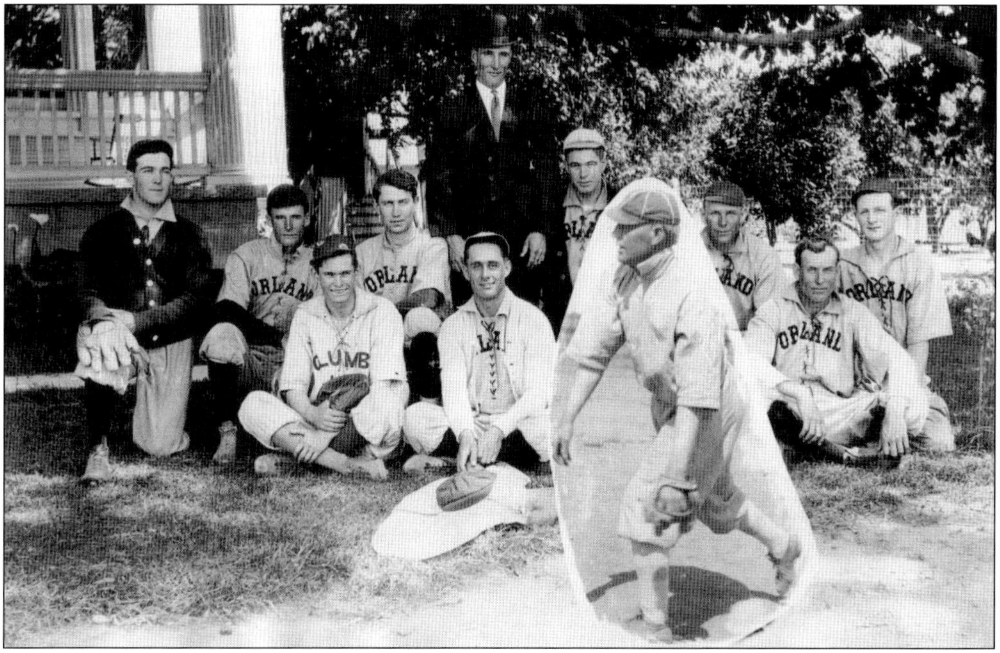

Beginning in the late 1800s, Orland played baseball up and down the Sacramento Valley. In 1912, the team was known as the Bearcats. In 1941, they were the Tigers. Various leagues were formed and dismantled depending on the popularity of the game and the politics of the time. The book *Land of Orland* has more pictures showing the teams and other recreational activities of the area. The inset picture is probably pitcher Charlie Thode of the 1923 or 1924 team. (Orland Historical and Cultural Society.)

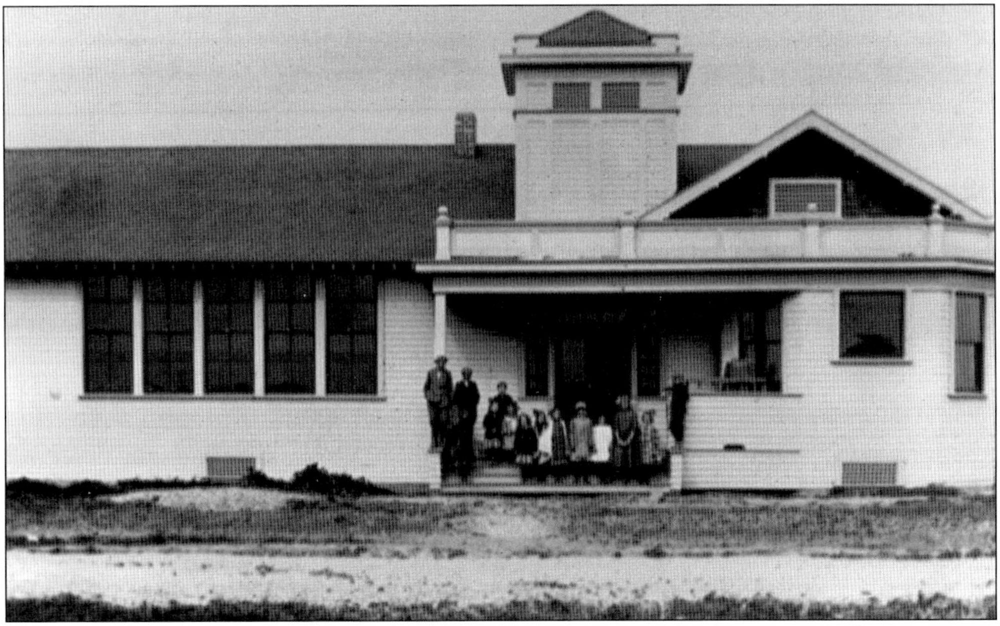

The community of Bayliss began as a camp established by the Sacramento Valley Irrigation project. The school, shown here in 1912, was built in 1911 and had two rooms. In the fall of 1953 as the student population continued to grow, construction began on a new building, to be called the "all-purpose room," which included a kitchen, cloakroom, and inside restrooms. In 1970, the Field Act required that the buildings be replaced. In 1983, the school was closed due to low enrollment. (Donna Klobas.)

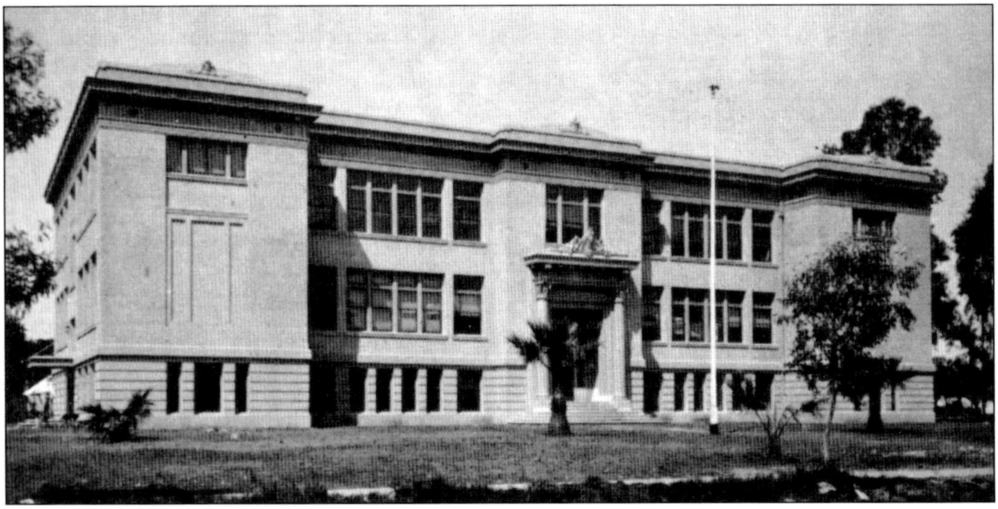

Glenn County High School was the first high school to be organized in Glenn County. Classes were held on the second floor of the Willows Grammar School building, which was located where Memorial Hall is now. The first high school graduation was held in 1897. The two graduates were Maud Potts and G.F. Fetherston. The high school building was built in 1903 and was located on Lassen Street on the site of the present shop building. As the student body grew, a new building was built in 1918. That school remained active until a fire destroyed it in 1941. Many residents recall that during the rebuilding, classes were held in houses on Murdock Street. (*Wagon Wheels*, September 1976.)

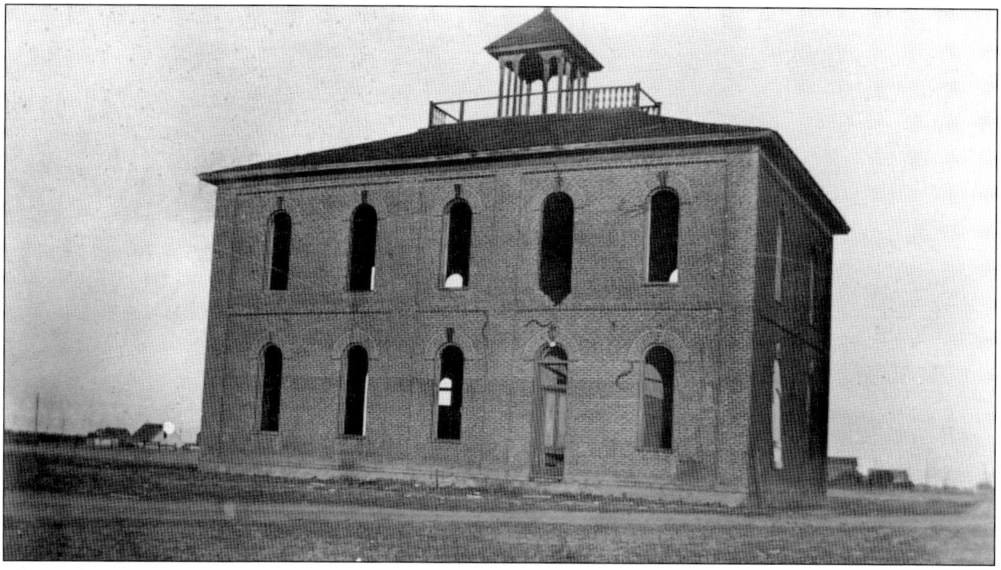

The Orland College was opened in 1882 on land donated by Albert Papst. It was located near where the Grange Hall currently is on Highway 32 in Orland. Prof. J.B. Patch was the first president. He raised money to have the structure built and did a lot of the work himself. The college closed in 1900. Bricks from the vacant structure (shown here) were used to build homes and an office in Orland. (Orland Historical and Cultural Society.)

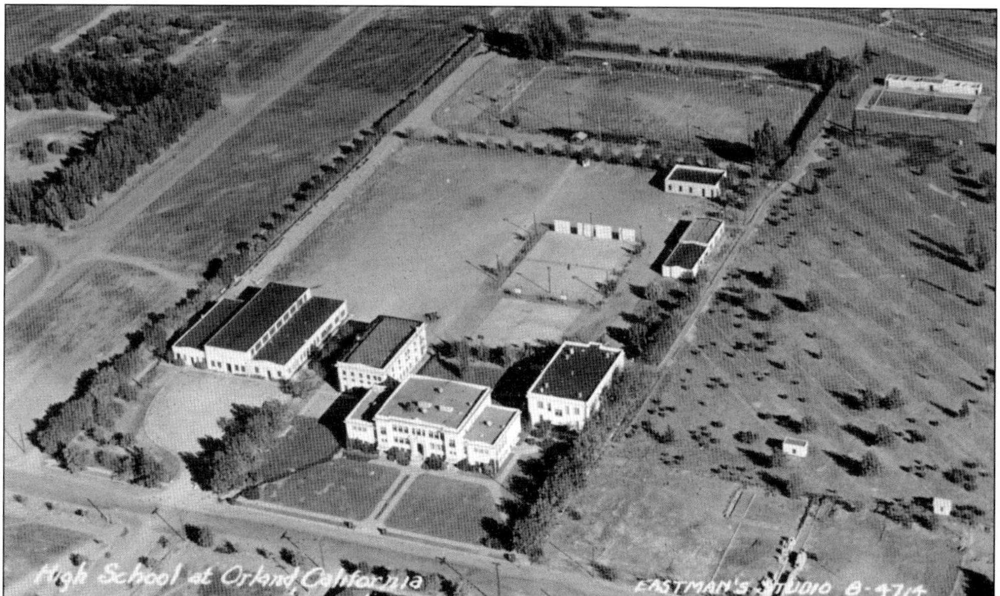

Orland High School was established in 1895. Frank Reager was the first principal, with 18 students. Classes were held in the second story of a wooden school building on Mill Street. A barn was built behind the school for the students' horses. As the student body grew, a new high school was built on the present site in 1916. Students assisted in building a new gym because the basketball team had won the Northern California High School Athletic pennant and there was a need for it. H.H. Busse built several of the concrete buildings, including the cafeteria. This Eastman postcard is dated 1946. (Author's collection.)

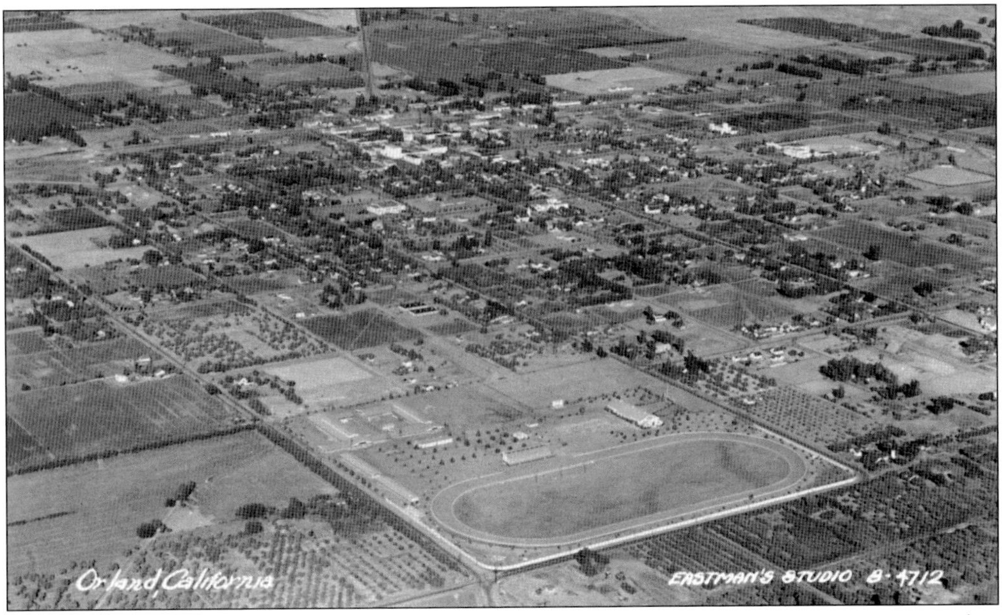

The Eastman's Originals Collection of historical postcards and negatives was sold to Anne Fisher in 1982. She donated the collection to the University of California, Davis, in 1994. This Eastman postcard of Orland is dated 1946. Note the diagonal road below the south (left) end of the race track. Prior to the creation of the town of Orland, this road connected the once-thriving foothill town of Newville to the shipping and navigation point at Monroeville on the Sacramento River. Both towns are now gone, but the road still cuts through the countryside. (Author's collection.)

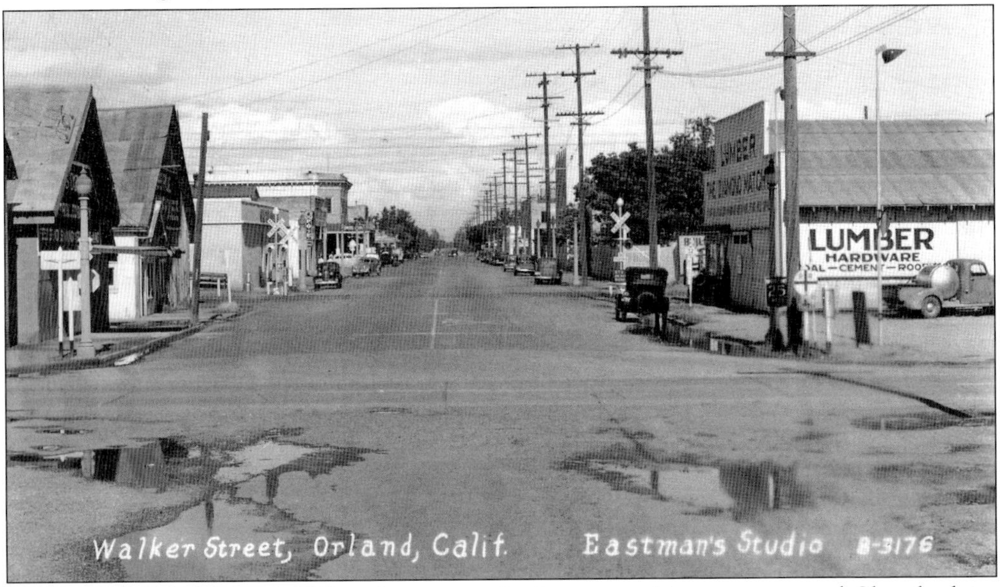

Orland was settled around 1875 and was part of a farm owned by a man named Chamberlain. The story goes that three pioneers of the town got together to petition for a post office, each suggesting a name for the new town: Leland (after Leland Stanford), Comstock, and Orland (the name of the birthplace in England of one of the pioneers, a Mr. Brown). The names were written on slips of paper and placed in a hat. An interested youth drew out the name of Orland. This view is looking west toward Chico on Walker Street. (Author's collection.)

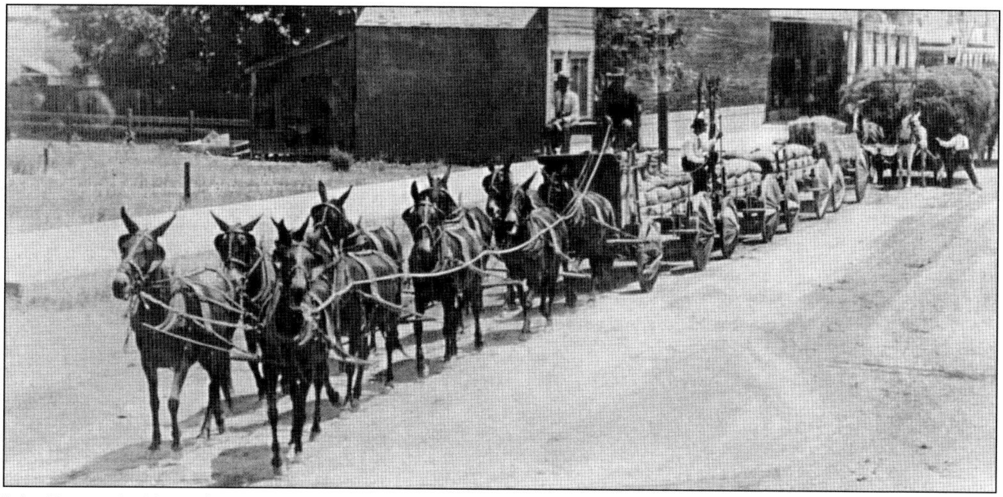

Mr. Burton's 10-mule-team wagon is coming from the Cushman Ranch in Newville with a load of wheat and baled straw. Behind them is a load of loose wheat or hay, which could be sold in Orland. (Hollis Burrow Spurlock.)

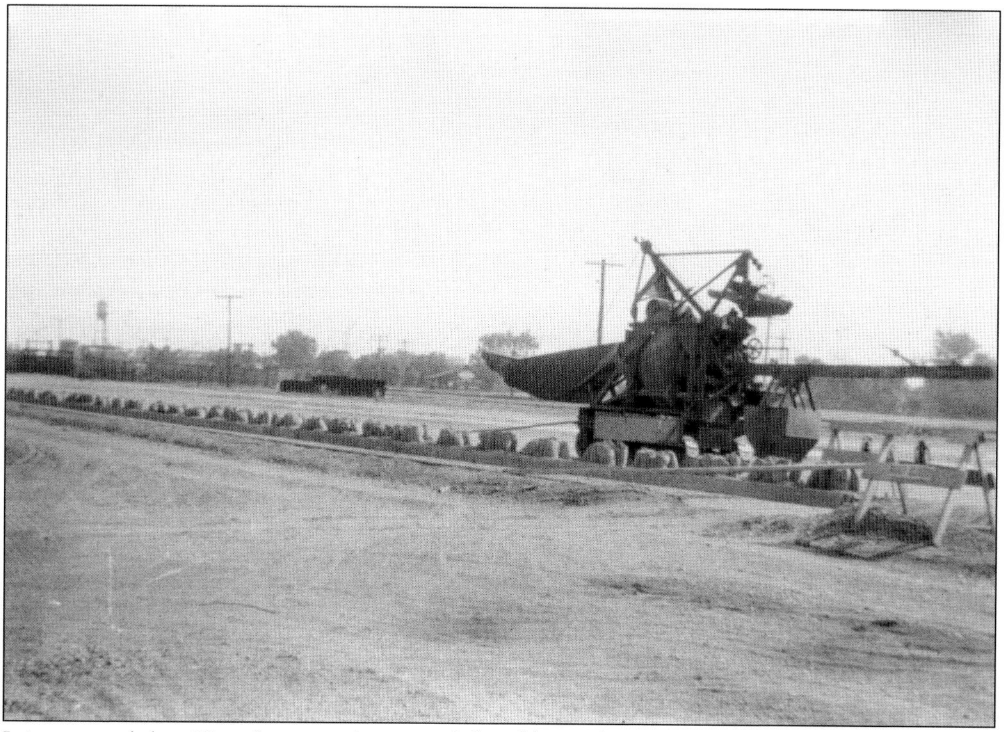

It is reported that 10-mule teams that were fed and housed at the Holtorf Livery Stable in Artois began the construction of Highway 99. These mule and oxen teams shared a time with the steamboats, barges, and ferries. That era slowly gave way to the automobile and the need for more utilitarian roadways. The highways became main thoroughfares and then the interstate was built in the mid-1900s. Highway 99W is pictured being paved in Orland around 1928. (Orland Historical and Cultural Society.)

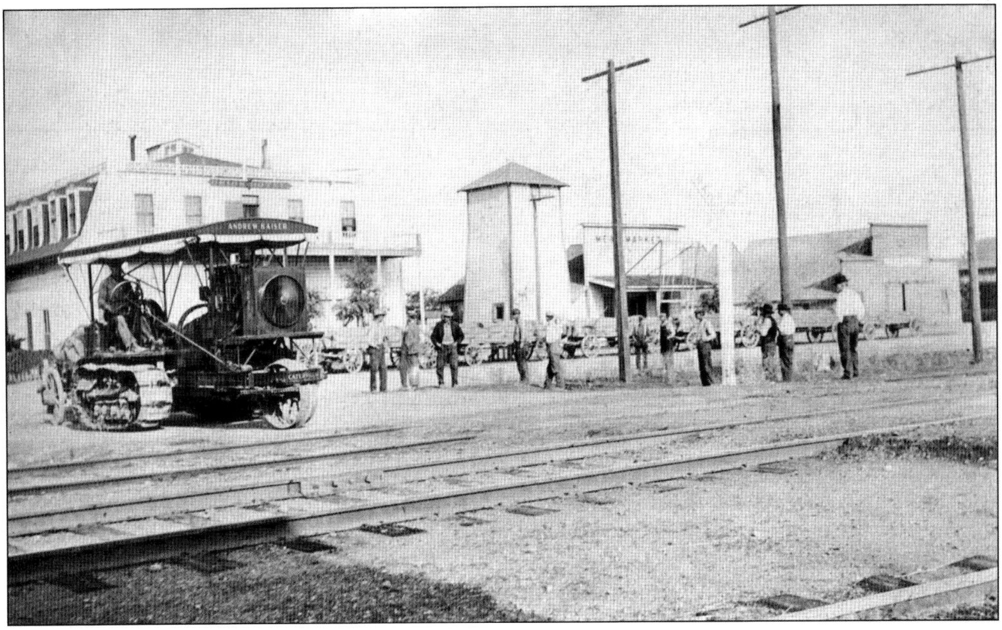

The farmland surrounding the Germantown area became quite productive during the late 1800s. In 1887, Justus Rogers reported that the wheat crop that season was very large, with heavy yields being reported from various parts of the county. Rogers noted the combined harvester held a prominent place during harvest. There was an attempt to corner the San Francisco wheat market, which inflated the price to $2.17 per hundredweight for a short period. The steam tractors, harvesters, grain wagons, and caterpillars that were owned by Germantown farmers, including Andrew Kaiser and George Mudd, were signs of the agricultural productivity of the era. Prior to these modern mechanizations, harvest on the Glenn Ranch alone would require 200–300 hundred men and 800 mules to put in and harvest the wheat. (Both, Laura Blevins.)

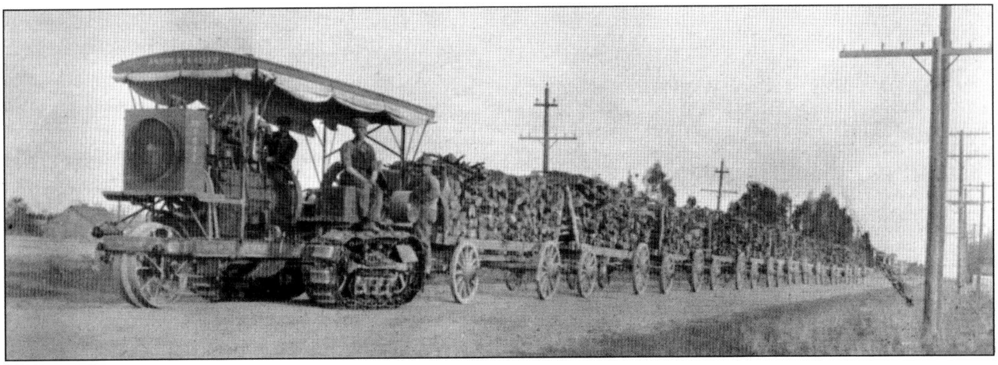

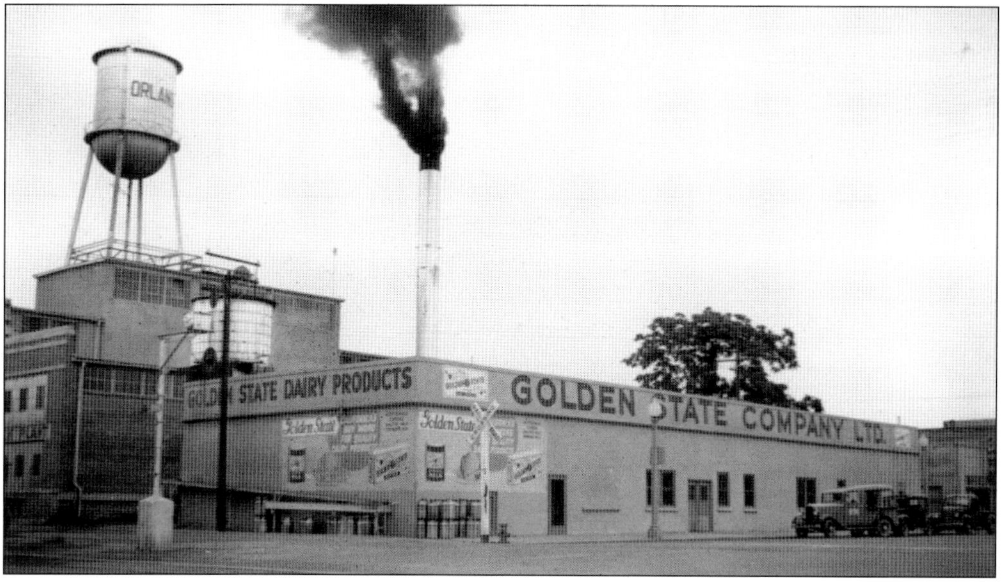

Glenn County's ability to grow quality irrigated alfalfa, a temperate climate, and the accessible and inexpensive lands led many dairymen from other parts of California to start their trade in Glenn County. Rumiano Cheese and the Orland Creamery were two early businesses that found that they had to grow to accommodate the increasing demand for dairy products. Glenn County was ranked fifth in the state in dairy production in 1925. Golden State bought the Orland Creamery in 1926. Remnants of the building can still be seen as part of Musco Olive. (Orland Historical and Cultural Society.)

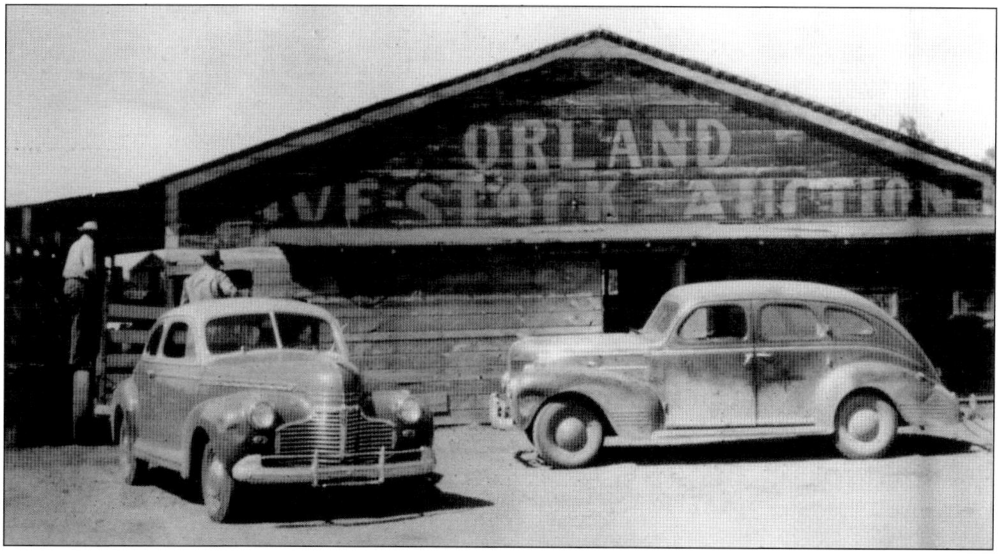

In 1947, Aaron Stockton partnered with his father, Ivan Stockton, to run the Orland Livestock Yards. Because the yards were conveniently located right off Highway 99 along South Street, ranchers from near and far had hauled their animals there since 1939. In 1955, Aaron Stockton took over sole proprietorship of the business. He was a self-taught auctioneer and donated much time to the Glenn County Fair Junior Livestock Auction, which benefitted the agricultural youth of the county. He sold the business to Ed Lacque in 1977. It burned down in 1979. (Lana Stockton Trovao.)

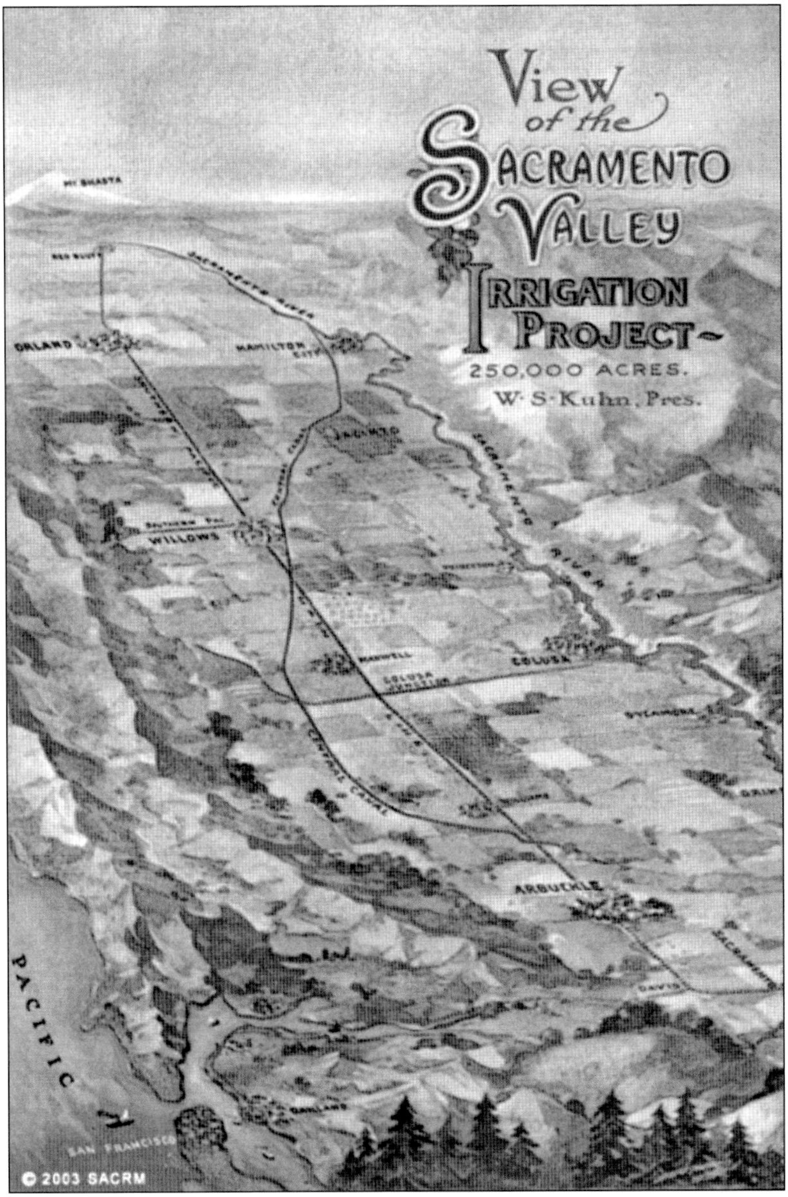

J.S. and W.S. Kuhn of Pittsburgh, Pennsylvania, formed the Sacramento Valley Irrigation Company in 1909. They had successfully constructed an irrigation system in the desert of southern Idaho and found that the Sacramento Valley was an excellent candidate for a similar system. Since 1860, Will S. Green had been a proponent of irrigation, but he did not foresee the land-marketing ploy that it would become. Advertising was extensive, positively publicizing Glenn and Colusa Counties, as well as California. This map is from a booklet that was created to formally announce the creation of the extensive irrigation project in the Sacramento Valley. The Kuhns touted the ideal conditions for the highest success in irrigation, which were a deep, rich soil, an abundance of water, the California climate, and the ability to grow a vast range of crops. They assured the use of the most permanent construction for the irrigation system and that every settler would "get a square deal" for his investment. The booklet showed pictures of a variety of beautiful crops and lovely homes to entice investors. (*Wagon Wheels*, 1964:1)

Four

IRRIGATION

Will Semple Green is known in Glenn and Colusa Counties as the "father of irrigation." He was born in Kentucky in 1832. His impressive story can be found in many terrific history books of the area. He began as editor of the *Colusa Sun* in 1863 and used this position to promote his crusade for irrigation. The impressive Sacramento River and other waterways and the failure of crops during drought years made him an advocate for the ability to harness that water for the betterment of the counties. He surveyed the land, became a proponent in the legislature, and served on committees and in companies to further the cause of irrigation. The irrigation system that is so central to Glenn County must also be attributed to two other men who worked on the system after Green died in 1905. Frank Seymour Reager was a primary figure in the Orland Project, and Charles Franklin Lambert drove the organization of the Glenn-Colusa District. (Justus H. Rogers.)

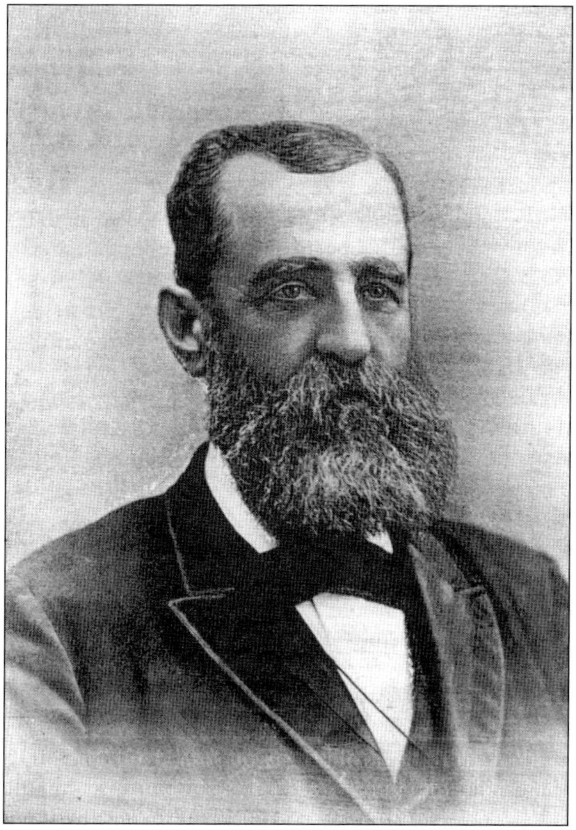

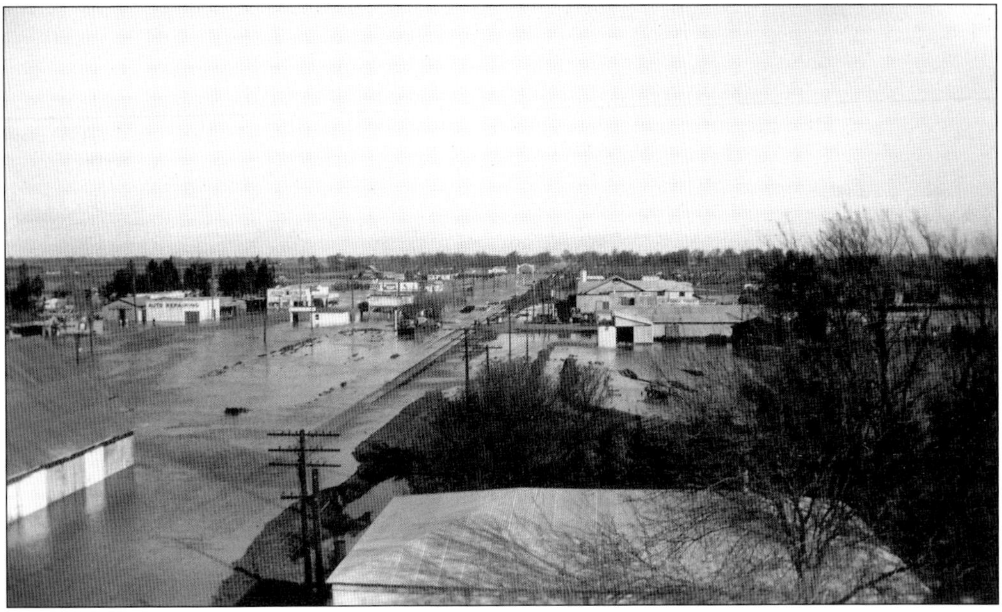

When the waters of Stony Creek left their banks, the result was miles of flooding along the creek. Floods continued even after the Orland Project was organized by the Reclamation Act of 1925, an irrigation project that eventually included three reservoirs and an extensive distribution system including diversion dams, main canals, and lateral canals that helped to contain the flooding. The photograph above may have been taken from the water tower, as it looks at the flooded roadway that heads north out of Orland. The photograph below was taken in the heart of Orland at the railroad tracks and Highway 32 (Sixth Street). (Both, Robert W. Johanningsmeier.)

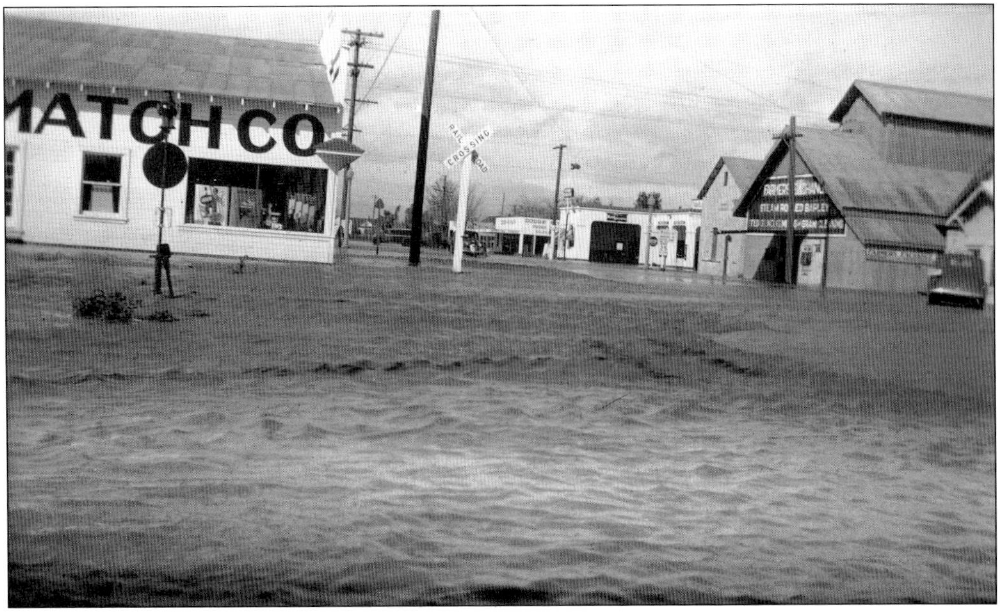

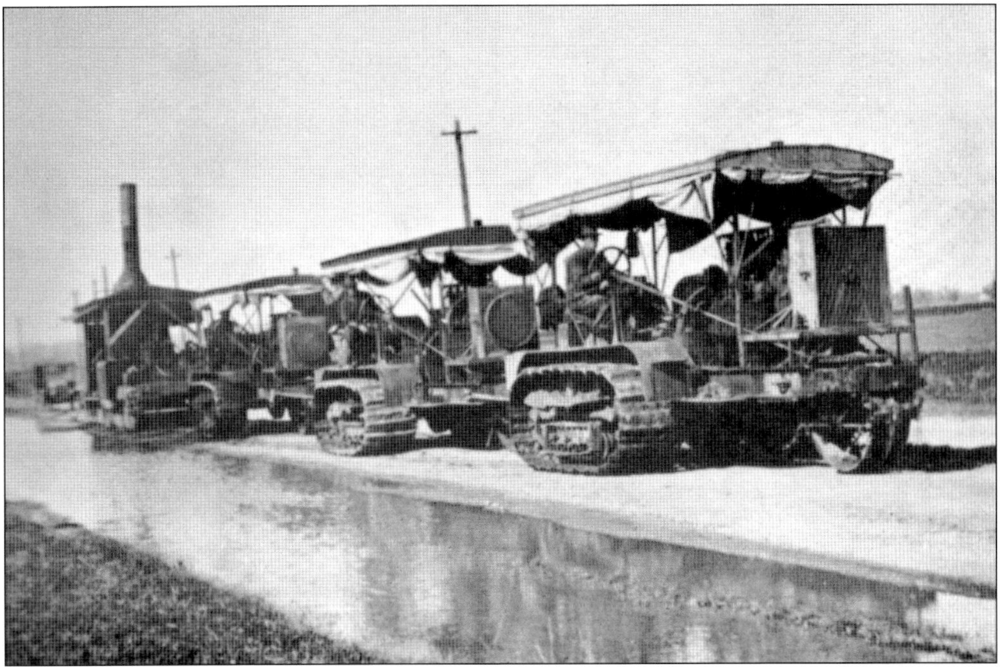

Roads were important to the development of the irrigation system. According to Cynthia F. Davis in *Where Water is King*, each quarter section was to have a road surrounding it and each 40 acres was to have a highway on two sides. Along Highway 45 in northern Glenn County, three tractors pull a donkey engine down the flooded roadway. A donkey engine is a steam-powered winch used to load and unload cargo. (*Wagon Wheels*, 1964:1.)

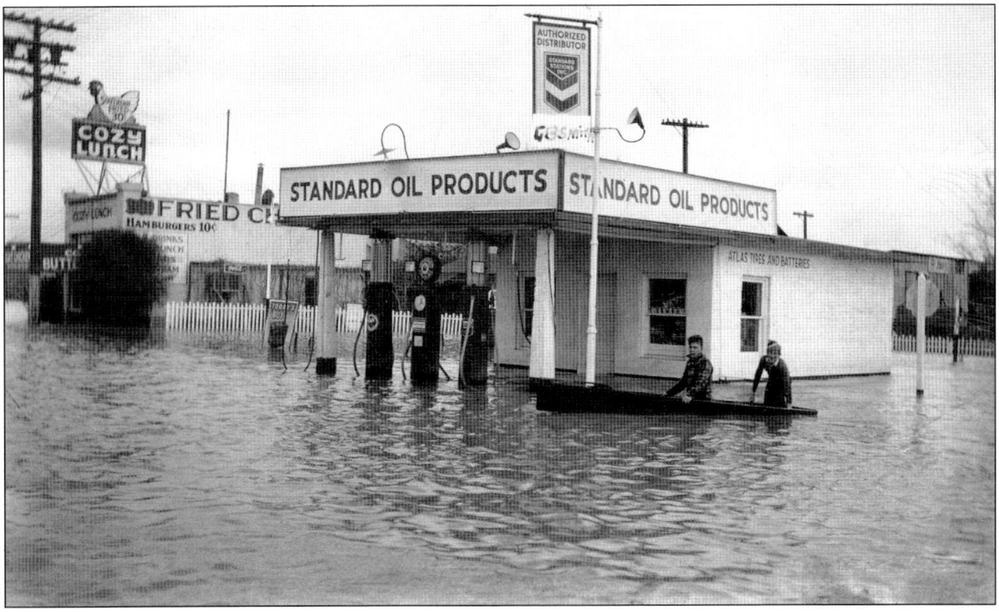

A heavy winter with continuous rains would cause extensive flooding, even in urban areas. Two boys have figured out that a canoe is the way to get around and it does not require gas. The diner next door probably had some flood damage to take care of prior to reopening. (Robert W. Johanningsmeier.)

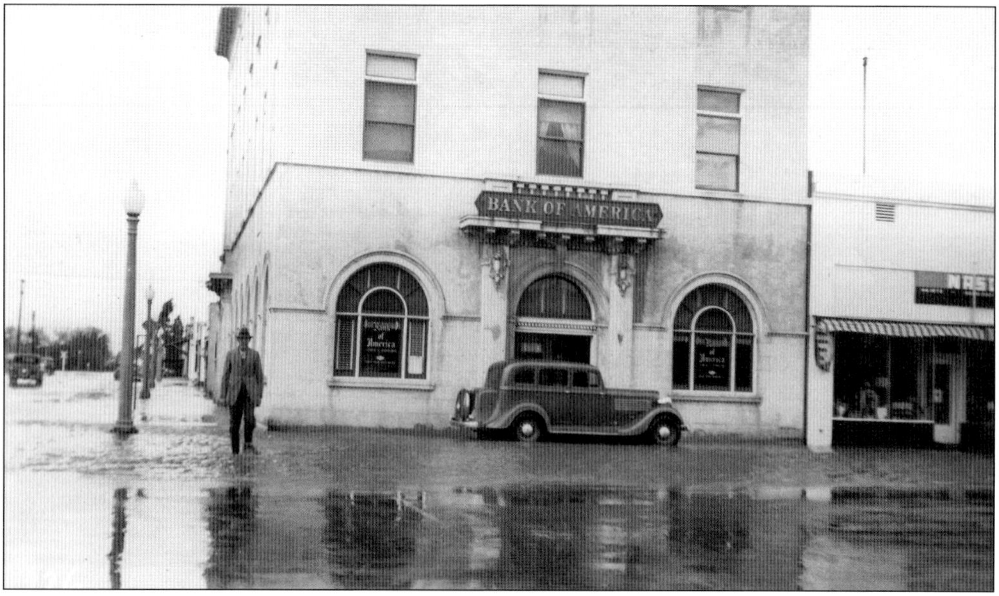

World War I created a food shortage, which allowed irrigated farm product prices to rise. Rice was found to be a successful crop on the previous grain ground, which had been farmed so extensively that it was almost useless. Rice growing was profitable until 1920, when the weather destroyed crops and the farming economy. Times remained difficult in Glenn County through the Great Depression. Landowners found it difficult to live and pay for irrigation. Many farmers turned over their land titles to a security holder, including banks (such as Bank of America in Orland), trusts, and insurance companies, to relieve their burden of payment. The security holders also sustained great losses. The Glenn-Colusa Irrigation District took possession of much of the land because it had been freed from any outstanding debts of the district. As time progressed, some landowners continued to pay assessments, thereby allowing the district to remain solvent. (Above, Robert W. Johanningsmeier; below, Hollis Burrows Spurlock.)

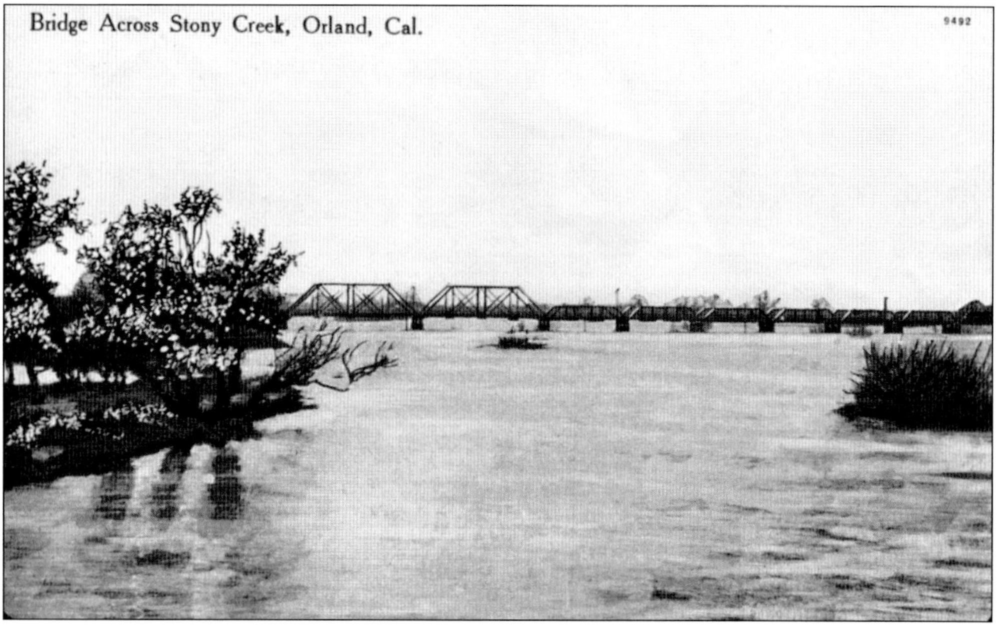

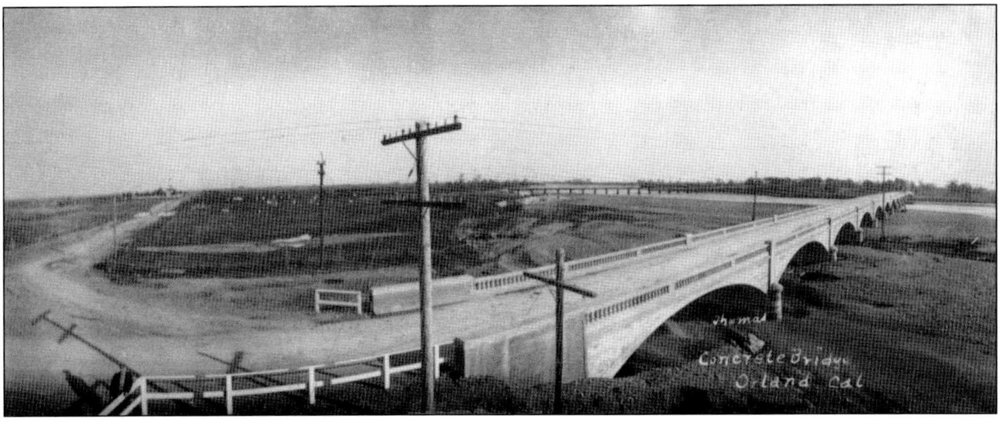

In 1913, a concrete bridge replaced the wooden bridge that crossed Stony Creek just north of Orland. As the irrigation project brought more people into Glenn County, a wider bridge that could handle the increased traffic was necessary on the active Highway 99W. The design and length of the bridge was also indicative of the need to pay attention to potential flood waters. (Orland Historical and Cultural Society.)

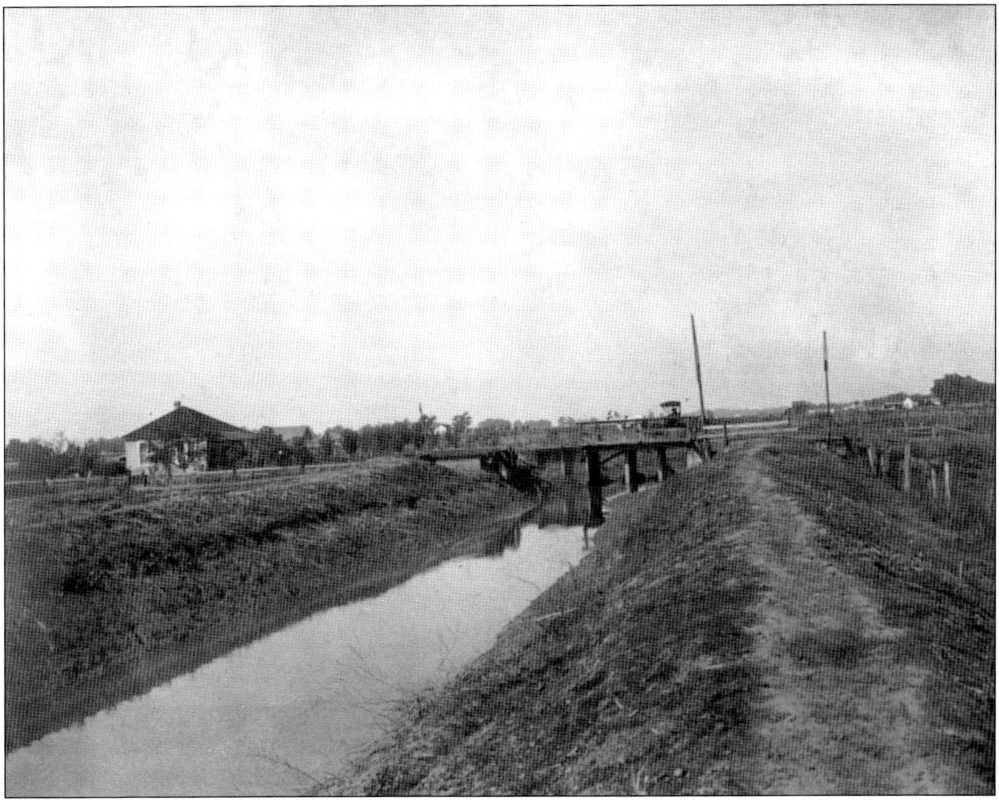

Will Green advocated in January 1887 to build canals along the sloughs and to build "immense headgates of solid masonry at the head of each canal." A survey for the canal was finished in September 1888. Green dragged a plow in the right-of-way and broke the first ground. Due to much opposition, litigation, and lack of funds, canals, such as the one shown here, were not completed until 1907. (Greg Steel.)

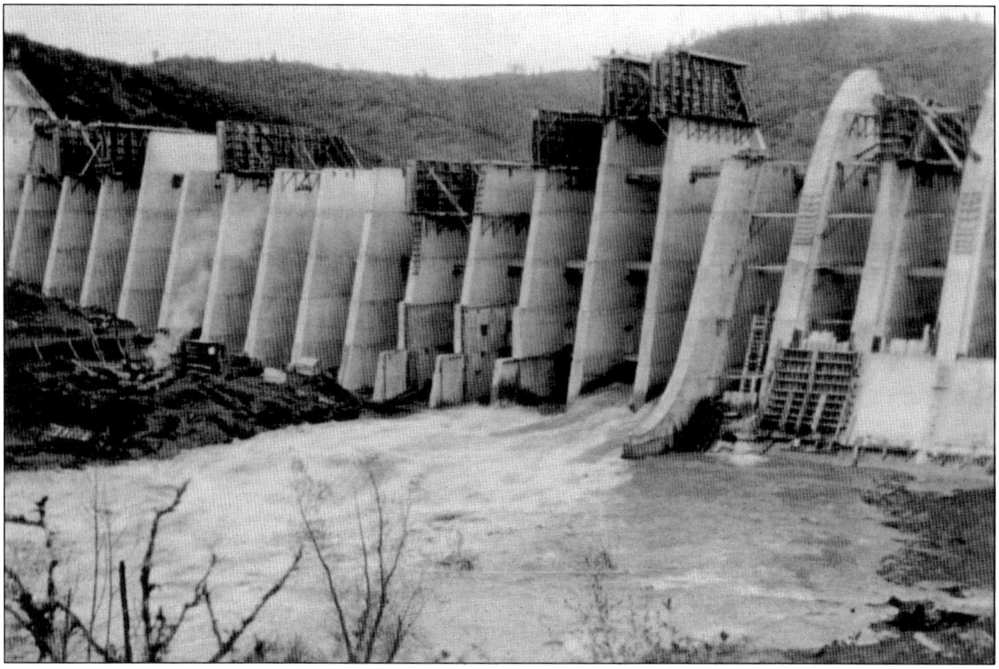

The Orland Water Users' Association formed to construct an irrigation project utilizing the waters of Stony Creek. Land and rights were purchased and construction began on the first phase, East Park Dam, in 1909. The dam was completed in 1910. Construction of Stony Gorge Dam began in late 1926 and was completed within two years. (Orland Historical and Cultural Society.)

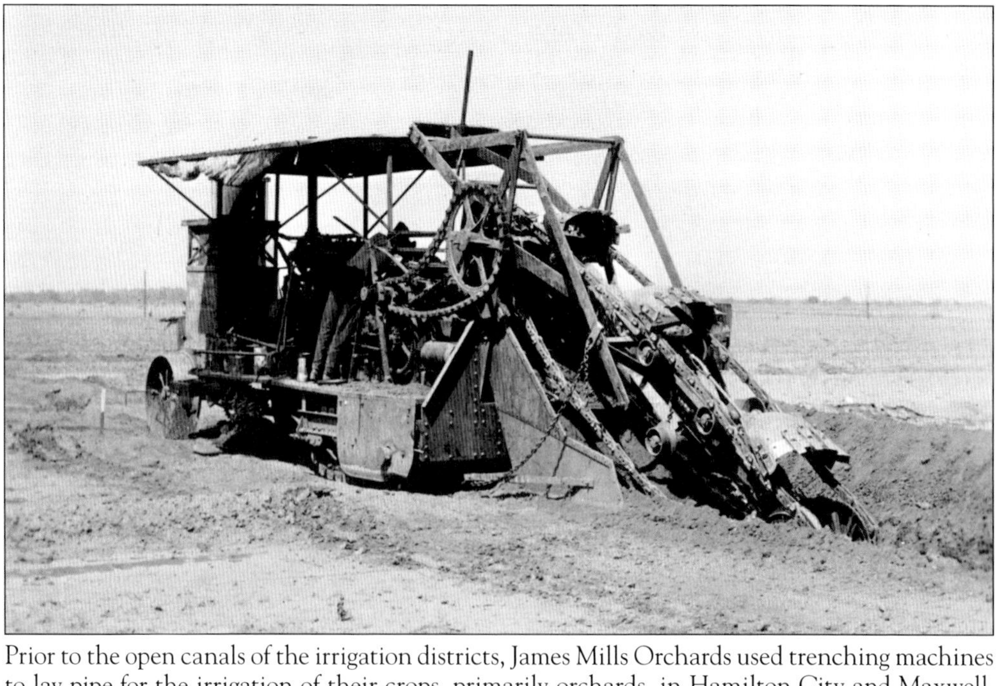

Prior to the open canals of the irrigation districts, James Mills Orchards used trenching machines to lay pipe for the irrigation of their crops, primarily orchards, in Hamilton City and Maxwell. According to the 1920 US Census, a group of laborers from Spain were the primary builders of the cement irrigation pipe. (Hamilton City Community Services District.)

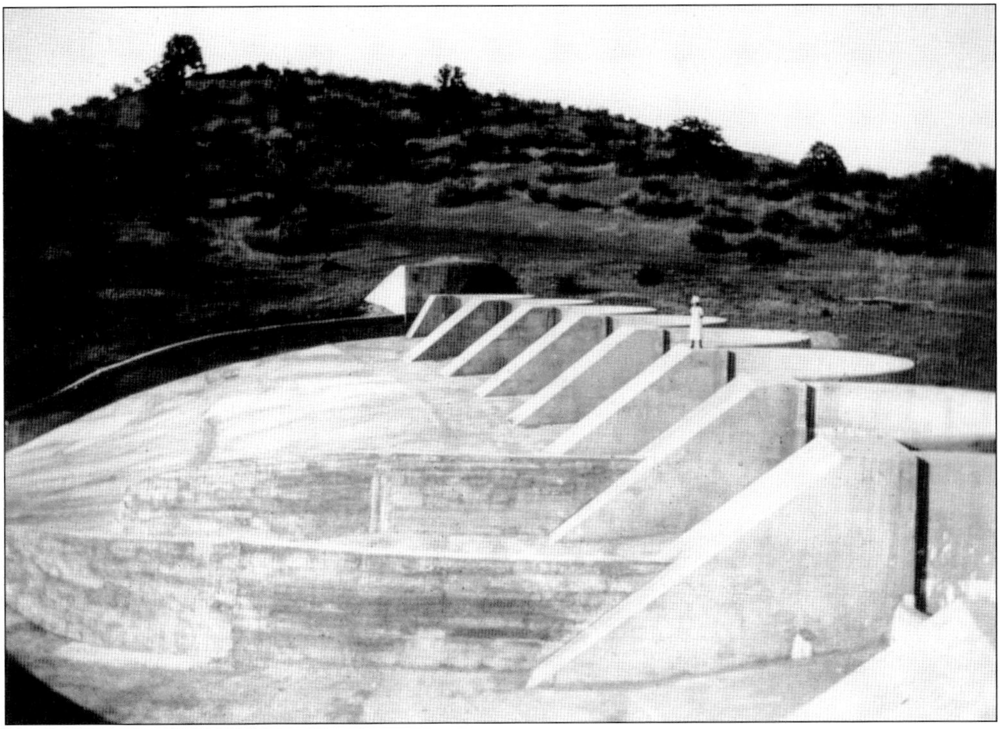

The Orland Project purchased land and property rights to the Stony Creek Irrigation Company for $25,000 and the Lemon Home Water, Power & Light Company for $15,250. The Stanley Contracting Company of San Francisco was awarded the construction project at a bid of $79,881.65. The final cost of the project was $155,000, and it was completed in June 15, 1910. East Park Dam spillway, pictured here, was photographed as the pride of the Orland Project. (Robert W. Johanningsmeier.)

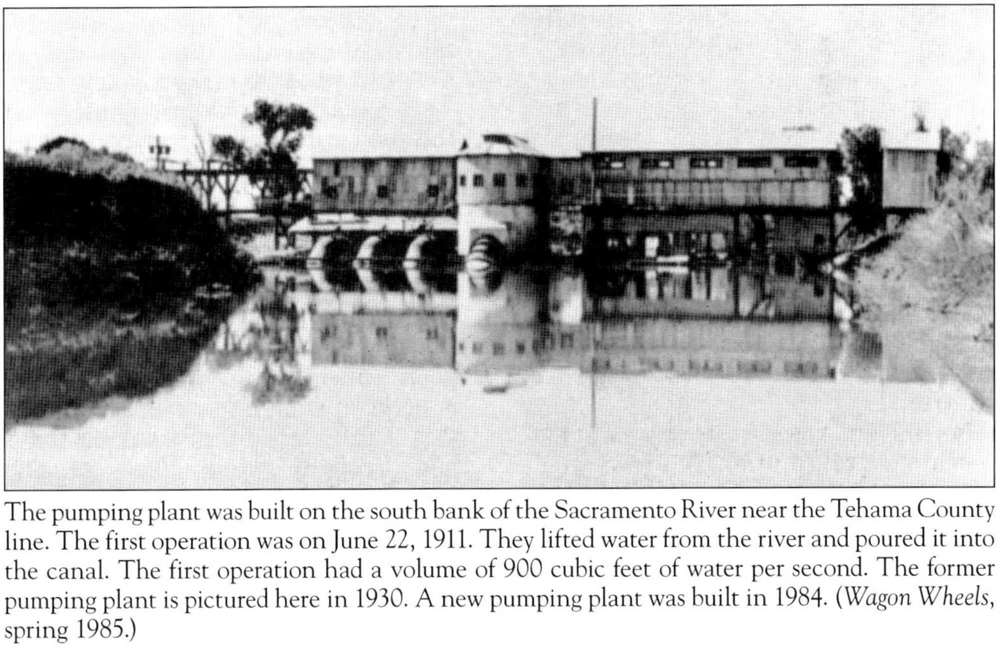

The pumping plant was built on the south bank of the Sacramento River near the Tehama County line. The first operation was on June 22, 1911. They lifted water from the river and poured it into the canal. The first operation had a volume of 900 cubic feet of water per second. The former pumping plant is pictured here in 1930. A new pumping plant was built in 1984. (*Wagon Wheels*, spring 1985.)

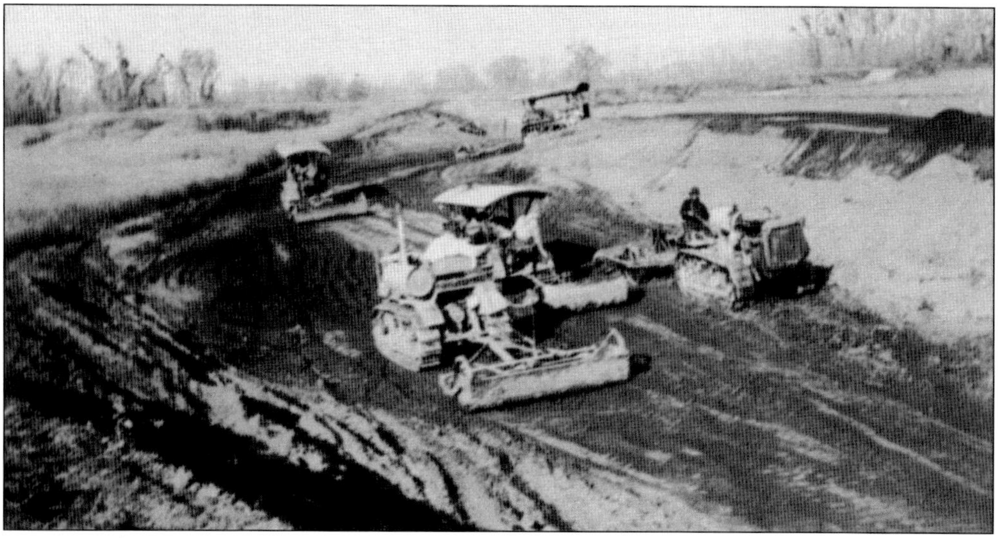

On December 22, 1919, the Glenn County Board of Supervisors authorized the Glenn-Colusa Irrigation District to enlarge the existing canal system in order to increase water flow capacity for the 1920 season. The rice crop was so successful in 1919 that the landowners were willing to contribute money for this purpose. According to the *Glenn Transcript*, it was "the first time in the history of Glenn and Colusa counties that a united front on any public enterprise has been secured." (Greg Steel.)

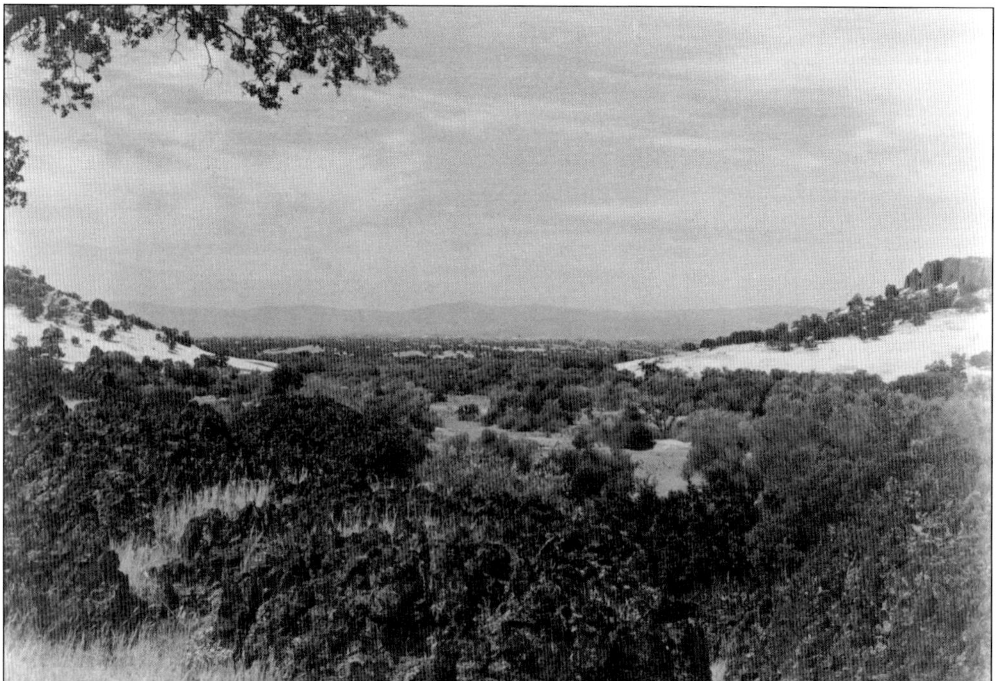

This photograph shows the Black Butte Dam. Written on the back of the photograph is, "Looking into reservoir area of Black Butte Dam, taken from right abutment site. The notch in the background is an alternate dam site. Present thinking places the dam at approximately the present Orland Project Diversion." (Orland Historical and Cultural Society.)

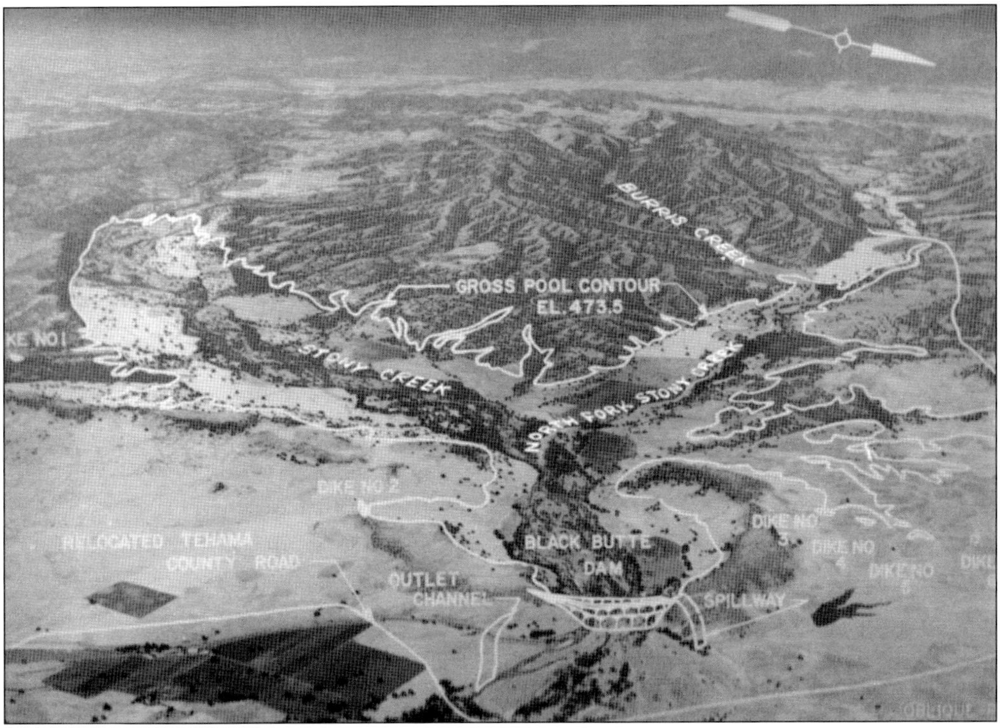

The US Reclamation Service had established itself in the Sacramento Valley with the development and construction of the Orland Project, including East Park and Stony Gorge reservoirs. The next step in reclamation was farther north on Stony Creek. This photograph shows the projected impact that the creation of a reservoir would have on the surrounding community. (Orland Historical and Cultural Society.)

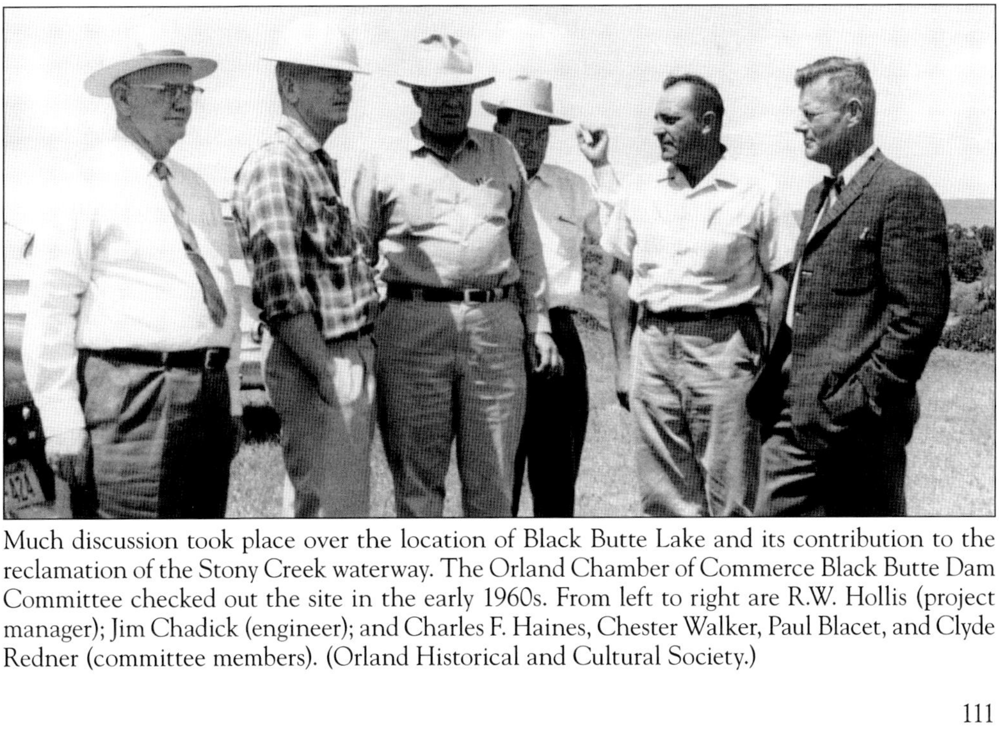

Much discussion took place over the location of Black Butte Lake and its contribution to the reclamation of the Stony Creek waterway. The Orland Chamber of Commerce Black Butte Dam Committee checked out the site in the early 1960s. From left to right are R.W. Hollis (project manager); Jim Chadick (engineer); and Charles F. Haines, Chester Walker, Paul Blacet, and Clyde Redner (committee members). (Orland Historical and Cultural Society.)

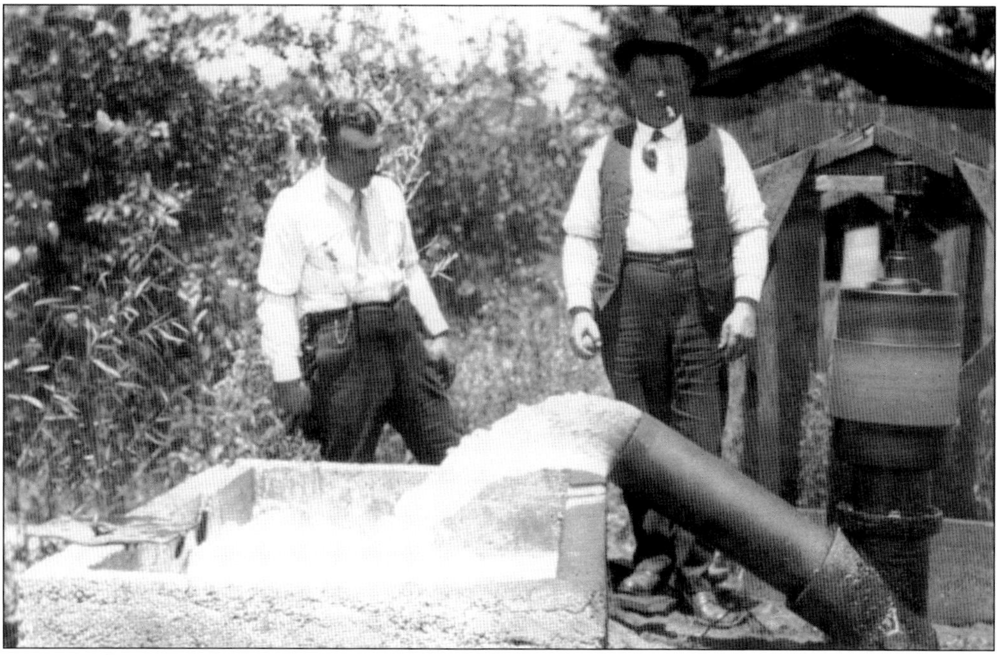

Since Will S. Green posted a notice to appropriate water rights of the Sacramento River in 1883, the irrigation system established in Glenn County has been in continual progression. The irrigation systems continue to provide water in the arid Sacramento Valley. Farmers continue to take advantage of the district water and, as pictured here in an orange orchard, to pump their own water. (Orland Historical and Cultural Society.)

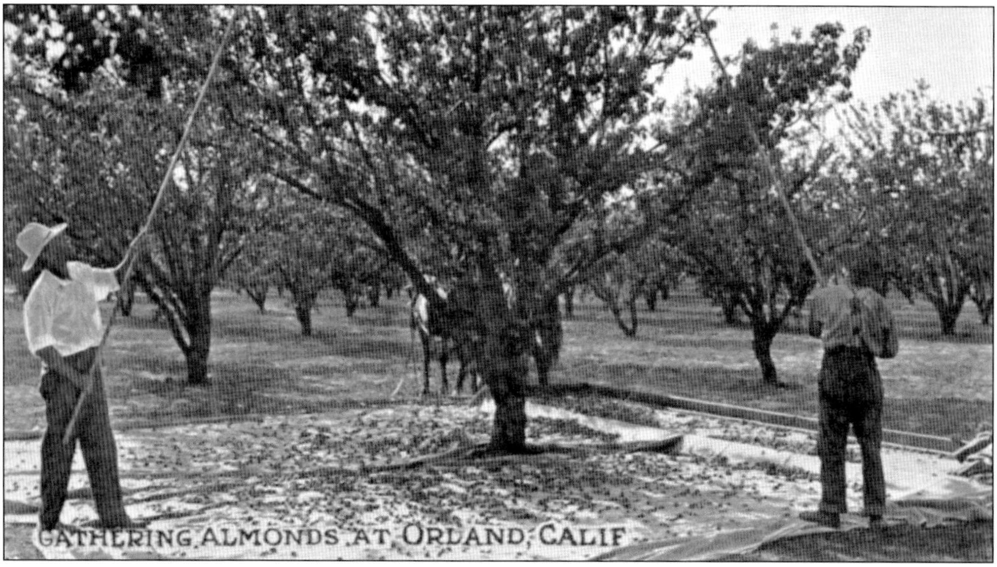

The vast agricultural area that we know as Glenn County continues to produce a variety of crops. These crops are ever-changing depending on markets, vagaries of weather, and the desire of the consumer. In 2011, Glenn County ranked 18th in overall agriculture out of 58 counties. The top five commodities produced were rice, almonds, walnuts, milk, and cattle and calves. As technology progresses, the current techniques of production and harvest will become as antiquated as knocking almond trees. (Author's collection.)

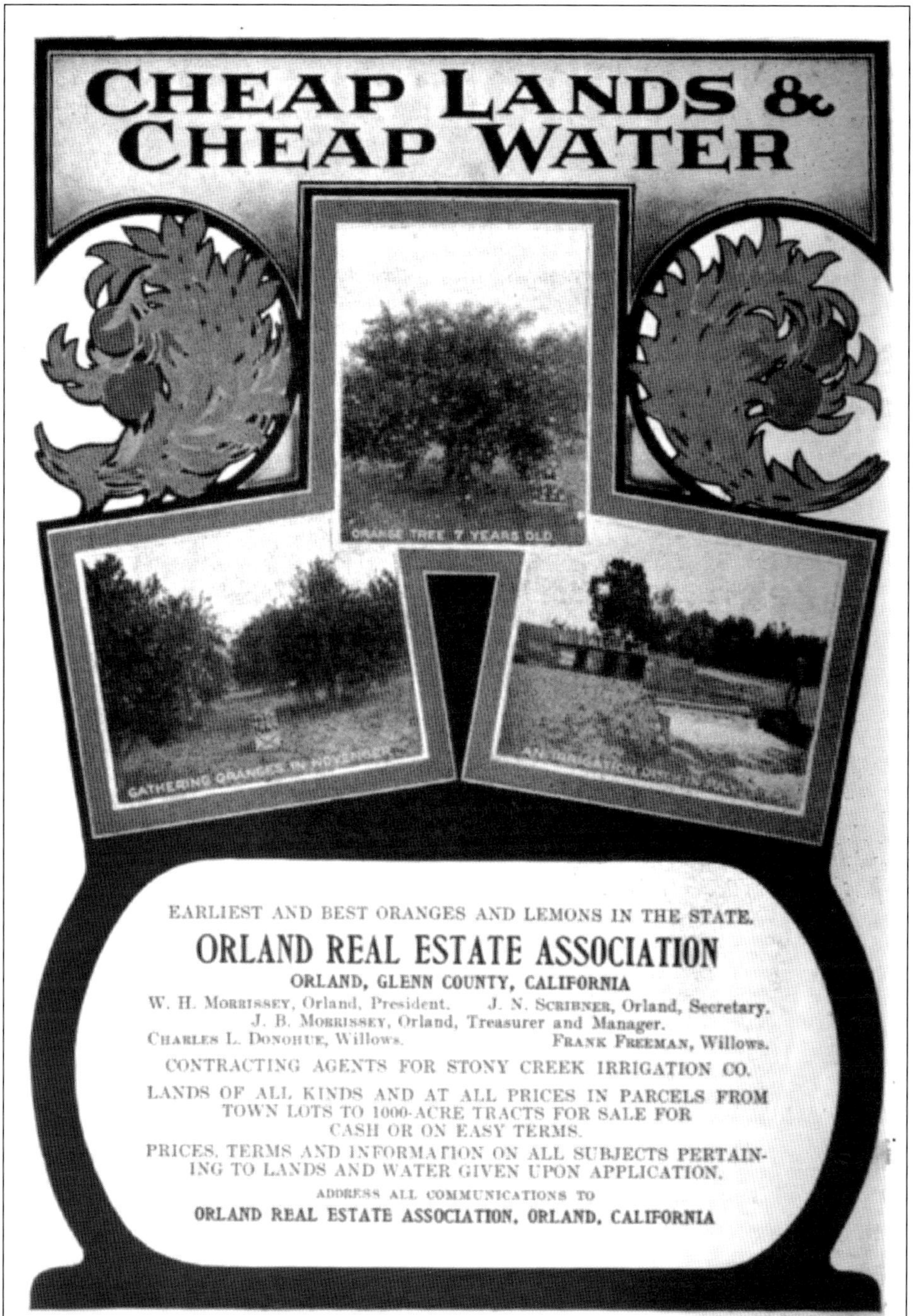

In 1915, *Sunset* magazine advertised Glenn County as a "prosperous and progressive paradise of peace and plenty." It extolled the virtues of its history and the promise of its future. The great wheat ranches of its early days made way for an increased population and farming opportunities. All of this happened because of Glenn County's great soil, temperate growing climate, steady water supply, good roads, railroad access, cheap land, modern conveniences, and handsome schools emphasizing agricultural, domestic science, and industrial education in high school courses. (Author's collection.)

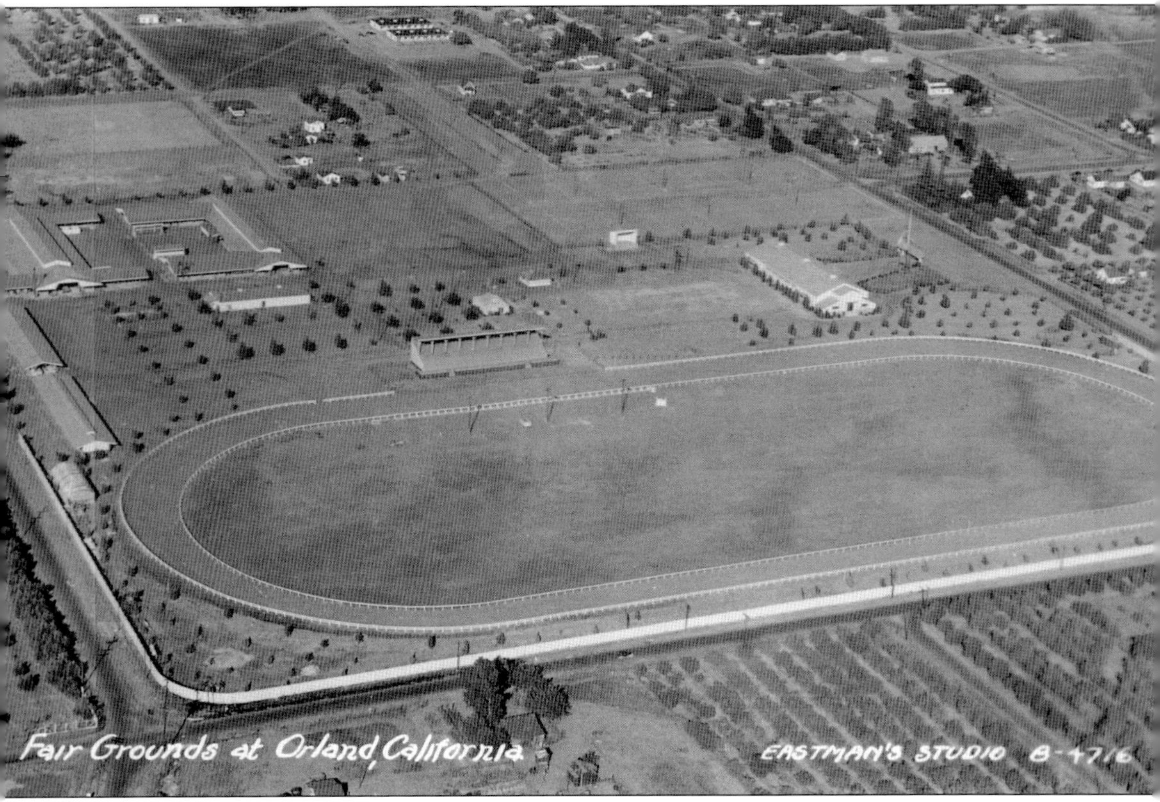

The new permanent 40-acre fairground facility located on East Yolo Street is pictured in this c. 1941 postcard. The structures were built by the Work Projects Administration. The track for horses was one half mile. The entrance on the north led fairgoers to Flaherty Hall. The bandstand, livestock facilities, and horse stalls are also familiar buildings. Eastman's Studios was a commercial photography and postcard studio based in Northern California. (Robert W. Johanningsmeier.)

Five

Fair

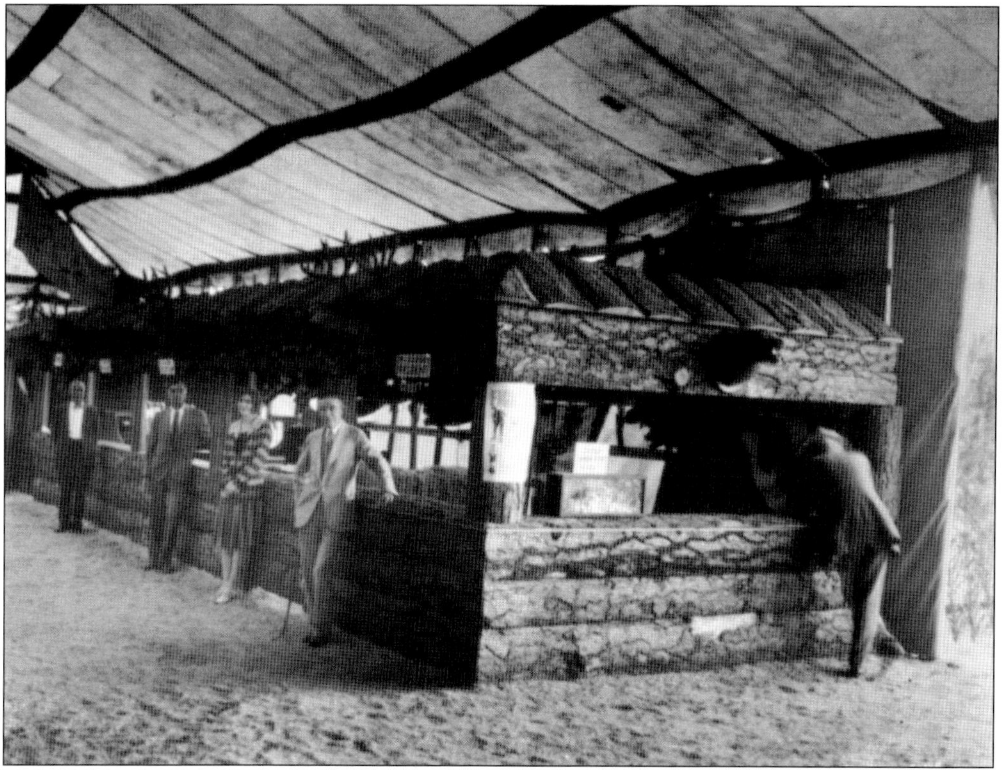

Through the enthusiastic directorship of John J. Flaherty, the Glenn County Fair grew from a temporary location in 1917 to its current permanent facility. Flaherty was elected president of the Glenn County Livestock and Agricultural Association upon the resignation of James Mills in February 1917. This picture is labeled, "Fair office under big top." Pictured around 1930, from left to right, are J.N. Tibessart (treasurer), E.A. Kirk (secretary-manager), Vera Vanderford (office secretary), and John J. Flaherty (president). (Orland Historical and Cultural Society.)

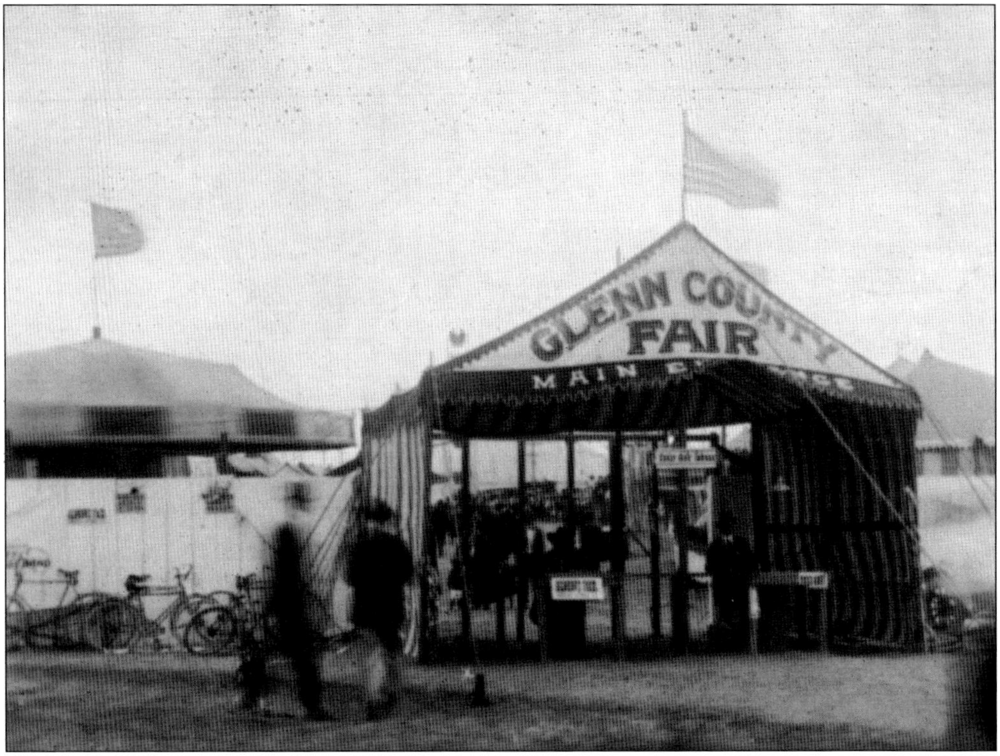

The first Glenn County Fair was held September 26–29, 1917, under the supervision of the Glenn County Livestock and Agricultural Association. The association's purpose was "to promote Livestock, Agricultural, Horticultural, and other interests of the County." John J. Flaherty wrote an open letter to the county encouraging people to enter their exhibits at the fair. (Orland Historical and Cultural Society.)

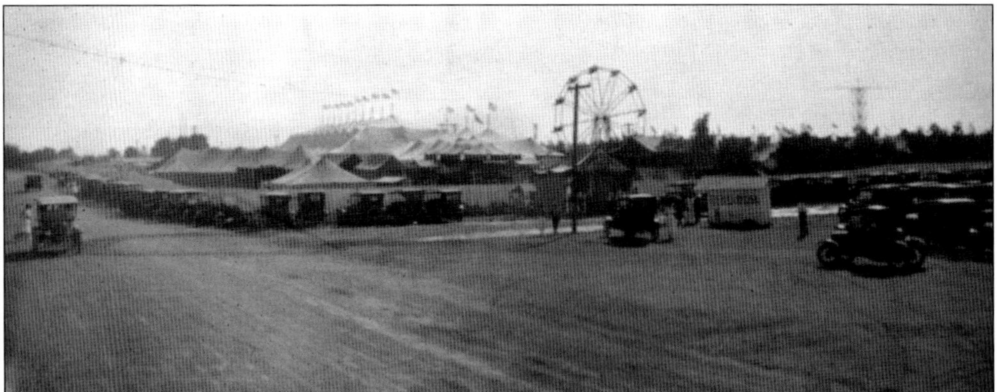

The first fair was located on the northwest corner of South Street and Highway 99W. Water pipes and sewer systems were installed to accommodate the four large tents. One tent enclosed livestock, one held poultry, and two were used for general exhibits. The Hedley Amusement Company, "the biggest and best aggregation of features on the Coast," provided amusements. Prior to opening, a tremendous north wind demolished the tents, tearing them into pieces. Sailmakers from San Francisco were called in to repair them, and the fair continued as planned. (Orland Historical and Cultural Society.)

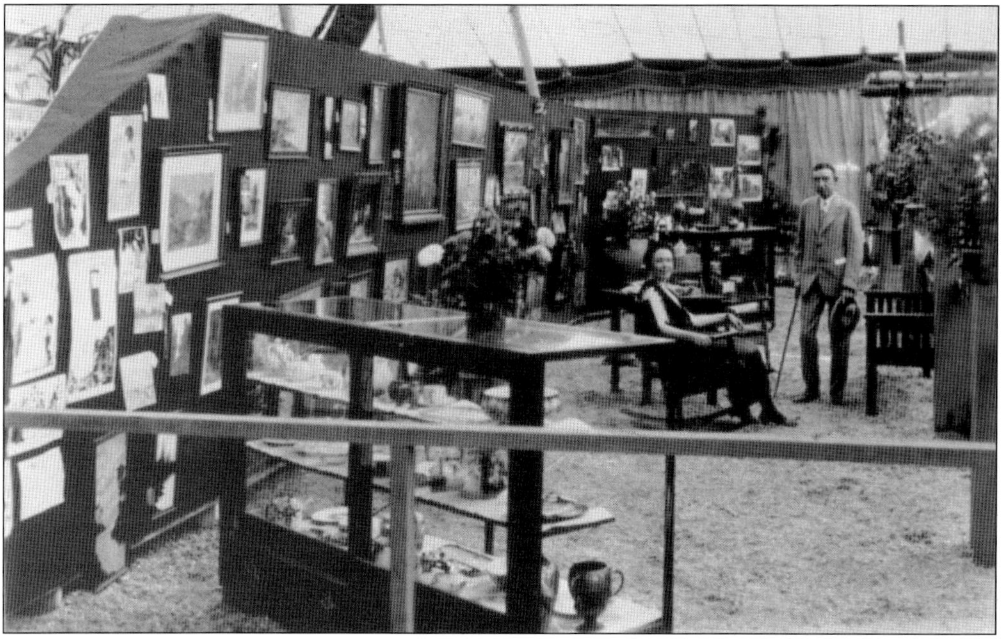

Glenn County was consistently recognized for its prize-winning crops. At the 1913 California Land Show in San Francisco, Glenn County was recognized for its "best exhibits of alfalfa plant, German millet, rhubarb, watermelon, alfalfa hay, fruiting spineless cactus, fish frozen in ice, grain in sheaves and fruit on branches." This photograph shows John Flaherty and Mrs. T.H. Brown at the Glenn County Fair in 1925. (Orland Historical and Cultural Society.)

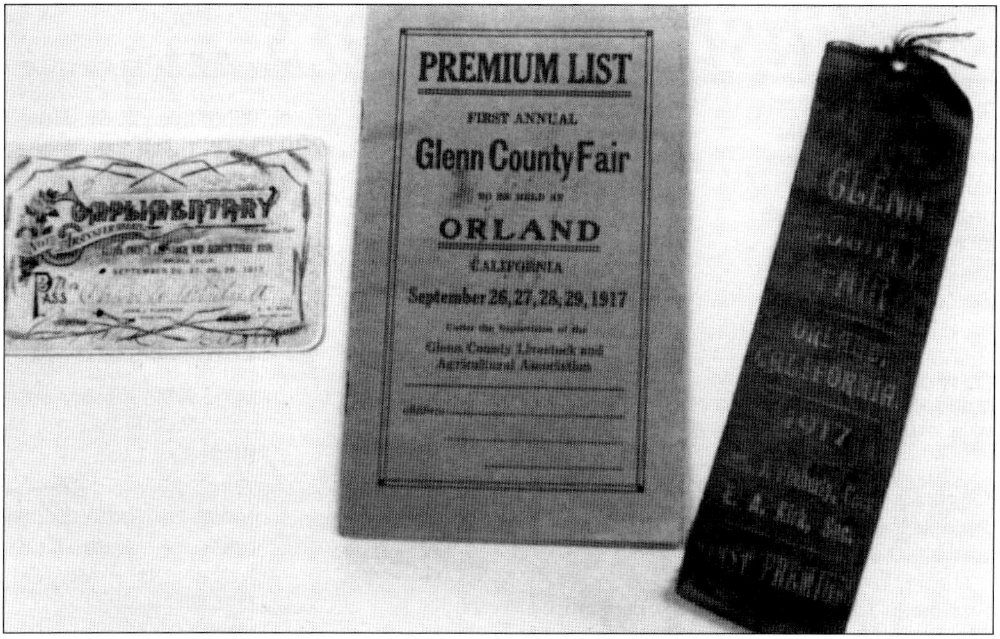

Memorabilia from the first Glenn County Fair in 1917 includes a complimentary pass, premium list, and a ribbon. The pass was made out to Charles Whitsett and signed by E.A. Kirk. The premium book was in such demand that it had to be printed a second time. The blue ribbon was given as a first prize for exceptional projects exhibited by county citizens. (Glenn County Fair.)

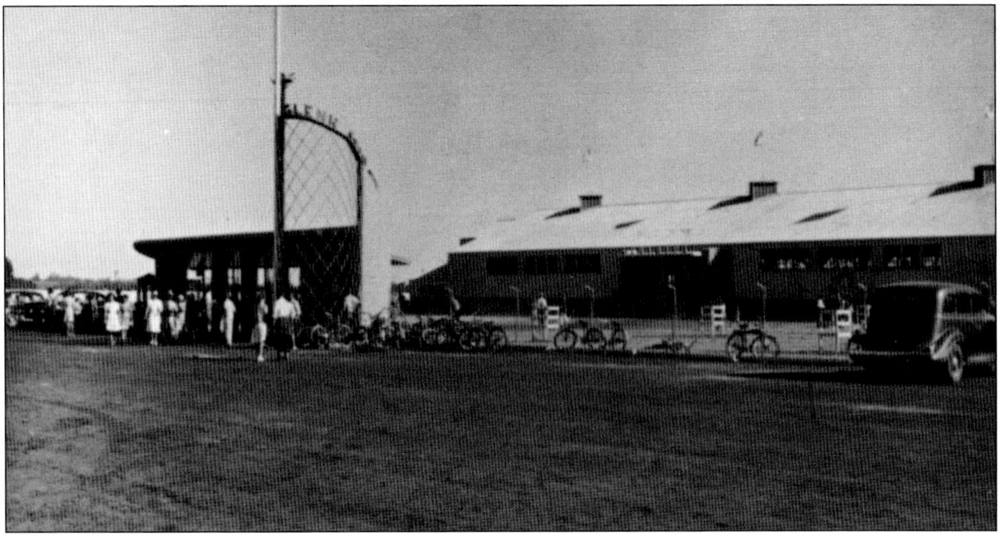

In 1941, a $200,000 facility was opened to celebrate the 25th anniversary of the Glenn County Fair. Using funds from pari-mutuel betting, 40 acres were purchased. The labor was provided by the Work Projects Administration. No Glenn County tax money was used for the facility. The opening gate shown here on the left is north of the building named Flaherty Hall, which honors the longtime president of the fair board, John Flaherty. (Orland Historical and Cultural Society.)

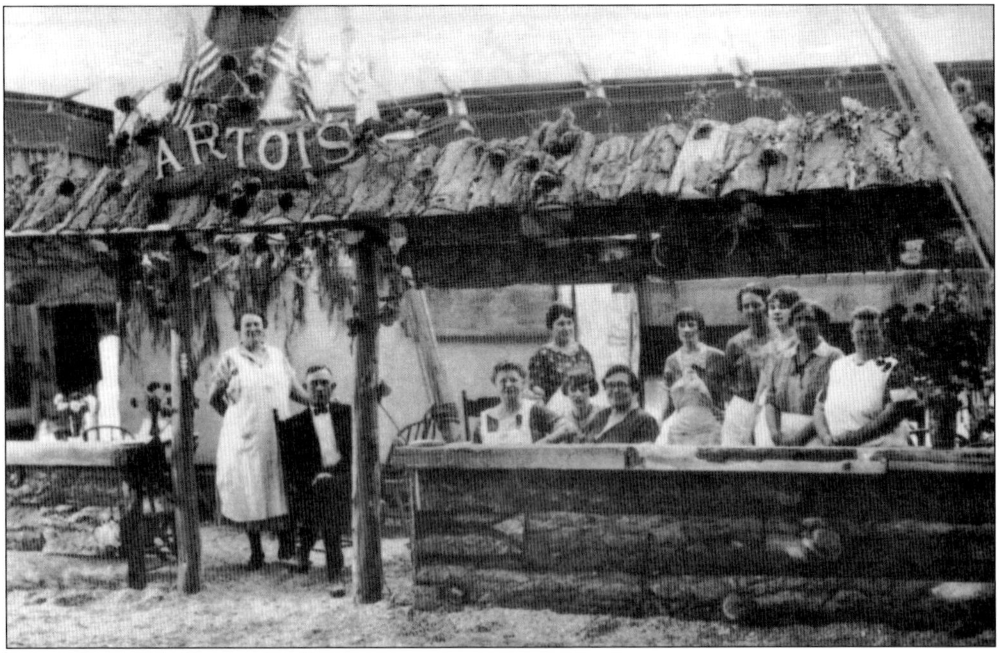

Potential advertisers were promised excellent rates and accommodations with the Southern Pacific to ensure the ease of transportation and display of an exhibit. A brochure advertising the fair stated that a business would be offered "the one great opportunity of the year . . . with the prosperous people of Glenn and surrounding counties." The Artois Ladies' Aid Food Concession took advantage of the offer. Pictured here at the 1920 fair in unknown order are Martha Peterich, Emma Rix Howard, Amanda von Bargen, Lorena Runge, Dora Pieper, Phil Veslage, Mary Holtorf, Lorna Prine, Agnes Rehse, Emma Peterich, and Alma Hinz. (Glenn County Fair.)

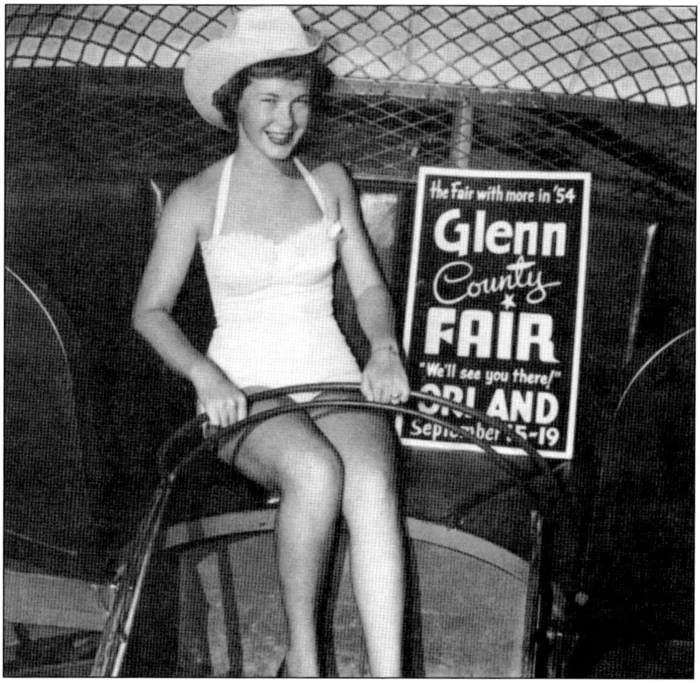

The first Miss Glenn County to be crowned was Shirley Mudd in 1954. Farryl Dean Luning of Red Bluff had been chosen queen of the fair in 1931. In a plan to raise out-of-town attendance, Luning and her 12 attendants were from different valley towns, so this was not truly a Miss Glenn County. Mudd was crowned with a wreath of laurels and given a ruby ring. (Glenn County Fair.)

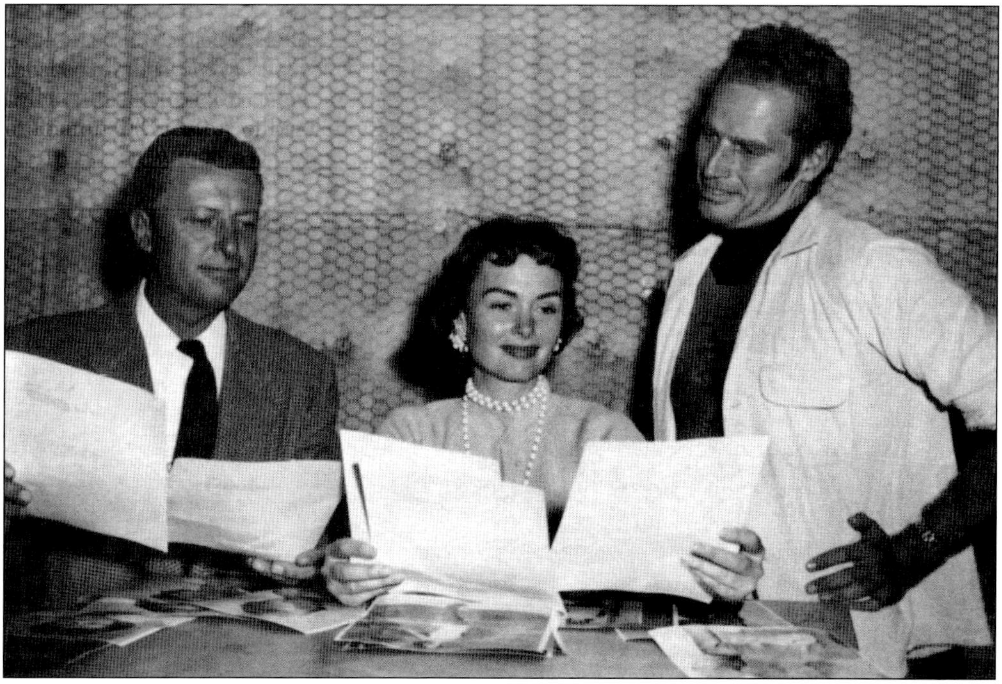

Celebrities were chosen to serve as judges for the first Miss Glenn County pageant at the 1954 Glenn County Fair. Max Factor Jr. (left) was the president of the Max Factor cosmetics empire based in Los Angeles. Actress Donna Reed (center) had just won the 1953 Academy Award for her performance as Lorene Burke in the war drama *From Here To Eternity*. Actor Charlton Heston would go on to perform as Moses in *The Ten Commandments* and Judah Ben-Hur in the movie *Ben-Hur*. (Glenn County Fair.)

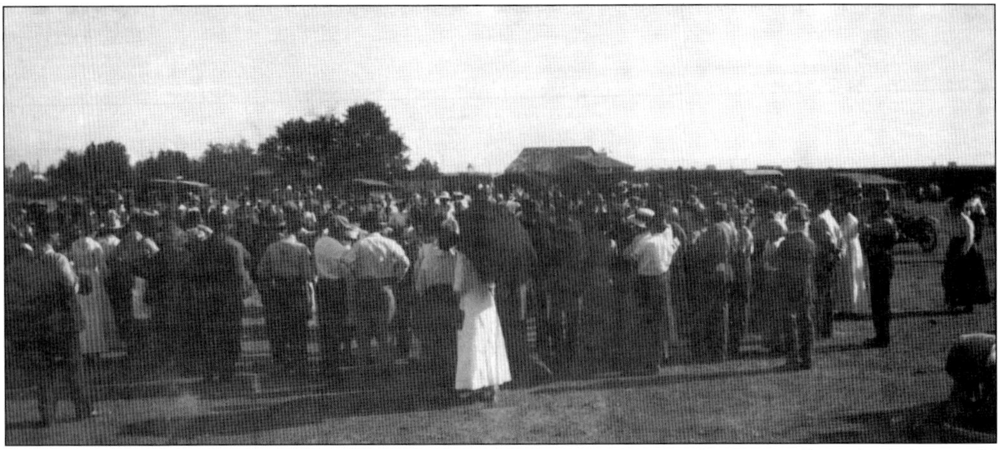

Prior to the new fairground facility, Future Farmers of America and 4-H youth and adults could exhibit their livestock at open-air events. This allowed the livestock raisers an opportunity to display the quality animals that they had been breeding. This crowd was watching a similar show in Orland that was sponsored by the Glenn County Farm Bureau. The show, in 1916, attracted 500 people and over 160 horses, dairy cattle, and pigs. (Glenn County Fair.)

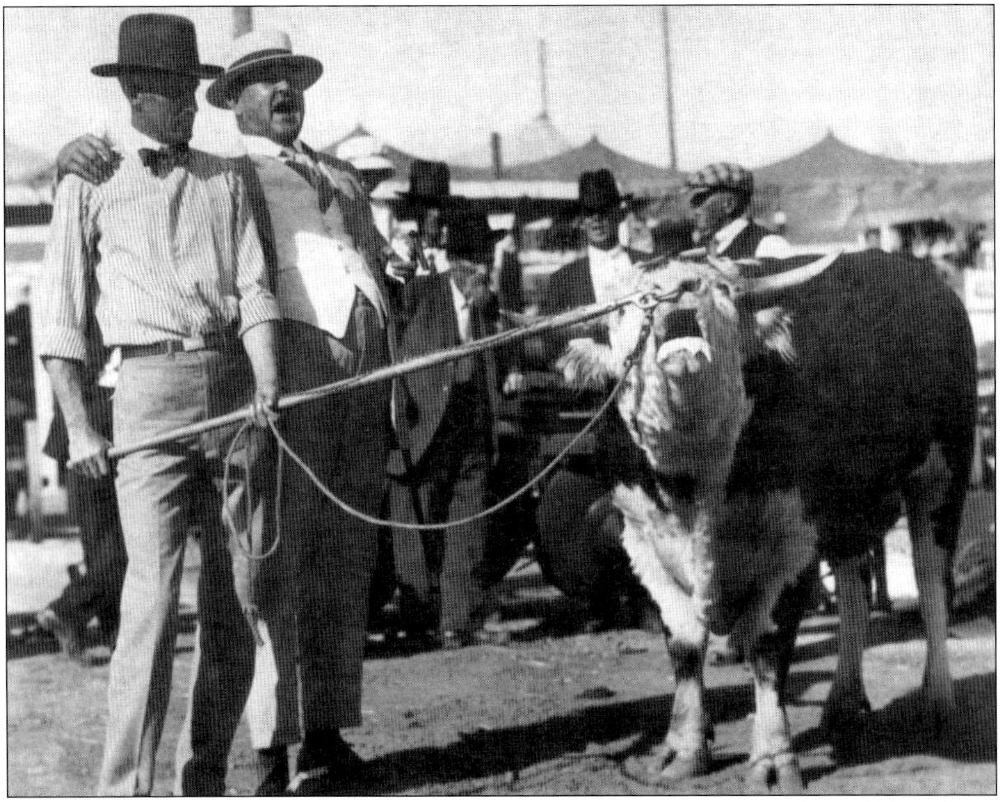

Livestock raisers desired to bring their animals to exhibit not only to show them off, but also to possibly sell them to a high bidder at auction. Likewise, farmers and ranchers looking to improve the quality of their herd would attend livestock shows in the hopes of purchasing new animals. The auctioneer pictured here is using his skills to try to obtain a good bid on this animal for the owner. Mr. Howard uses a ring stick to pose the animal. (Glenn County Fair.)

The new permanent facilities were situated between East Yolo Street on the north, Papst Avenue on the east, Walnut Avenue on the west, and South Street on the south. The site contained 40 acres. Permanent structures were built for livestock and poultry exhibits. Future Farmers of America and 4-H livestock exhibitors were treated to a new venue. (Orland Historical and Cultural Society.)

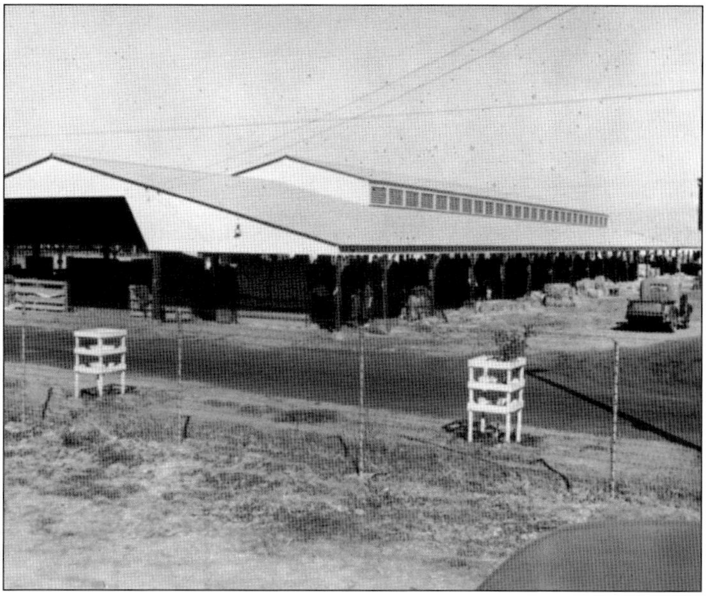

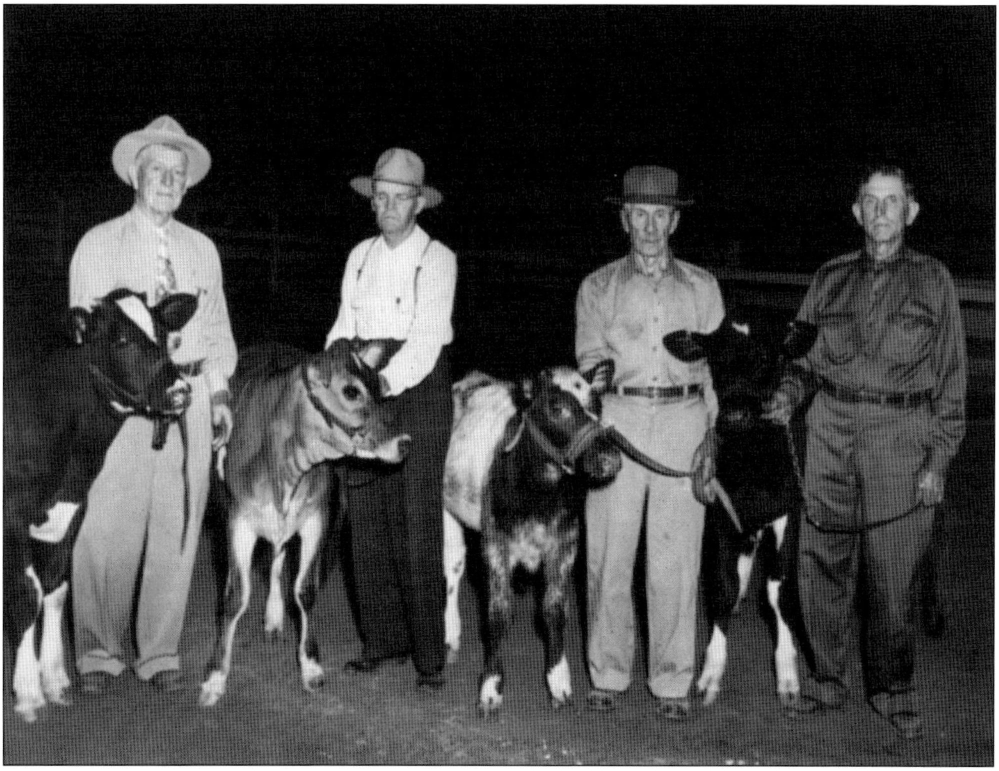

Although dairy cattle have been a permanent fixture in Glenn County for family use, it was not until the completion of the river branch canal and the subdivision of large holdings into intensive farms in 1907 that dairying became a firmly established industry in the county. A quality dairy animal can be promoted and sold through shows like the Glenn County Fair, as shown here in 1953. From left to right are Jack Cook, Charlie Whitsett, Bob Yates, and Bert Bills. (Orland Historical and Cultural Society.)

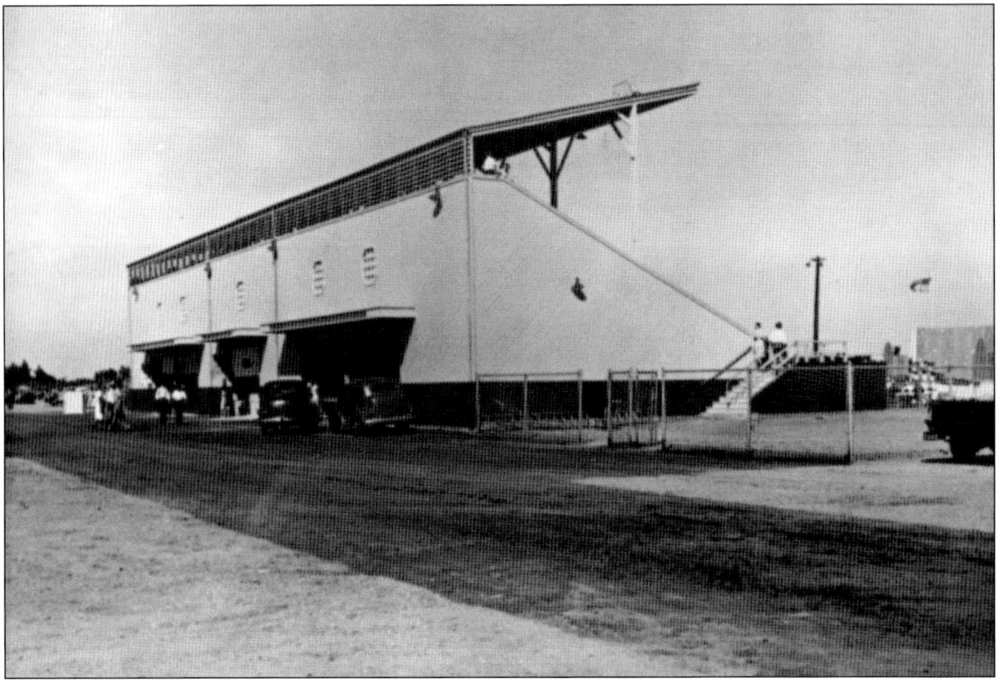

In 1941, the 40-acre facility was opened to fairgoers. The permanent structures included a dance pavilion, a main exhibit hall, a half-mile track, and the largest grandstand of any adjoining county. (Orland Historical and Cultural Society.)

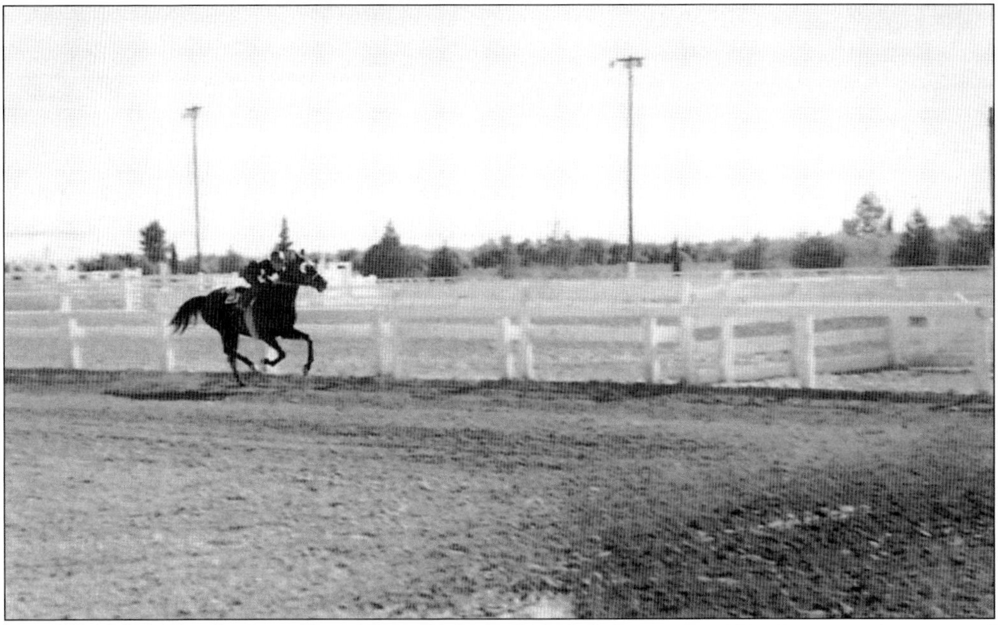

The main event for the first Glenn County racetrack was horse racing. The fairground contained stalls for the horses and was an ideal place for training. Many Glenn County residents raised and raced horses. Most of the local trainers campaigned their horses at Golden Gate, Tanforan, Bay Meadows, Ferndale, and the fair circuit. Here trainer and owner Dee Kirkpatrick of Orland gallops a horse on the track at the Glenn County Fairgrounds around 1962. (Sherrie Cooper.)

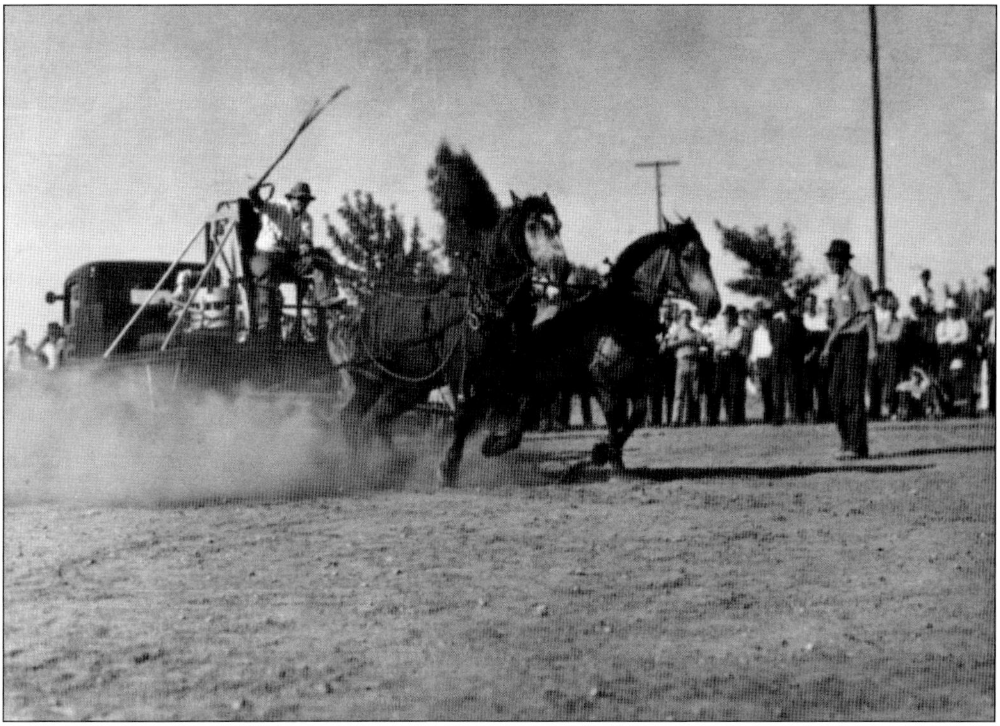

County fairs were a great place for the community to come together to exhibit their goods and to compete against others. Margaret Manner is shown here in a horse-pulling contest in 1936. Margaret competed in numerous contests, entering in the middle to heavyweight divisions. (Orland Historical and Cultural Society.)

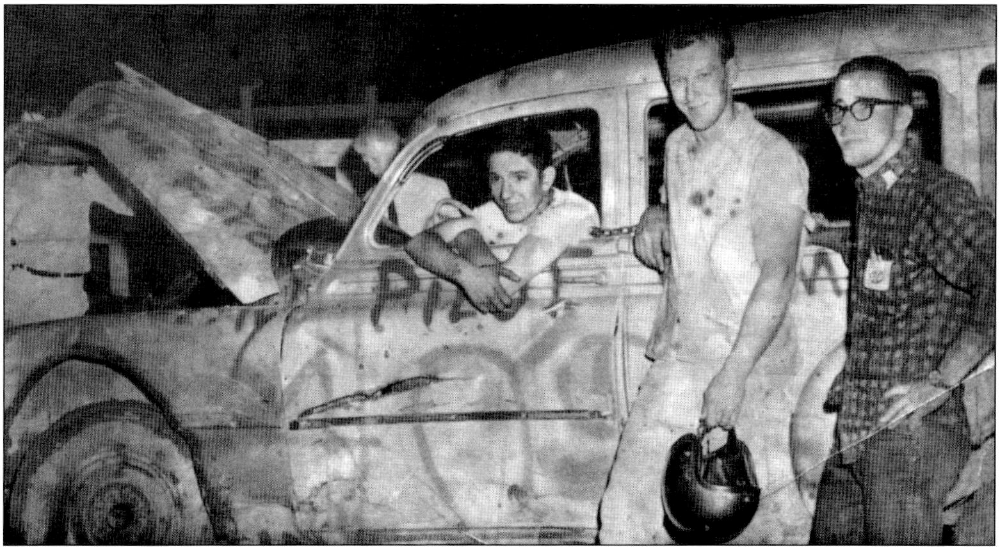

The destruction derby was debuted at the Glenn County Fair in 1965. It proved to be one of the most popular attractions, drawing near-capacity crowds. Drivers from all over Northern California competed. Ken Gilmore of Orland drove a station wagon to tie the race with Loren Elliott of Redding in 1965. From left to right are David Cufaude and Dan Cufaude (near the hood), Gilmore (in the car), Loren Elliott, and Bob Silveira. (Glenn County Fair.)

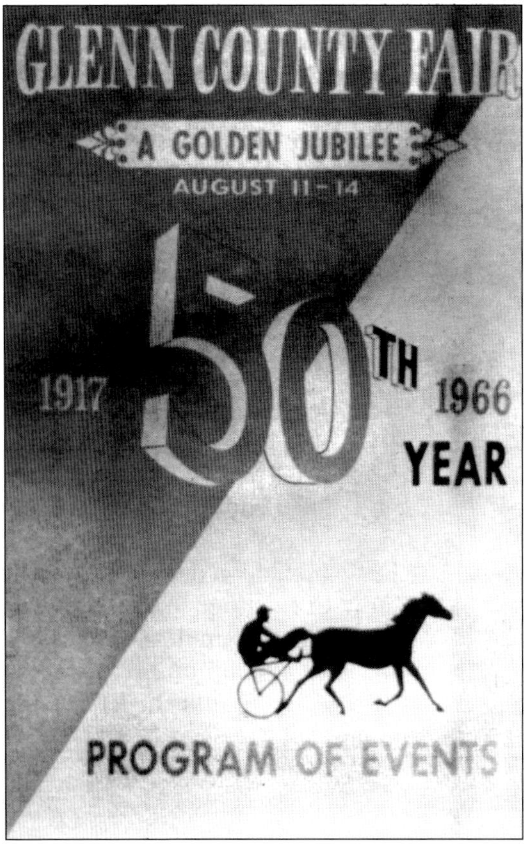

The golden jubilee 50th anniversary was celebrated in 1966. The program of events included the destruction derby, battle of the teen bands, Pinky and Chimp (a woman balanced on a sword), a gold nugget collection owned by Bank of America, a junior livestock show and auction, and full exhibit halls. The previous attendance record, set in 1964, was broken that year with 42,774 in attendance during the four-day fair. (Glenn County Fair.)

Trainer and owner Dee Kirkpatrick sits astride Tippy Tin, grandson of Sea Biscuit. Although Dee was never a jockey, he owned and trained horses and made his livelihood in racing. Dee lost his hearing due to meningitis when he was about five years old. He attended Orland Public Schools and then attended a school for the deaf in the East. (Sherrie Cooper.)

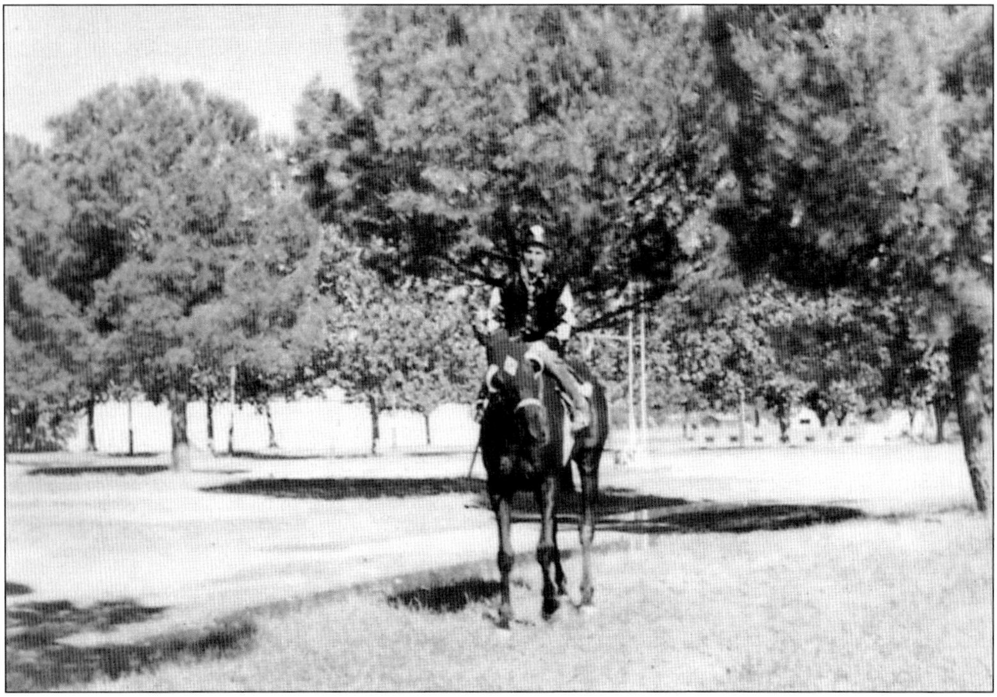

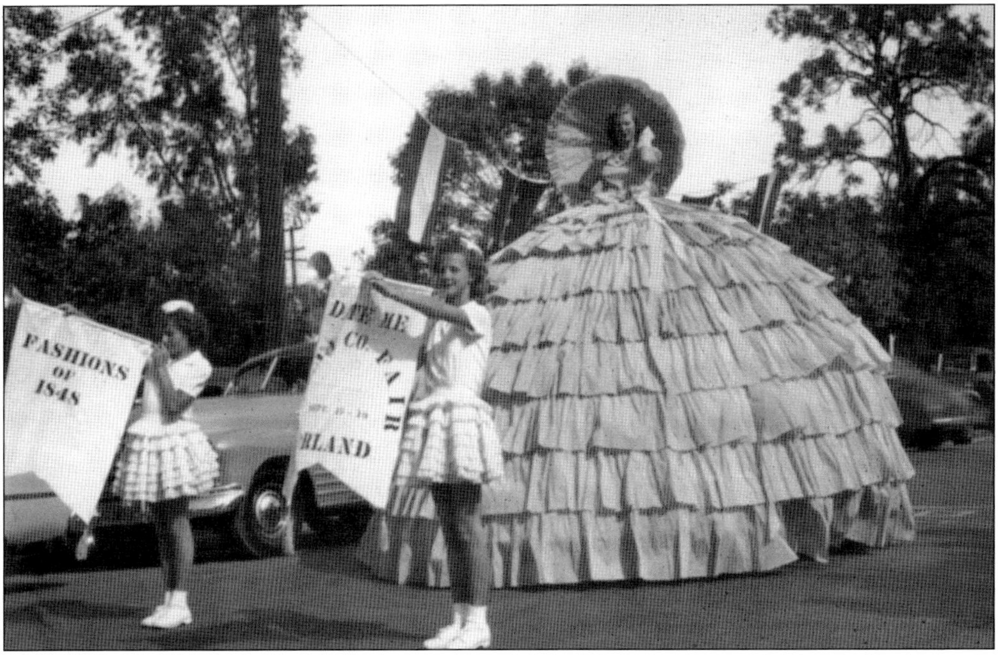

Beginning with the first fair in 1917, each Glenn County Fair was preceded by a school parade. As time progressed, civic organizations and businesses had entries. In 1920, a plane led the school parade (a photograph of this parade can be seen in *Land of Orland*). In 1941, floats, four bands, and over 3,500 students participated in the parade. This 1948 entry featured a vintage fashion float with student marchers. (Orland Historical and Cultural Society.)

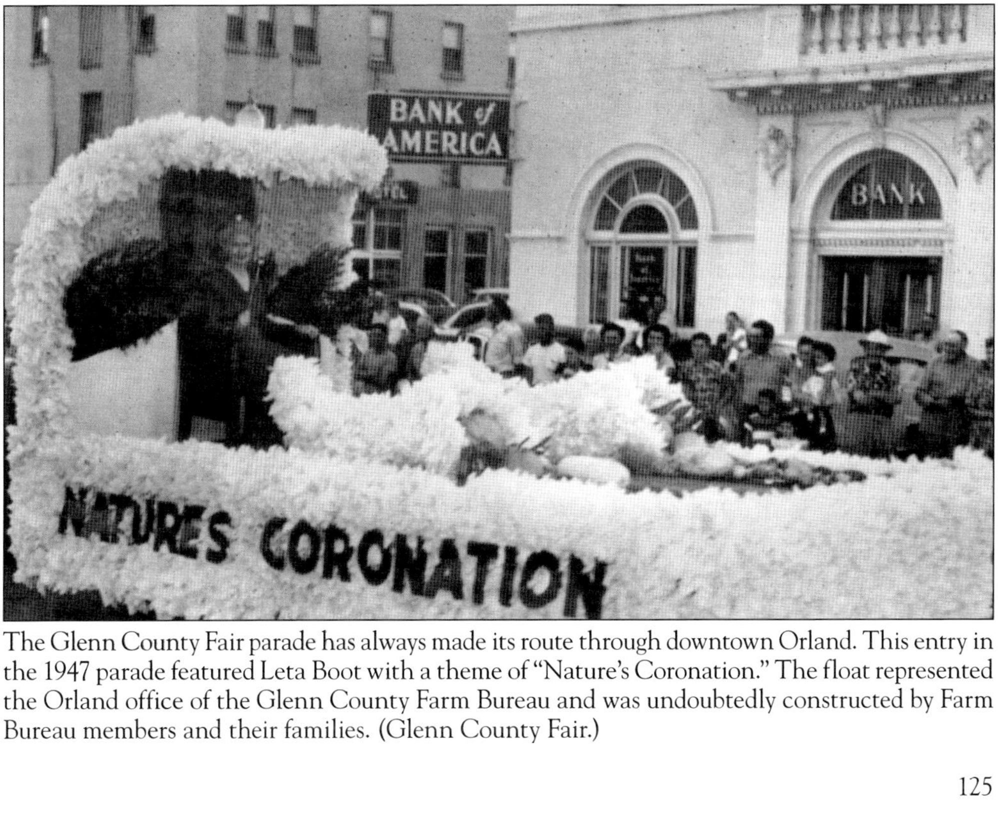

The Glenn County Fair parade has always made its route through downtown Orland. This entry in the 1947 parade featured Leta Boot with a theme of "Nature's Coronation." The float represented the Orland office of the Glenn County Farm Bureau and was undoubtedly constructed by Farm Bureau members and their families. (Glenn County Fair.)

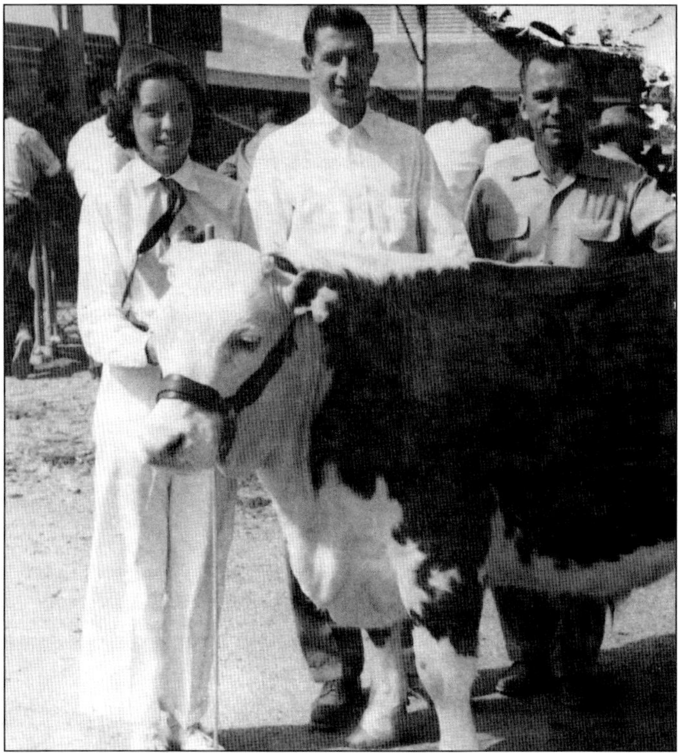

The first junior livestock auction (JLA) of the Glenn County Fair was held in 1955. The JLA was created to support the 42nd District Agricultural Association's mission to support and promote agriculture and enhance the advancement of education. Glenn County 4-H and Future Farmer of America members exhibit and sell the livestock they raised specifically for the fair. Pictured here are Donna Stockton (left), who exhibited the 4-H Grand Champion Steer and sold it to Bill Zielesch (center) and Vern Graham (right). (Glenn County Fair.)

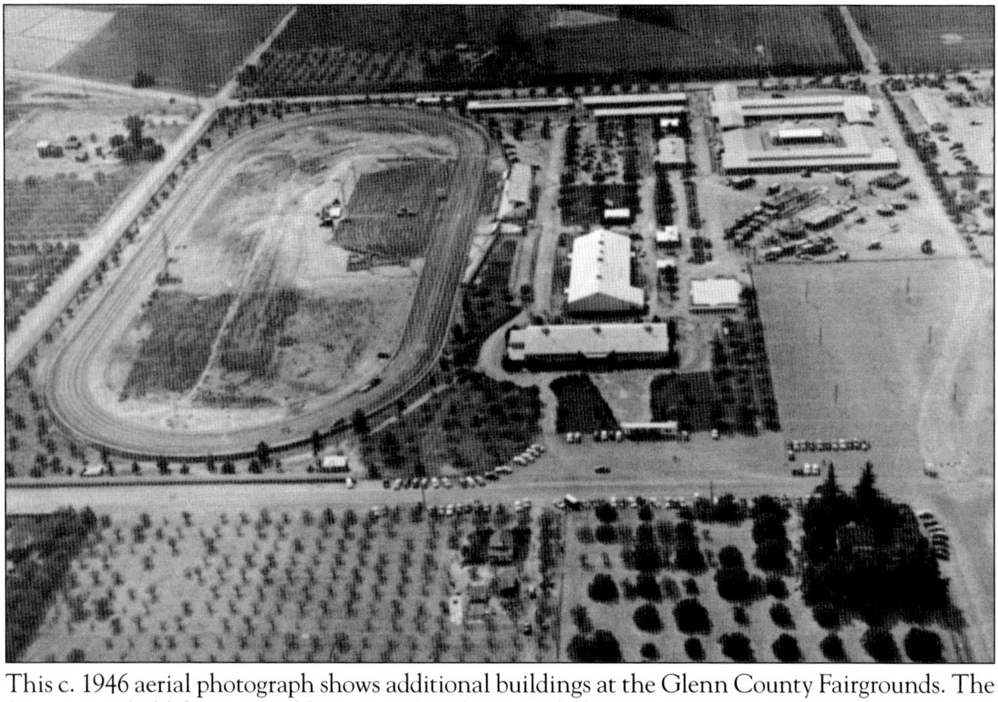

This c. 1946 aerial photograph shows additional buildings at the Glenn County Fairgrounds. The fair was not held during World War II. This photograph depicts preparations prior to the opening of the fair. Readers familiar with these fairgrounds will note which buildings are still in existence and which no longer exist. (Orland Historical and Cultural Society.)

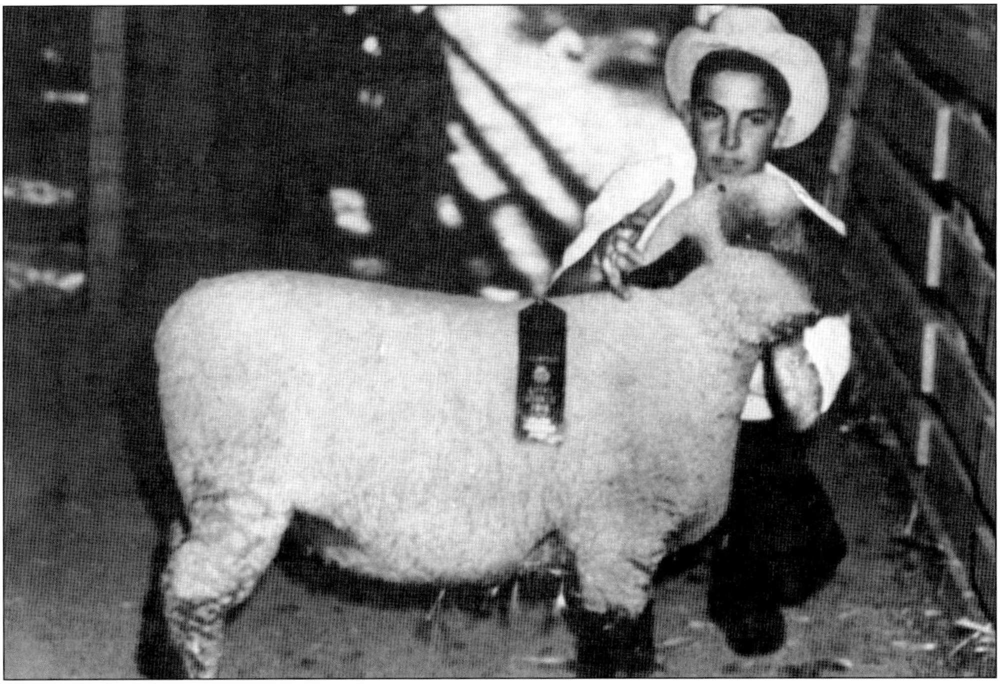

The Future Farmers of America (FFA) and 4-H programs both began in 1928. Ray Lyon was instrumental in both programs in Glenn County and is pictured here in 1949 as an Orland FFA member with his champion ewe. As an integral part of Glenn County, he was an Orland High School agriculture instructor, and a 4-H dairy and forage crop advisor. Known as "Mr. 4-H," he retired in 1994 with the title of county director advisor, emeritus. (Glenn County Fair.)

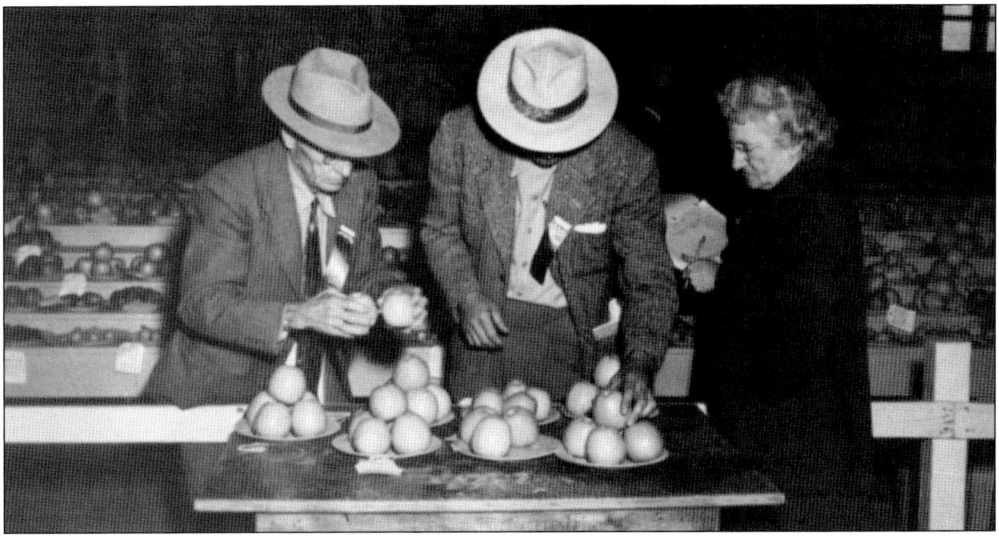

Since the inception of the Glenn County Fair, children and adults alike have flocked on opening day to the exhibit buildings to see what the fruits of their labor have been awarded. From canvas tents to permanent buildings, the exhibits are the main attraction. Ribbons were given as the first premium while cash prizes were added in later years. Joe Smith was in charge of the fruit and vegetable displays for many years. Here, he is one of three volunteer judges inspecting apples in Flaherty Hall around 1941. (Orland Historical and Cultural Society.)